B E Y O N D   G R O W T H

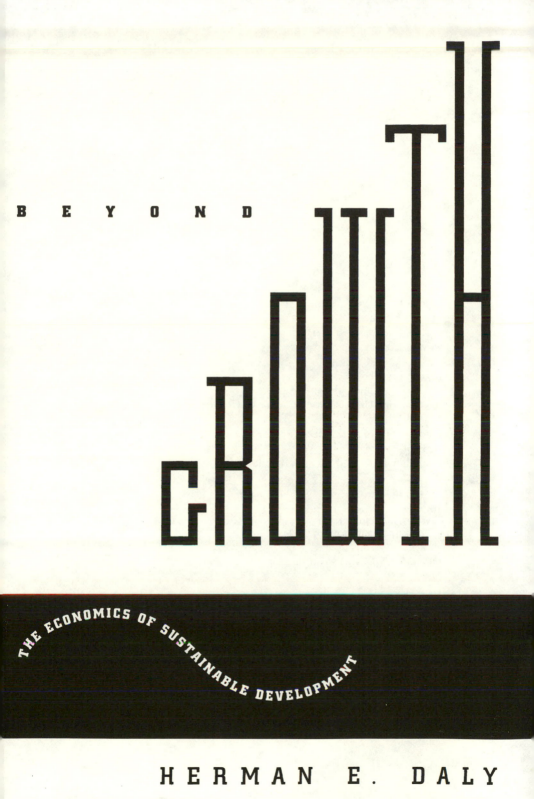

BEYOND GROWTH

THE ECONOMICS OF SUSTAINABLE DEVELOPMENT

HERMAN E. DALY

BEACON PRESS • BOSTON

Beacon Press
25 Beacon Street
Boston, Massachusetts 02108-2892
www.beacon.org

Beacon Press books
are published under the auspices of
the Unitarian Universalist Association of Congregations.

15 14 13 12 11   17 16 15 14 13

Text design by John Kane
Composition by Wilsted & Taylor

Library of Congress Cataloging-in-Publication Data

Daly, Herman E.
    Beyond growth: the economics of sustainable development / Herman
    Daly.
        p.   cm.
    Includes bibliographical references and index.
    ISBN 978-0-8070-4709-5 (paper)
    1. Sustainable development.   I. Title.
    HC79.E5D324   1996
    333.7—dc20   95-51311

Contents

Acknowledgments

On the title page my name appears as sole author of this book. However, I have had a number of silent partners who are at least collaborators, if not co-authors. Over the past decade or so they have taught and helped me a great deal. The International Society for Ecological Economics has provided a supporting community of thought and scholarship, and in particular my partnership with Robert Costanza in founding that organization, and its journal, *Ecological Economics*, has been very rewarding. My partnership with John B. Cobb, Jr., in writing *For the Common Good* was another very fortunate and instructive friendship for me. During my six years at the World Bank I was lucky to have Robert Goodland as mentor, partner, and friend, as well as Salah El Serafy and a number of the members of "the loyal opposition of environmentalists" within the World Bank. More recently, at the University of Maryland I have benefited from discussions with my new colleagues Robert Nelson, Robert Sprinkle, Mark Sagoff, and David Crocker, and especially from the support of Peter G. Brown. This book also owes much of its coherence to the thoughtful editorial advice of Andrew Hrycyna, and to the careful and helpful copyediting of Chris Kochansky. Most of all, Marcia Damasceno Daly, my life partner and wife, has provided constant help, wisdom, and goodness for thirty-three years.

BEYOND GROWTH

Introduction

The Shape of Current Thought on Sustainable Development

Although there is an emerging political consensus on the desirability of something called sustainable development, this term—touted by many and even institutionalized in some places—is still dangerously vague. Apparent agreement masks a fight over what exactly "sustainable development" should mean—a fight in which the stakes are very high.

The power of the concept of sustainable development is that it both reflects and evokes a latent shift in our vision of how the economic activities of human beings are related to the natural world—an ecosystem which is finite, non-growing, and materially closed. The demands of these activities on the containing ecosystem for regeneration of raw material "inputs" and absorption of waste "outputs" must, I will argue, be kept at ecologically sustainable levels as a condition of sustainable development. This change in vision involves replacing the economic norm of quantitative expansion (growth) with that of qualitative improvement (development) as the path of future progress. This shift is resisted by most economic and political institutions, which are founded on traditional quantitative growth and legitimately fear its replacement by something as subtle and challenging as qualitative development. The economics of development without—and beyond—growth needs to be worked out much more fully. There are enormous forces of denial aligned against this necessary shift in vision and analytic effort, and to overcome these forces requires a deep philosophical clarification, even religious renewal.

Sustainable development is a term that everyone likes, but nobody is sure of what it means. (At least it sounds better than "unsustainable nondevelopment.") The term rose to the prominence of a mantra—or a shibboleth—following the 1987 publication of the U.N.-sponsored Brundtland Commission report, *Our Common Future*, which defined the term as development which meets the needs of the present without sacrificing the ability of the future to meet its needs. While not vacuous by any means, this definition was sufficiently vague to allow for a broad consensus. Probably that was a good political strategy at the time—a consensus on a vague concept was better than disagreement over a sharply defined one. By 1995, however, this initial vagueness is no longer a basis for consensus, but a breeding ground for disagreement. Acceptance of a largely undefined term sets the stage for a situation where whoever can pin his or her definition to the term will automatically win a large political battle for influence over our future.

Some would like to abandon the concept of sustainable development altogether, arguing that it adds nothing to standard economics and is too vague to ever be useful.[1] But most important concepts are not subject to analytically precise definition—think of democracy, justice, welfare, for example. Important concepts are more dialectical than analytic, in the sense that they have evolving penumbras which partially overlap with their "other." Analytic concepts have no overlap with their other, so the law of contradiction holds—that is, B cannot be both A and non-A. But for dialectical concepts there are cases in which it makes sense to say that B is both A and non-A.[2] For example, there is an age at which we are both young and old; a tidal salt marsh is both land and sea; a credit card is both money and non-money. If all our concepts were analytic we could not deal with change and evolution. Analytically defined species could never evolve if they at no time and in no way overlapped with their other. All important concepts are dialectically vague at the margins. I claim that sustainable development is at least as clear an economic concept as money itself. Is money really $M1$ or $M2$, or is it $M1a$? Do we count Eurodollar-based loans in the U.S. money supply? How liquid does an asset have to be before it counts as "quasi-money"? Yet the human mind is clever. Not only can we handle the concept of money, we would have a hard time without it. The same, I suggest, is true for the concept of sustainable development. If economists reject this concept because it is dialectical rather than analytical, then they should also stop talking about money.

While accepting the inherent overlap and vagueness of all dialectical concepts, there still remains much room for giving content to and sharpening the analytical cutting power of the idea of sustainable development. For one thing, the Brundtland definition tells us only that sustainable development means development which does not impoverish the future. This statement implies something about what "sustainable" means in this context, but it does not even try to define "development." Is there a difference between economic development and economic growth? Does growth mean growth in the total value of goods and services produced during a given time period (GNP, or gross national product)? Or does it mean growth in the rate of flow of matter and energy through a given economic system (physical throughput)? These are some of the issues to be addressed in this book. But before doing so it is useful to recognize that the issues addressed by the concept of sustainable development existed and were actively discussed long before the term itself became customary.

For over twenty-five years the concept of a steady-state economy has been at the center of my thinking and writing.[3] John Stuart Mill, back in 1857, discussed this idea under the label "stationary state," by which he meant a condition of zero growth in population and physical capital stock, but with continued improvement in technology and ethics. Following Mill and the classical economists, I have always thought that this concept was most relevant to "developed" or "mature" economies. During the six years that I worked for the World Bank (1988–1994), I was therefore surprised to see a very similar idea, now called "sustainable development," become the dominant ideal for the less developed countries (the South), but *not* for the mature, developed countries (the North). In my view, while sustainability is certainly relevant to the South, the critical issue is for the North to attain sustainability in the sense of a level of resource use that is both sufficient for a good life for its population and within the carrying capacity of the environment if generalized to the whole world. Population growth and production growth must not push us beyond the sustainable environmental capacities of resource regeneration and waste absorption. Therefore, once that point is reached, production and reproduction should be for replacement only. Physical growth should cease, while qualitative improvement continues.

Sustainable Development and Classical Economics

The classical economists thought that the economy would naturally end up in the stationary state, with wages at a subsistence level and the surplus all going to landlords as rent, with nothing left over for the capitalist's profit, and therefore no motive for further growth. Most of the classical economists dreaded the stationary state as the end of progress, but Mill welcomed it, recognizing that "a stationary condition of capital and population implies no stationary state of human improvement," and that in fact there would be more likelihood of "improving the art of living ... when minds ceased to be engrossed by the art of getting on." Unlike many classical economists, Mill believed that the laws governing production did not rigidly determine distribution—so that the subsistence-level wage was not a necessary feature of the stationary state. In today's jargon, Mill was arguing for sustainable development—development without growth—that is, qualitative improvement without quantitative increase. But Mill's writings on the stationary state were forgotten, and most economics Ph.D.s from the past two decades have never heard of this concept because their teachers, who had heard of it, rejected it as unworthy of transmission.

The limits that the classical economists saw were basically demographic and ecological—Malthus's iron law of wages and Ricardo's law of increasing differential rent (resulting from the increased competition of a growing population for a fixed amount of land that differs in quality) combined to bid up the premium paid for superior land (rent) and keep wages at subsistence. In their era there was not such an awareness of overall ecological limits as there is today, although that factor was not entirely absent from their theories. There was more emphasis on a distributive limit as all the surplus ended up in the unproductive hands of land-lords—but that accumulation itself resulted from demographic pressure of the growing laboring class and the ecological fact of the differential fertility of land that gave rise to increasing rent on lands of better quality.

Unlike that of the classical economists, today's standard (neoclassical) economic theory begins with nonphysical parameters (technology, preferences, and distribution of income are all taken as givens) and inquires how the physical variables of quantities of goods produced and resources used must be adjusted to fit an equilibrium (or an equilibrium rate of growth) determined by those nonphysical parameters. The nonphysical, qualitative conditions are given and the physical, quantitative magnitudes must adjust. In neoclassical theory this "adjustment" almost always involves growth. Today's newly emerging paradigm (steady state, sustainable development), however, begins with physical parameters (a finite world, complex ecological interrelations, the laws of thermodynamics) and inquires how the nonphysical variables of technology, preferences, distribution, and lifestyles can be brought into feasible and just equilibrium with the complex biophysical system of which we are a part. The physical quantitative magnitudes are what is given, and the nonphysical qualitative patterns of life become variables. This emerging paradigm is more like classical than neoclassical economics in that adjustment is by qualitative development, not quantitative growth.

With the Industrial Revolution, the idea of a stationary state, and classical economics in general, was retired to history. Neoclassical economics, with its subjectivist theory of value, shifted attention away from resources and labor and onto utility, exchange, and efficiency. The subjectivist and marginalist revolution, with its marginal utility theory of value, was certainly an improvement in the understanding of prices and markets. But that gain came at the cost of pushing physical factors too far into the background. Classical considerations of the "real cost" dimension of value (labor and resources) were eclipsed. Today the classical ghost of the stationary state has returned to the ball, uninvited, in the costume of sustainable development. Like Mill, I welcome its presence. And, like Mill, I am in the minority among economists, most of whom resist the very idea, as will be seen in the discussions that follow.

If development means anything concretely it means a process by which the South becomes like the North in terms of consumption levels and patterns. But current Northern levels and patterns are not generalizable to the whole world, assuming anything remotely resembling even our best existing technology, without exceeding ecological carrying capacity—that is, without consuming natural capital and thereby diminishing the capacity of the earth to support life and wealth in the future. It is clear that we already consume natural capital and count it as current income in our national accounts. One need only try to imagine 1.2 billion Chinese with automobiles, refrigerators, washing machines, and so on, to get a picture of the ecological consequences of generalizing advanced Northern resource consumption levels across the globe. Add to that the ecological consequences from agriculture when the Chinese begin to eat higher on the food chain—more meat, less grain. Each pound of meat requires diversion of roughly ten pounds of grain from humans to livestock, with similarly increased pressure on grasslands and the conversion of forests to pasture.

Might such expansion destroy the ecological capacity of the earth to support life in the future? Perhaps, because such a "liquidation" can be "optimal" in the economists' models. The dominant model excludes ecological costs altogether, but even those models that recognize ecological costs, if they are based on present value maximization, also can lead to "optimal" liquidation. The higher the discount rate, the sooner the liquidation. This anomaly sometimes makes neoclassical economists uneasy, but not always. Their usual assumption is that additional man-made capital substitutes for liquidated natural resources. One place where reality is forcing reconsideration of these models is in the World Bank, probably the world's largest and most generous employer of economists.

Sustainable Development and the World Bank

Certainly the World Bank would be the proper institution to recognize the ecological contradictions in the world's economic development plans, and to call attention to the need for the North to stop growth in resource throughput in order to both reserve for the people of the South the remaining ecological space needed for growth to satisfy their vital needs and set a generalizable and replicable example of sustainable development. The World Bank's best opportunity to date for doing this was through its 1992 World Development Report, entitled *Development and the Environment*. I worked in the Environment Department of the World Bank during that time, and although I was not part of the team that wrote the report, I did have an opportunity to comment on various early drafts and to observe the whole effort from close range.

While the 1992 report made a number of contributions, especially in calling attention to the public health consequences of the environmental degradation of water and air, it nevertheless failed to address the biggest question. Environmental deterioration was held to be mainly a consequence of poverty, and the solution proposed was the same as the World Bank's solution to other economic problems, namely more growth. And this meant not only growth in the South, but also in the North, for how else could the South grow if it could not export to Northern markets and receive foreign investments from the North? And how could the North provide foreign investment and larger markets for the South if it in turn did not grow? While the World Bank's report acknowledged a few conflicts between growth and environment here and there, the world was seen to be full of "win-win" opportunities for both increasing growth as usual and improving the environment. The message was both a reaffirmation of the Bank's faith in economic growth and a denial of the existence of any fundamental ecological limits to that growth: problems reside mainly in the South, solutions are to be found mainly in the North. This formulation is politically convenient, at the very least, since the Bank is creditor to the South and debtor to the North. It is always easier to preach to your debtors than to your creditors.

The evolution of the manuscript of *Development and the Environment* is revealing. An early draft contained a diagram entitled "The Relationship Between the Economy and the Environment." It consisted of a square labeled "economy," with an arrow coming in labeled "inputs" and an arrow going out labeled "outputs"—nothing more. I suggested that the picture failed to show the environment, and that it would be good to have a large box containing the one depicted, to represent the environment. Then the relation between the environment and the economy would be clear—specifically, that the economy is a subsystem of the environment and depends upon the environment both as a source of raw material inputs and as a "sink" for waste outputs.

The next draft included the same diagram and text, but with an unlabeled box drawn around the economy like a picture frame. I commented that the larger box had to be labeled "environment" or else it was merely decorative, and that the text had to explain that the economy is related to the environment as a subsystem within the larger ecosystem and is dependent on it in the ways previously stated. The next draft omitted the diagram altogether.

By coincidence, a few months later the chief economist of the World Bank, Lawrence H. Summers, under whom the report was being written, happened to be on a conference panel at the Smithsonian Institution, discussing the book *Beyond the Limits* (Donella H. Meadows et al.), which Summers considered worthless. In that book there was a diagram showing the relation of the economy to the ecosystem, a diagram exactly like the one I had suggested (and like the one in figure 3, page 49). During the question-and-answer time I asked the chief economist if, looking at that diagram, he felt that the question of the size of the economic subsystem relative to the total ecosystem was an important one, and whether he thought economists should be asking the question, What is the optimal scale of the macro economy relative to the environment? His reply was immediate and definite: "That's not the right way to look at it."

Reflecting on these two experiences has reinforced my belief that the main issue in the sustainable development controversy truly does revolve around what economist Joseph Schumpeter called "preanalytic vision." My preanalytic vision of the economy as subsystem leads immediately to the questions, How big is the subsystem relative to the total system? How big can it be without disrupting the functioning of the total system? How big should it be? What is its optimal scale beyond which further growth would be antieconomic, would cost more than it's worth? The World Bank's chief economist had no intention of being sucked into addressing these subversive questions, so he dismissed the viewpoint that gave rise to them.

Summers's dismissal was rather peremptory, but so, in a way, was my response to the diagram showing the economy receiving inputs from nowhere and exporting wastes to nowhere. That is not the right way to look at it, I felt, and any questions arising from that incomplete picture—say, how to make the economy grow as fast as possible by speeding up the flow of energy and materials through it—were not the right questions. Unless one has the preanalytic vision of the economy as subsystem, the whole idea of sustainable development—of a subsystem being sustained by a larger system whose limits and capacities it must respect—makes no sense whatsoever. On the other hand, a preanalytic vision of the economy as a box floating in infinite space allows people to speak of "sustainable *growth*"—a clear oxymoron to those who see the economy as a subsystem. The difference between these two visions could not be more fundamental, more elementary, or more irreconcilable.

It is interesting that such a huge issue should be at stake in a simple picture. Once you draw the boundary of the environment around the economy, you have said that the economy cannot expand forever. You have said that John Stuart Mill was right, that populations of human bodies and accumulations of capital goods cannot grow forever, that at some point quantitative growth must give way to qualitative development as the path of progress.

I believe we are at that point today. But the World Bank cannot say that—at least not yet. It cannot acknowledge limits to growth because growth is seen as the solution to poverty. Historically there is a lot of truth in this view. If we now recognize that growth is physically limited, or even economically limited in that it is beginning to cost more than it is worth at the margin, then how will we lift poor people out of poverty? The answer is painfully simple: by population control, by redistribution of wealth and income, and by technical improvements in resource productivity. In sum, not by growth, but by development. However, in most circles population control and redistribution are considered politically impossible. Increasing resource productivity is considered a good idea until it conflicts with capital and labor productivity, until we realize that in the developed countries we have bought high productivity and high incomes for capital and labor—and thus a reduction in class conflict—by using resources lavishly, in other words, by sacrificing resource productivity. Yet resources are the limiting factor in the long run, and therefore they are the very factor whose productivity economic logic says should be maximized. The temptation to denial becomes politically overwhelming.

When we draw that containing boundary of the environment around the economy we move from "empty-world" economics to "full-world" economics—from a world where inputs to and outputs from the economy are unconstrained, to a world in which they are increasingly constrained by the depletion and pollution of a finite environment. Economic logic stays the same—economize on the limiting factor. But the perceived pattern of scarcity changes radically—the identity of the limiting factor shifts from man-made capital to our remaining natural capital, from fishing boats to the populations of fish remaining in the sea—therefore policies must change radically. That is why there is such resistance to a simple picture. The fact that the picture is both so simple and so obviously realistic explains why it cannot be contemplated by the growth economists, why they must continue to insist, "That's not the right way to look at it!"

In the end, the World Bank's report *Development and the Environment* proved unable to face the most basic question: Is it better or worse for the South if the North continues to grow in its own resource use? The standard answer is that it is better because growth in the North increases markets for Southern exports, as well as funds for aid and investment by the North in the South. The alternative view is that Northern growth makes things worse by preempting the remaining resources and ecological space needed to support economic growth in the South up to a sufficient level, and that it also increases global income inequality and world political tensions. This view urges continued *development* in the North, but not *growth*. These two answers to the basic question cannot both be right. And the absence of that fundamental question from World Bank's policy research represents a failure of both nerve and intellect, as well as a continuing psychology of denial regarding limits to growth.

A small environmental resistance movement within the Bank tried to get the above question into *Development and the Environment*, not in any central way, because that was clearly impossible, but just as a half-page box raising the issue for future reflection. We were not successful because the orthodox economists correctly realized that reflection on this question was much too dangerous to their whole enterprise. It was as if we were building a skyscraper and, having reached the twentieth floor, some of us were pointing out that the whole structure was out-of-plumb and that if we were to go up another twenty stories it would fall. Architects and investors hate redoing foundations. Orthodox economists have solved all the foundational problems of development theory, they believe, and they have made their professional reputations on the basis of those solutions. They now wish to focus on advanced, "cutting-edge" issues and build this leaning tower of Babel ever higher, making ad hoc corrections as we go. Forget that silly diagram—that's not the right way to look at it.

Having failed to fundamentally influence *Development and the Environment*, our environmental resistance group put together its own alternative statement, which we tried unsuccessfully to publish within the Bank and then published with UNESCO.[4] Among our contributors were two Nobel Laureate economists (Jan Tinbergen and Trygve Haavelmo), and the preface was an endorsement by the environment ministers of two of the Bank's major borrowing countries (José Lutzenburger of Brazil, and Emil Salim of Indonesia). But the Bank could not possibly publish it because it was based on that simple but threatening diagram. I mention the two Nobel Laureate economists not to suggest that counting Nobelites on each side of an issue is the way to resolve it—by that criterion the World Bank's position would easily win—but just to show that not all economists are unwilling to rethink the assumptions of their discipline. The Norwegian version of the little book even had a nice foreword by Prime Minister Gro Harlem Brundtland, chairman of the famous Brundtland Commission, which had put the whole idea of sustainable development on the agenda. But the World Bank simply could not take it seriously.

Although the World Bank was on record as officially favoring sustainable development, the near vacuity of the phrase made this a meaningless affirmation. Attempts of the environmental resistance group to give the concept a clear definition were vigorously countered. The party line was that sustainable development was like pornography—we'll know it when we see it, but it's too difficult to define. Our simple definition—development without growth beyond environmental carrying capacity, where development means qualitative improvement and growth means quantitative increase—just confirmed the orthodox economists' worst fears about the subversive nature of the idea, and reinforced their resolve to keep it vague.

One way to render any concept innocuous is to expand its meaning to include everything. By 1991 the phrase had acquired such cachet that everything had to be sustainable, and the relatively clear notion of environmental sustainability of the economic subsystem was buried under "helpful" extensions such as social sustainability, political sustainability, financial sustainability, cultural sustainability, and on and on. We expected any day to hear about "sustainable sustainability." Any definition that excludes nothing is a worthless definition. Yet if one objects to including culture in the definition of sustainable development one is accused of denying the importance of culture. Pretty soon sustainable development was being defined to include even the right to peaceable assembly. The right to peaceable assembly is a good thing, but it is not useful to include all good things in the definition of sustainable development. The term had acquired such vogue that everyone felt that their favorite cause had to be a part of the definition or else be implicitly condemned to oblivion, and this natural confusion was abetted by those in the Bank who wanted to keep the concept vague, to dull its sharp edges enough to keep it from cutting into business as usual—that is, pushing loans in the interest of export-led growth and global integration.

I should say in defense of the World Bank that its environmental standards are generally higher than those of most of its member countries. Only the Netherlands and the Scandinavian countries are really in a position to tell the Bank to improve its environmental standards. The other thing that must be said in the

Bank's defense is that it is like the church—trying to do good in the world according to what its clergy learned in seminary. But the "seminaries" are teaching bad theology. Bank economists, whether from Cameroon or California, all get their training in a handful of academic economics departments, and all learn basically the same economic theology. Frequent academic advisors to the Bank (its chief economist is also usually brought in from academia) keep renewing the flawed theology, reminding everyone, when necessary, that "that's not the right way to look at it." I have suggested to friends at Greenpeace that in addition to protesting Bank projects, they should at least once a year go hang a black shroud on the building that houses the MIT economics department (or that of Chicago, Stanford, Oxford, Cambridge, etc.).

Sustainable Development and Academia

In 1994 I decided to leave the World Bank to return to academia. I certainly had no illusion that I was leaving blindness and corruption behind and entering a realm of truth and honesty. I had been in academia before. If I had harbored such an illusion it would have quickly been dispelled by an experience with the MIT Press that taught me that prestigious universities can sometimes be less committed to free speech and open debate than commercial publishers.[5]

There is a better side to academia than the one just mentioned. In 1995, eleven important academic economists and ecologists signed a statement entitled "Economic Growth, Carrying Capacity, and the Environment," and published it in the policy forum section of the journal *Science*.[6] There was an explicit agreement among these important thinkers to the effect that (1) "*the* [environmental] *resource base is finite*," (2) "*there are limits to the carrying capacity of the planet*," and (3) "*economic growth is not a panacea for* [diminishing] *environmental quality*" (italics added). That such obvious propositions still face sufficient opposition to require such a defensively crafted consensus is a sad but accurate commentary on the current state of the academic disciplines of both economics and ecology.

One might have hoped that the authors would have carried the third insight a bit further to consider whether economic growth, in addition to being a false cure, might not also be a major *cause* of environmental degradation—along with population growth, which also gets short shrift. To make this case they would have had to separate economic growth (defined as expansion of GNP) into its quantitative, physical component (resource throughput growth) and its qualitative, nonphysical component (resource efficiency improvement). They might then have reached a further consensus that total throughput growth is indeed the major cause of environmental degradation, while improvements in resource efficiency, by allowing a reduction in throughput or a more benign mix of products, are sparing of the environment. Perhaps they would have then agreed to advocate development (improvement in resource efficiency) without growth (expansion of resource throughput)—sustainable development. They might have pointed out that growth in this physical sense can be antieconomic, or negative—that, at the margin, throughput growth may cause environmental costs to increase faster than production benefits, thereby making us poorer, not richer. No one is against being richer, but some of us are against becoming poorer as a result of antieconomic growth masquerading as economic growth.[7] But this is the best to come from mainstream academia, and it is much better than what one hears from most orthodox economists, so one should be grateful.

It has, of course, occurred to me that maybe the orthodox economists are right, and that perhaps we dissidents really are looking at things in the wrong way. So I do try from time to time to see things in the light of their preanalytic vision, and in the light of other visions as well. It requires effort to go against my basic "default settings," and I am sure the same is true for the growth economists. But let me share some reflections on alternative visions for integrating economics and ecology, for relating the subsystem to the total system.

There are, I believe, three alternative strategies for integrating the economy and the ecosystem that have been discussed in the public forum.[8] First, the strategy of "economic imperialism," in which the subsystem, the economy, expands until everything is included. The subsystem becomes identical to the total system, everything is economy and everything has a price. Internalization of externalities has been carried to the limit and nothing remains external to the economy. This seems to be the implicit strategy of neoclassical economics.

The second strategy is to shrink the economy boundary to nothing so that everything is ecosystem. This I call ecological reductionism. All human valuations and choices are held to be explicable by the same evolutionary forces of chance and necessity that presumably control the natural world. Relative values correspond to embodied energy content, and economies, like ecosystems, are governed by the dictates of survival. Some follow this position to its logical conclusion, and view—or at least affect to view—human extinction as no more significant than the extinction of any other species. This seems to be the implicit strategy of those many biologists and ecologists who operate on a philosophy of scientific materialism.

The third strategy is the one adopted here—to view the economy as a subsystem of the ecosystem and to recognize that while it is not exempt from natural laws, neither is it fully reducible to explanation by them. The human economy cannot be reduced to a natural system. There is more to the idea of value than embodied energy or survival advantage. But neither can the economy subsume the entire natural system under its managerial dominion of efficient allocation. This vision of the earth as an alchemist's centrally planned terrarium, with nothing wild or spontaneous but everything base transformed into gold, into its highest instrumental value for humans, is a sure recipe for disaster.

We cannot get rid of the subsystem boundary, either by expanding it to include the whole system or by collapsing it to include nothing. Too many critical distinctions are lost in either strategy. Therefore we must be concerned with drawing the boundary properly so that we include neither too much nor too little, so that we include and exclude the right things. For now, however, the most pressing need is to stop the exponential expansion of this subsystem boundary under the current regime of economic imperialism—but without falling prey to the seductions of ecological reductionism.

We have a long way to go. The World Bank is still dedicated to expanding the boundary by economic growth as traditionally defined. Academic economists are probably even more dedicated to economic growth. And of course the U.S. government is yet even more committed to growth as a goal. But there are some signs of change. Although Clinton and Gore won on a growth platform, Al Gore as senator had written a very insightful book on problems of environment and economic growth.[9] We also have the President's Council on Sustainable Development, whose pronouncements merit attention as an authoritative statement of exactly where we are—and how far we have yet to go.

Sustainable Development and U.S. Politics

To get a concrete idea of the degree of political consciousness in the United States regarding sustainable development, we can look at the President's Council on Sustainable Development and their fifteen proclaimed principles on the issue.[10]

The council is to be commended for coming up with an initial list of principles and inviting comment, even though *fifteen* principles, where two or three would have sufficed, does not inspire confidence. It is not easy to get consensus on such a difficult issue from such a diverse committee, one which by design and necessity includes members of many different interest groups. Getting consensus on a principle frequently requires reduction of the principle to vacuity—the less you say, the less there is to disagree with. And the less each principle says, the greater is the felt need to add another principle. Still, the council came up with some principles that, while not crystal clear and specific, are not totally vacuous either. And even if some do appear a bit empty or repetitive, this is a further invitation for citizens to provide additional specificity and content, and thus further the discussion.

Below I quote each of the fifteen principles, and add a brief comment aimed at moving the principle toward more specificity and clarity. In most cases my comment would not receive the consensus accorded the original principle precisely because of the added specificity. Although it would be possible to impose a stricter order on the discussion than the one inherent in these fifteen principles, I think it is important to accept them as our framework, even if a loose one, in order to see the extent of present consensus and understanding in all its incompleteness, and to avoid any possible misrepresentation by paraphrase or summary. References to discussions in the remaining chapters of the book that are relevant to some of the principles helps to fill out the introductory function of this essay.

> 1. *We must preserve and, where possible, restore the integrity of natural systems—soils, water, air, and biological diversity—which sustain both economic prosperity and life itself.*

Yes, indeed. Restoring natural systems requires reducing our physical demands on those systems (as sources and sinks for the economy) in order to allow them to recuperate. Continuing expansion of the scale of the human economy will require the takeover of ever more of the habitat of other species and is inconsistent with maintaining biodiversity and ecological life-support systems.

Chapters 1, 2, and 4 contribute to this discussion.

> 2. *Economic growth, environmental protection, and social equity should be interdependent, mutually reinforcing national goals, and policies to achieve these goals should be integrated.*

Maybe these goals *should* be mutually reinforcing, but frequently they conflict. To sort out conflicts and harmonies we must distinguish *growth* (quantitative increase by assimilation or accretion of materials) from *development* (qualitative improvement, realization of potential). The construct "gross national product" conflates these two totally different things, as does the usual concept of economic growth, thought of as growth in GNP. Quantitative increase of the scale of the economy by assimilation or accretion of material from the finite environment is not sustainable. Qualitative improvement and realization of potential may well continue forever—at least we cannot specify any obvious limits to its sustainability. Sustainable development therefore is development without growth—that is without throughput growth beyond the regeneration and absorption capacities of the environment. The path of future progress is development, not growth. This distinction must be made or confusion is inevitable.

Further discussion will be found in Chapters 1, 2, and 5.

> 3. *Along with appropriate protective measures, market strategies should be used to harness private energies and capital to protect and improve the environment.*

Yes, the market should certainly be the main mechanism for solving the problem of efficient allocation of resources. There are two prior problems that have to be solved politically as the precondition for the market to work in this way. We must politically and socially limit the total scale of resource throughput for key resources to a level that is sustainable. This provides a sustainable scale. Second, the rights to deplete or pollute up to the scale limit are no longer free goods, but valuable assets. Who owns them? The just distribution of initial ownership has to be settled socially. Only after these context questions of a sustainable scale and a just distribution have been settled socially can the individualistic market solve the question of efficient allocation. We must use the market to solve the allocation question, but we cannot expect it to solve the scale and distribution questions.

This will be elaborated in Chapters 2 and 15.

4. Population must be stabilized at a level consistent with the capacity of the earth to support its inhabitants.

This is crucial. For clarity we should add, ". . . support its inhabitants at a level of per capita wealth sufficient for a good life." We cannot precisely define "a good life," but most would agree with Malthus that it should be such as to permit one to have a glass of wine and a piece of meat with one's dinner. Even if one is a teetotaler or a vegetarian that level of affluence is desirable, and would serve by itself to rule out populations at or above today's level. What really must be stabilized is total consumption, which of course is population times per capita consumption. Both of the latter factors must be reduced.

The nation, not the earth, will be the effective unit in which population and consumption are controlled. Different nations will make different choices: some will not control either population or consumption, others will. Of those that do control total consumption, some will choose high per capita consumption and low population, others will choose the reverse. Free migration, or even free trade with free capital mobility, will undercut any national policies of self-discipline and restraint in consumption and population growth. The current thrust toward economic globalization is, short of the unappealing prospect of world government, likely to be contrary to sustainable development. Setting a successful national example for possible emulation may be the best contribution our own nation can make toward global sustainable development.

These issues are discussed in Chapters 8 and 9.

5. Protection of natural systems requires changed patterns of consumption consistent with a steady improvement in the efficiency with which society uses natural resources.

What is needed in the first instance are *reduced levels* of consumption, not just *changed patterns*. We certainly must improve the efficiency with which society uses resources (development), but the best way to do that is to limit the level of resource throughput (growth), thereby forcing progress onto the path of development rather than growth, as suggested in comment on point 2.

See Chapter 3 for additional discussion.

6. *Progress toward elimination of poverty is essential for economic progress, equity, and environmental quality.*

Elimination of poverty, in the absence of growth (which so far has failed to reduce poverty anyway), will have to come from greater sharing, more population control, and development in the sense of the term here defined. The political difficulty of facing up to sharing, population control, and qualitative development as the real cures to poverty will sorely tempt politicians to resurrect the impossible goal of growth—more for all with sacrifice by none, for ever and ever, world without end, amen. No doubt they will want to call it "sustainable growth"!

Chapters 14 and 15 deal with equity and distribution.

7. *All segments of society should equitably share environmental costs and benefits.*

Yes. This should be done through internalization of environmental costs into prices so that the polluter and the depleter pay. One powerful way to move in this direction is to shift the tax base from income (value added) to throughput (that to which value is added). Why tax what we want more of—employment and income? Why not tax what we want less of—depletion and pollution? This shift could be revenue neutral, and supplemented with a stiff income tax on very high incomes and a negative tax on very low incomes in order to maintain progressivity. Since we have to raise public revenue somehow, and since almost all taxes are distortionary, why not induce the "distortions" we want instead of those we do not want? Equity is served because the polluter and the depleter pay, yet the inevitable regressivity of a consumption tax is countered by a negative income tax on very low incomes and a high tax on very high incomes.

Chapters 5 and 15 deal with related matters.

8. *All economic and environmental decision-making should consider the well-being of future generations, and preserve for them the widest possible range of choices.*

The goal of preserving the range of choice of the present for future generations is certainly central to sustainable development, but it cannot be effected by piecemeal individualistic consideration of the effect of all micro economic and environmental decisions on the future. Protecting the range of options for the future has to be a macro, social decision, effected through a macro policy such as limiting the scale of throughput. Urging individuals to consider the future generations in their personal economic decisions is necessary but not sufficient.

> 9. *Where public health may be adversely affected, or environmental damage may be serious or irreversible, prudent action is required in the face of scientific uncertainty.*

Irreducible uncertainty about the environmental effects of new technologies or substances are real economic costs. Like other costs, they should be included in the price and paid for by the consumer of the commodity that has imposed the cost, rather than thrown on the general public. This could be better accomplished by requiring an assurance bond in the amount of possible damage, to be posted up front and then returned over time as experience reduces the uncertainty about damage. Currently the burden of uncertainty is too much borne by the public at large. Our liability laws operate only after the fact, and even then inability to pay is frequent.

> 10. *Sustainable development requires fundamental changes in the conduct of government, private institutions, and individuals.*

Yes. Some specific changes have been suggested in my comments here on these fifteen principles. While conduct or behavior needs to change, frequently the underlying principle remains the same. For example, it is an accepted principle in economics that in accounting income we must deduct for depreciation of capital in order to keep productive capacity intact. This principle remains, and only needs to be extended to natural capital as well as manmade. Depletion of natural capital is a cost and should be counted in the macro System of National Accounts, in micro project evaluation, and in the international balance of payments. See Chapters 2, 6, and 7.

> 11. *Environmental and economic concerns are central to our national and global security.*

True, especially in the sense that countries that are living within a non-growing biophysical budget that is environmentally sustainable are much less likely to go to war with each other than countries that are expanding their consumption of and dependence upon resources belonging to other countries, or to mankind in general—petroleum in the Middle East, for example, or atmospheric capacity to absorb CO_2 or SO_2.
Chapter 10 is relevant here.

12. *Sustainable development is best attained in a society in which free institutions flourish.*

Yes. We must keep in mind that free institutions include not only the institution of individual freedom in the competitive marketplace (freedom from monopoly), but also the social, collective freedom to democratically enact rules for the common good. As emphasized above, the market solution to the efficient allocation problem presupposes a political solution to the problems of sustainable scale and just distribution.

13. *Decisions affecting sustainable development should be open and permit informed participation by affected and interested parties, that requires a knowledgeable public, a free flow of information, and fair and equitable opportunities for review and redress.*

In relation to the above, the old GATT (General Agreement on Tariffs and Trade) and the new WTO (World Trade Organization) are highly suspect, and require considerable changes to come into conformity with this requirement for transparency and other principles of sustainable development.
See Chapters 10 and 11.

14. *Advances in science and technology are beneficial, increasing both our understanding and range of choices about how humanity and the environment relate. We must seek constant improvements in both science and technology in order to achieve eco-efficiency, protect and restore natural systems, and change consumption patterns.*

No one can oppose the advancement of knowledge, but by now it should be clear that not every new technology that comes down the pike is a net benefit to the human race. As E. J. Mishan put it, "While new technology is unrolling the carpet of increased choice before us by the foot, it is often simultaneously rolling it up behind us by the yard." We need technologies of development, technologies that more efficiently digest a given resource throughput, not the technologies of growth, of larger jaws and a bigger digestive tract. And, once again, instead of vaguely calling for "changed consumption patterns" we need to specify "reduced consumption levels" of resources and environmental services. Once the level of resource throughput is reduced to a sustainable level, the pattern of consumption will automatically adapt, thanks to the market. Controlling the pattern directly would require abrogation of the market and would not limit the level of consumption.

17

15. *Sustainability in the United States is closely tied to global sustainability. Our policies for trade, economic development, aid, and environmental protection must be considered in the context of the international implications of these policies.*

The connection between sustainability and international trade is important, but rather different I think from what the council has in mind. Nearly all policies for sustainability involve internalizing external environmental and social costs at the national level. This makes prices higher. Therefore free trade with countries that do not internalize these costs, or do it to a much lesser extent, is not feasible. In such cases there is every reason for protective tariffs. Such tariffs would be protecting not an inefficient industry or firm but an efficient national policy of cost internalization. Free trade among differing regimes of cost internalization will result in a standards-lowering competition, leading to a situation in which more and more of total world product is produced in countries that do a less and less complete job of counting costs. Hardly a movement toward global efficiency! The current thrust toward economic globalization by free trade, free capital mobility, and free (or at least uncontrolled) migration is in effect the erasure of national boundaries for economic purposes. This greatly undercuts the ability of nations to put into effect any policies in support of sustainable development, including population control and including domestic enforcement of international treaties that may have been signed in support of efforts to combat irreducibly global environmental problems. The power vacuum created by the weakening of national communities will be filled by the transnational corporations, which, in the absence of a world government, will be unconstrained by any community interests.

Further discussion of these issues is contained in Chapters 5, 10, and 11.

Sustainable Development, Science, and Religion

I will end this introductory essay with some reflections on the rather low sense of urgency and level of ethical motivation inspired by sustainable development—in the World Bank, academia, the U.S. government, and most other national governments. Of course there are individual exceptions in each of these domains, prophetic voices that cry in the wilderness. But why do these cries evoke so little response in so much wilderness? What is required to break out of our default position of denial?

Some prominent scientists turned part-time prophets calling for environmental repentance have asked themselves this same question. Some of them have decided that science has the techniques but is unable to ignite sufficient moral fervor to induce the public to accept and finance policies that apply these techniques. They thought that it would be worth a try to appeal to religion to supply the missing moral fervor as a basis for political consensus. This resulted, in May of 1992, in the "Joint Appeal by Science and Religion on the Environment," led by the eminent scientists Carl Sagan, Edward O. Wilson, and Stephen Jay Gould, along with a few religious leaders, and hosted by then Senator Al Gore. The three scientists are quite well known for their affirmations of scientific materialism and consequent renunciations of any religious interpretation of the cosmos, as well as for their highly informed and genuine concern about the environment. Their rationale for courting the religious community was that while science had the understanding on which to proceed, it lacked the moral inspiration to act and to inspire others to act. Or, in a frequently used metaphor, religion was asked to supply the moral compass, while science would supply the vehicle.

I attended the conference, and was vaguely troubled at the time by what seemed to me a somewhat less than honest appeal by the scientists to a somewhat credulous group of religious leaders. A year or so later I read a book by theologian John F. Haught, who had also been present, and discovered that he had precisely articulated my vague doubts.

In *The Promise of Nature*, Haught wondered aloud

> whether it is completely honest for them [the scientists] to drink in this case so lustily from the stream of moral fervor that flows from what they have consistently taken to be the inappropriate and even false consciousness of religious believers. . . . The well-intended effort by the skeptics to co-opt the moral enthusiasm of the religious for the sake of ecology is especially puzzling, in view of the fact that it is only because believers take their religious symbols and ideas to be disclosive of the *truth* of reality that they are aroused to moral passion in the first place. If devotees thought that their religions were *not* representative of the way things *really* are, then the religions would be ethically impotent. . . .
>
> It is hard to imagine how any thorough transformation of the habits of humans will occur without a corporate human confidence in the ultimate worthwhileness of our moral endeavors. And without a deep trust in reality itself, ecological morality will, I am afraid, ultimately languish and die. Such trust . . . must be grounded in a conviction that the universe carries a meaning, or that it is the unfolding of a "promise". A commonly held sense that the cosmos is a significant process, that it unfolds something analogous to what we humans call "purpose", is, I think an essential prerequisite of sustained global and intergenerational commitment to the earth's well-being.[11]

Haught's point, of course, is that Sagan, Wilson, and Gould proclaim the cosmology of scientific materialism, which considers the cosmos an absurd accident, and life within it to be no more than another accident ultimately reducible to dead matter in motion. In their view there is no such thing as value in any objective sense, or purpose, beyond short-term survival and reproduction, which are purely instinctual and thus ultimately mechanical. Calling for a moral compass in such a world is as absurd as calling for a magnetic compass in a world in which you proclaim that there is no such thing as magnetic north. A sensitive compass needle is worthless if there is no external lure toward which it is pulled. A morally sensitive person in a world in which there is no lure of objective value to pull and persuade this sensitized person toward itself is like the compass needle with no external magnetic force to act on it.

One might reply that objective value does not exist externally, but is an internal affair created by humans (or by God in humans only) and projected or imposed by humans on the external world. This is the solution of dualism, and has been dominant since Descartes. Purpose, mind, and value enter the world discontinuously in human beings; all the rest is mechanism. Such a view, however, is contrary to the evolutionary understanding of kinship of human beings with other forms of life that is affirmed by science. For mind, value, and purpose to be real, they must, in an evolutionary perspective, already be present to some degree in the world out of which humans evolved, or else they must be the object of a special creation. The latter, of course, is not acceptable to science and the theory of evolution. Scientific materialism resolves the dilemma by denying the reality of purpose, mind, and value in human beings as well as in the external world. The subjective feelings that we refer to as purpose or value are mere epiphenomena, ultimately explainable in terms of underlying physical structures and motions.

The main alternative to scientific materialism, one that still takes science seriously, is the process philosophy of Alfred North Whitehead. This view is radically empirical. What we know most concretely and directly, unmediated by the senses or by abstract concepts, is our inner experience of purpose. That should be the starting point, the most well known thing, in terms of which we try to explain less well known things. To begin with highly abstract concepts such as electrons and photons, and to explain the immediate experience of purpose as an "epiphenomenon" incidentally produced by the behavior of these abstractions, is an example of what Whitehead called "the fallacy of misplaced concreteness." I do not wish to pretend that Whiteheadean philosophy is easy, or without problems of its own, but merely to say that for me it strains credulity a lot less than scientific materialism.

Gould himself has noted, "We cannot win this battle to save species and environments without forging an emotional bond between ourselves and nature as well—for we will not fight to save what we do not love."[12] But is it possible to love an accident? Rather, is it possible for an accident to love an accident? For an accident to fight to save another accident? I doubt it, but I do not doubt that it is possible for people who call themselves scientific materialists to fall in love with the world they study and have come to know intimately. God's world is lovable, and scientists often fall in love with it much more deeply than theologians! But should they not confess that love, and ask themselves how it is that they could have fallen in love with something their science tells them is an accident? In their daily life are they particularly fond of random events, or do they find them annoying? There is something fundamentally silly about biologists teaching on Monday, Wednesday, and Friday that everything, including our sense of value and reason, is a mechanical product only of genetic chance and environmental necessity, with no purpose whatsoever, and then on Tuesday and Thursday trying to convince the public that they should love some accidental piece of this meaningless puzzle enough to fight and sacrifice to save it.

The absurdity is highlighted by the scientists' recognition that they have nothing to appeal to in their effort to rouse public support other than religiously based values that they themselves consider unfounded! Are they not temporarily living by the fruit of the tree whose taproot they have just cut? As Haught puts it,

> Such thinkers consider any vision of purpose in the universe to be archaic and illusory. . . . Indeed it is rare to find scientists, literati or philosophers publicly claiming that our universe has any point to it or that any transcendent purpose influences its evolution. But can this cosmic pessimism adequately nourish the vigorous environmental activism that many of these same thinkers, now hand in hand with members of the religious community, are calling for today?[13]

To call this a "quite ingenuous proposal," as Haught does, is to be kind. It also should be surprising (and flattering beyond merit) to members of the religious community that the scientists should assume that the majority of today's religious people will in fact be led by their beliefs to care about the environment, when to date that has not happened. It is indeed a paradox that people whose professed beliefs give them no good reason to be environmentalists are usually trying harder to save the environment than are people whose beliefs give them every good reason to be environmentalists! The scientists are implicitly calling for a religious reformation, not just a moral compass that magically functions in an amoral universe—to point the scientists in the direction of public funds to save the environment.

As Alfred North Whitehead observed,

> Many a scientist has patiently designed experiments for the purpose of substantiating his belief that animal operations are motivated by

no purposes. He has perhaps spent his spare time writing articles to prove that human beings are as other animals so that purpose is a category irrelevant for the explanation of their bodily activities, his own activities included. Scientists animated by the purpose of proving that they are purposeless constitute an interesting subject for study.[14]

We might add that religious persons animated by a belief in the Creator God, yet happily participating in the destruction of Creation, also constitute an interesting subject for study.

During the meeting in Washington, D.C., of the Joint Appeal, the void of purpose was frequently glossed over in discussions with the phrase "for our children." But of course if we are accidents then so are they, and the dilemma is not resolved by pushing it one generation forward. I recall that one woman was evidently so annoyed by the sentimentality of this constant and cloying invocation of "our children" that she took the microphone to say that she had no children, and was she to understand, therefore, that she had no reason to care about the future of God's Creation? I believe the woman was a reporter or photographer, not even an official participant, but I thought her intervention was on target. To read some biologists you would think that whoever does not manage to propel their genes into the next generation might as well never have lived!

Environmentalists and advocates of sustainable development really must face up to deep philosophical and religious questions about why their efforts ultimately make sense. Neither vague pantheistic sentimentality about Gaia, nor the ad hoc wishful invention of instincts like "biophilia" can withstand much philosophical criticism. But they are welcome first steps away from pure scientific materialism. I find the thinking of a minority of Christian thinkers influenced by Whitehead, such as John B. Cobb, Jr., John F. Haught, and Charles Birch, to offer a much more solid base than either scientific materialism or traditional theology for loving nature enough to fight to save it. Many other traditional religions share with Christianity a theology of Creation (not the same as the literalist sect doctrine of "scientific creationism"), so the theological basis for something like "biophilia" as a persuasive virtue rather than a mechanical instinct is widely affirmed. All traditional religions are enemies of the same modern idolatry—that accidental man, through economic growth based on science and technology, is the true creator, and that the natural world is just a pile of instrumental, accidental stuff to be used up in the arbitrary projects of one purposeless species. If we cannot assert a more coherent cosmology than that, then we might as well close the store and all go fishing— at least while the fish last.

For the above reasons I felt that it was absolutely necessary to include Part 7, on religion and ethics, in this book, in addition to the other more usual sections on economic theory, operational policy, national accounts, population, international trade, and the recent history of economic thought on sustainability. I put this topic last not because I think it least important—I think it is most important—but because I am least qualified to deal with it, and because in our society, where political correctness has come to include an antireligious attitude, it will likely be the most controversial part. As a strategy of building consensus it is probably good to keep the most controversial issues for last, even if they are ultimately the most important. But it would be quite dishonest not to bring them up at all.

Economic Theory and Sustainable Development

Introduction

Sustainability has had a hard time breaking into economic theory because the economics of the past fifty years has been overwhelmingly devoted to economic growth. The term "economic growth" has in practice meant growth in gross national product. All problems are to be solved, or at least ameliorated, by an ever growing GNP. It is the only magnitude in all of economics that is expected to grow forever—never to reach an economic limit at which the marginal costs of further growth become greater than the marginal benefits. In microeconomics every enterprise has an optimal scale beyond which it should not grow. But when we aggregate all microeconomic units into the macroeconomy, the notion of an optimal scale, beyond which further growth becomes antieconomic, disappears completely!

There are several reasons for this. First, all microeconomic activities are seen as parts of a larger whole, and it is the relationship to the larger whole that limits the scale of the part to some proper or optimal size. The macroeconomy is not seen as a part of anything larger—rather it *is* the whole. It can grow forever, and by so doing it removes the temporary constraints on each of its sectors that result from bottlenecks imposed by shortages in other complementary sectors of the economy. As long as the proportions are right, the total, and its parts, can grow forever. Each firm may still reach an optimal scale due to managerial limits, but the industry or sector can grow forever by adding new firms. Prices measure relative scarcity and guide us in keeping everything in the right proportion relative to everything else—but there is no recognition of any absolute scarcity limiting the scale of the macroeconomy.

The chapters of Part 1 are based on the preanalytic vision that the macroeconomy is not the whole, but is itself a subsystem of a larger finite and nongrowing ecosystem, and consequently that the macroeconomy too has an optimal scale. A necessary requirement for this optimal scale is that the economy's

27

throughput—the flow beginning with raw material inputs, followed by their conversion into commodities, and finally into waste outputs—be within the regenerative and absorptive capacities of the ecosystem. The whole idea of sustainable development is that the economic subsystem must not grow beyond the scale at which it can be permanently sustained or supported by the containing ecosystem.

There is much confusion about what, precisely, is supposed to grow as GNP grows. Many people speak of the "dematerialization of the economy" and the possibility that GNP can grow forever without encountering physical limits, because it is measured in value units rather than in physical units. Perhaps the best example of this is the development of computers—newer generations use less matter and energy to perform more complicated operations. The value of services increases, but the matter and energy required for those services diminishes. In this book such qualitative improvement in the state of the arts is referred to as "development"; increasing the number of computers, of whatever vintage, is referred to as "growth." GNP accounting does not distinguish growth from development —both lead to an increase in the GNP, an increase in the value of annual goods and services, and are counted as "economic growth." But conflating qualitative improvement and quantitative increase in the same value index leads to much confusion.

GNP will be looked at more closely in Part 3, on national accounts. For now it must at least be said that although GNP is not a simple physical magnitude, it is nevertheless, a value-based *index* of an aggregate of goods and services which *are* physical. Aggregation by prices into a value index does not annihilate physical dimensions. In fact, in calculating *real* GNP, economic statisticians go to great lengths to eliminate changes that are not due to increase in physical units of output. Value is $P \times Q$ and the price index, P, is held constant so that changes in value will reflect only changes in the quantity index, Q, which are physical. Even services represent the service of some*body* or some*thing* for some time period, and consequently have a physical dimension.

To the extent that "dematerialization" is just an extravagant term for increasing resource productivity (reducing the throughput intensity of service) then by all means we should push it as far as we can. Much excellent work is done by people who use the term in this restricted sense (at the Wuppertal Institute in Germany, for instance). But the notion that we can save the "growth forever" paradigm by dematerializing the economy, or "decoupling" it from resources, or substituting information for resources, is fantasy. We can surely eat lower on the food chain, but we cannot eat recipes!

But one really does not have to argue that point. We can simply distinguish growth (quantitative expansion) from development (qualitative improvement), and urge ourselves to develop as much as possible, while ceasing to grow, once the regenerative and absorptive capacities of the ecosystem are reached (sustainable development). Those who believe in dematerialization should have even less reason to oppose this policy than those who are worried about physical limits.

A word is in order about what I have omitted from Part 1, but might have included. The relation of economics and entropy is mentioned, but not discussed in detail. For this the reader is referred to the magisterial work of the late Nicholas Georgescu-Roegen, *The Entropy Law and the Economic Process.*[1] A summary of his contribution is provided in Chapter 13, but it will be helpful to briefly outline here Georgescu-Roegen's insights regarding entropy and economics.

The main thrust of Georgescu-Roegen's ideas can be summarized in his "entropy hourglass" analogy (see figure 1).

Figure 1. *Entropy hourglass (Georgescu-Roegen)*

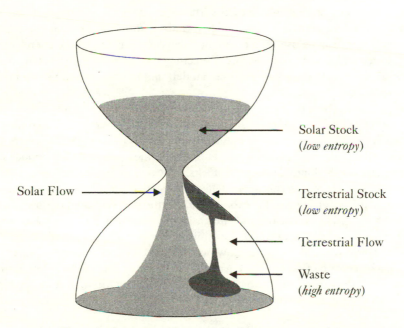

First, the hourglass is an isolated system: no sand enters, no sand exits.

Second, within the glass there is neither creation nor destruction of sand, the amount of sand in the glass is constant. This, of course, is the analog of the first law of thermodynamics—conservation of matter / energy.

Third, there is a continuing running-down of sand in the top chamber, and an accumulation of sand in the bottom chamber. Sand in the bottom chamber has used up its potential to fall and thereby do work, it is high-entropy or unavailable (used up) matter/energy. Sand in the top chamber still has potential to fall—it is low-entropy or available (still useful) matter/energy. This is the second law of thermodynamics: entropy (or "used-up-ness") increases in an isolated system. The hourglass analogy is particularly apt since entropy is time's arrow in the physical world.

The analogy can be extended by considering the sand in the upper chamber to be the stock of low-entropy energy in the sun. Solar energy arrives to earth as a flow whose amount is governed by the constricted middle of the hourglass, which limits the rate at which sand falls, the rate at which solar energy flows to earth. Suppose that over ancient geologic ages some of the falling sand had gotten stuck against the inner surface of the bottom chamber, but at the top of the bottom chamber, before it had fallen all the way. This becomes a terrestrial dowry of low-entropy matter/energy, a stock that we can use up at a rate of our own choosing. We use it by drilling holes into its surface through which the trapped sand can fall to the bottom of the lower chamber. This terrestrial source of low-entropy matter/energy can be used at a rate of our own choosing, unlike the energy of the sun, which arrives at a fixed flow rate. We cannot "mine" the sun to use tomorrow's sunlight today, but we can mine terrestrial deposits and, in a sense, use up tomorrow's petroleum today.

There is thus an important asymmetry between our two sources of low entropy. The solar source is stock-abundant, but flow-limited. The terrestrial source is stock-limited, but flow-abundant (temporarily). Peasant societies lived off the abundant solar flow; industrial societies have come to depend on enormous supplements from the limited terrestrial stocks.

Reversing this dependence will be an enormous evolutionary shift. Georgescu-Roegen argued that evolution has in the past consisted of slow adaptations of our "endosomatic organs" (heart, lungs, etc.), which run on solar energy. But the present path of evolution has shifted to rapid adaptations of our "exosomatic organs" (cars, airplanes, etc.), which depend on terrestrial low entropy. The uneven ownership of exosomatic organs and of the terrestrial stocks of low entropy from which they are made, compared to the egalitarian distribution of ownership of endosomatic capital, is for Georgescu-Roegen the root of social conflict in industrial societies.

One more thing. Unlike a real hourglass, this one cannot be turned upside down! Its central feature is what Georgescu-Roegen called the "metabolic flow," the entropic throughput of matter/energy by which the economy depends on its environment. This dependence is completely abstracted from in the neoclassical economist's starting point, the circular flow of exchange value.

Chapter 1

Moving to a Steady-State Economy

Sustainable development, I argue, necessarily means a radical shift from a growth economy and all it entails to a steady-state economy, certainly in the North, and eventually in the South as well. My first task has to be to elaborate the case for that theoretical and practical shift in worldview. What are the main theoretical and moral anomalies of the growth economy, and how are they resolved by the steady state? And what are the practical failures of the growth economy, viewed as forced first steps toward a steady state?

It is necessary to define what is meant by the terms "steady-state economy" (SSE) and "growth economy." Growth, as here used, refers to an increase in the physical scale of the matter/energy throughput that sustains the economic activities of production and consumption of commodities. In an SSE the aggregate throughput is constant, though its allocation among competing uses is free to vary in response to the market. Since there is of course no production and consumption of matter/energy itself in a physical sense, the throughput is really a process in which low-entropy raw materials are transformed into commodities and then, eventually, into high-entropy wastes. Throughput begins with depletion and ends with pollution. Growth is quantitative increase in the physical scale of throughput. Qualitative improvement in the use made of a given scale of throughput, resulting either from improved technical knowledge or from a deeper understanding of purpose, is called "development." An SSE therefore can develop, but cannot grow, just as the planet earth, of which it is a subsystem, can develop without growing.

The steady state is by no means static. There is continuous renewal by death and birth, depreciation and production, as well as qualitative improvement in the stocks of both people and artifacts. By this definition, strictly speaking, even the stocks of artifacts or people may occasionally grow temporarily as a result of technical progress that increases the durability and repairability (longevity) of artifacts. The same maintenance flow can support a larger stock if the stock becomes longer-lived. The stock may also decrease, however, if resource quality declines at a faster rate than increases in durability-enhancing technology.

The other crucial feature in the definition of an SSE is that the constant level of throughput must be ecologically sustainable for a long future for a population living at a standard or per capita resource use that is sufficient for a good life. Note that an SSE is not defined in terms of gross national product. It is not to be thought of as "zero growth in GNP."

Ecological sustainability of the throughput is not guaranteed by market forces. The market cannot by itself register the cost of its own increasing scale relative to the ecosystem. Market prices measure the scarcity of individual resources relative to each other. Prices do not measure the absolute scarcity of resources in general, of environmental low entropy. The best we can hope for from a perfect market is a Pareto-optimal allocation of resources (i.e., a situation in which no one can be made better off without making someone else worse off). Such an allocation can be achieved at any scale of resource throughput, including unsustainable scales, just as it can be achieved with any distribution of income, including unjust ones. The latter proposition is well known, the former less so, but equally true. Ecological criteria of sustainability, like ethical criteria of justice, are not served by markets. Markets singlemindedly aim to serve allocative efficiency. Optimal *allocation* is one thing; optimal *scale* is something else.

Economists are always preoccupied with maximizing something: profits, rent, present value, consumers' surplus, and so on. What is maximized in the SSE? Basically the maximand is life, measured in cumulative person-years ever to be lived at a standard of resource use sufficient for a good life. This certainly does not imply maximizing population growth, as advocated by Julian Simon (1981), because too many people simultaneously alive, especially high-consuming people, will be forced to consume ecological "capital" and thereby lower the carrying capacity of the environment and the cumulative total of future lives. Although the maximand is human lives, the SSE would go a long way toward maximizing cumulative life for all species by imposing the constraint of a constant throughput at a sustainable level, thereby halting the growing takeover of habitats of other species, as well as slowing the rate of drawdown of geological capital otherwise available to future generations.

I do not wish to put too fine a point on the notion that the steady state maximizes cumulative life over time for all species, but it certainly would do better in this regard than the present value-maximizing growth economy, which drives to extinction any valuable species whose biological growth rate is less than the expected rate of interest, as long as capture costs are not too high (Clark 1976).

Of course many deep issues are raised in this definition of the SSE that, in the interests of brevity, are only touched on here. The meanings of "sufficient for a good life" and 'sustainable for a long future" have to be left vague. But any economic system must give implicit answers to these dialectical questions, even when it refuses to face them explicitly. For example, the growth economy implicitly says that there is no such thing as sufficiency because more is always better, and that a twenty-year future is quite long enough if the discount rate is 10%. Many would prefer explicit vagueness to such implicit precision.

Moving from Growthmania to the Steady State in Thought: Theoretical and Moral Anomalies of the Growth Paradigm That Are Resolved by the Steady State

The growth economy runs into two kinds of fundamental limits: the biophysical and the ethicosocial. Although they are by no means totally independent, it is worthwhile to distinguish between them.

Biophysical Limits to Growth   The biophysical limits to growth arise from three interrelated conditions: finitude, entropy, and ecological interdependence. The economy, in its physical dimensions, is an open subsystem of our finite and closed ecosystem, which is both the supplier of its low-entropy raw materials and the recipient of its high-entropy wastes. The growth of the economic subsystem is limited by the fixed size of the host ecosystem, by its dependence on the ecosystem as a source of low-entropy inputs and as a sink for high-entropy wastes, and by the complex ecological connections that are more easily disrupted as the scale of the economic subsystem (the throughput) grows relative to the total ecosystem. Moreover, these three basic limits interact. Finitude would not be so limiting if everything could be recycled, but entropy prevents complete recycling. Entropy would not be so limiting if environmental sources and sinks were infinite, but both are finite. That both are finite, plus the entropy law, means that the ordered structures of the economic subsystem are maintained at the expense of creating a more-than-offsetting amount of disorder in the rest of the system. If it is largely the sun that pays the disorder costs, the entropic costs of throughput, as it is with traditional peasant economies, then we need not worry. But if these entropic costs (depletion and pollution) are mainly inflicted on the terrestrial environment, as in a modern industrial economy, then they interfere with complex ecological life-support services rendered to the economy by nature. The loss of these services should surely be counted as a cost of growth, to be weighed against benefits at the margin. But our national accounts emphatically do not do this.

Standard growth economics ignores finitude, entropy, and ecological interdependence because the concept of throughput is absent from its preanalytic vision, which is that of an isolated circular flow of exchange value (see figure 2, page 47), as can be verified by examining the first few chapters of any basic textbook

(Daly 1985; Georgescu-Roegen 1971). The physical dimension of commodities and factors is at best totally abstracted from (left out altogether) and at worst assumed to flow in a circle, just like exchange value. It is as if one were to study physiology solely in terms of the circulatory system without ever mentioning the digestive tract. The dependence of the organism on its environment would not be evident. The absence of the concept of throughput in the economists' vision means that the economy carries on no exchange with its environment. It is, by implication, a self-sustaining isolated system, a giant perpetual motion machine. The focus on exchange value in the macroeconomic circular flow also abstracts from use value and any idea of purpose other than maximization of the circular flow of exchange value.

But everyone, including economists, knows perfectly well that the economy takes in raw material from the environment and gives back waste. So why is this undisputed fact ignored in the circular flow paradigm? Economists are interested in scarcity. What is not scarce is abstracted from. Environmental sources and sinks were considered infinite relative to the demands of the economy, which was more or less the case during the formative years of economic theory. Therefore it was not an unreasonable abstraction. But it is highly unreasonable to continue omitting the concept of throughput after the scale of the economy has grown to the point where sources and sinks for the throughput are obviously scarce, even if this new absolute scarcity does not register in relative prices. The current practice of ad hoc introduction of "externalities" to take account of the effects of the growing scale of throughput that do not fit the circular flow model is akin to the use of "epicycles" to explain the departures of astronomical observations from the theoretical circular motion of heavenly bodies.

Nevertheless, many economists hang on to the infinite-resources assumption in one way or another, because otherwise they would have to admit that economic growth faces limits, and that is "unthinkable." The usual ploy is to appeal to the infinite possibilities of technology and resource substitution (ingenuity) as a dynamic force that can continuously outrun depletion and pollution. This counterargument is flawed in many respects. First, technology and infinite substitution mean only that one form of low-entropy matter/energy is substituted for another, within a finite and diminishing set of low-entropy sources. Such substitution is often very advantageous, but we never substitute high-entropy wastes for low-entropy resources in net terms. Second, the claim is frequently made that reproducible capital is a near-perfect substitute for resources. But this assumes that capital can be produced independently of resources, which is absurd. Furthermore, it flies in the teeth of the obvious complementarity of capital and resources in production. The capital stock is an agent for transforming the resource flow from raw material into a product (Georgescu-Roegen 1971). More capital does not substitute for less resources, except on a very restricted margin. You cannot make the same house by substituting more saws for less wood.

The growth advocates are left with one basic argument: resource and environmental limits have not halted growth in the past and therefore will not do so in the future. But such logic proves too much, namely, that nothing new can ever happen. A famous general survived a hundred battles without a scratch, and that was still true when he was blown up.

Earl Cook offered some insightful criticism of this faith in limitless ingenuity in one of his last articles (Cook 1982). The appeal of the limitless-ingenuity argument, he contended, lies not in the scientific grounding of its premises nor in the cogency of its logic but rather in the fact that

> the concept of limits to growth threatens vested interests and power structures; even worse, it threatens value structures in which lives have been invested. . . . Abandonment of belief in perpetual motion was a major step toward recognition of the true human condition. It is significant that "mainstream" economists never abandoned that belief and do not accept the relevance to the economic process of the Second Law of Thermodynamics; their position as high priests of the market economy would become untenable did they do so. [Cook 1982, p. 198]

Indeed it would. Therefore, much ingenuity is devoted to "proving" that ingenuity is unlimited. Julian Simon, George Gilder, Herman Kahn, and Ronald Reagan trumpeted this theme above all others. Every technical accomplishment, no matter how ultimately insignificant, is celebrated as one more victory in an infinite series of future victories of technology over nature. The Greeks called this hubris. The Hebrews were warned to "beware of saying in your heart, 'My own strength and the might of my own hand won this power for me' " (Deut. 8:17). But such wisdom is drowned out in the drumbeat of the see-no-evil "optimism" of growthmania. All the more necessary is it then to repeat Earl Cook's trenchant remark that "without the enormous amount of work done by nature in concentrating flows of energy and stocks of resources, human ingenuity would be onanistic. What does it matter that human ingenuity may be limitless, when matter and energy are governed by other rules than is information?" (Cook 1982, p. 194).

Ethicosocial Limits   Even when growth is, with enough ingenuity, still possible, ethicosocial limits may render it undesirable. Four ethicosocial propositions limiting the desirability of growth are briefly considered below.

1. *The desirability of growth financed by the drawdown of geological capital is limited by the cost imposed on future generations.* In standard economics the balancing of future against present costs and benefits is done by discounting. A time

discount rate is a numerical way of expressing the value judgment that beyond a certain point the future is not worth anything to presently living people. The higher the discount rate, the sooner that point is reached. The value of the future to future people does not count in the standard approach.

Perhaps a more discriminating, though less numerical, principle for balancing the present and the future would be that the basic needs of the present should always take precedence over the basic needs of the future but that the basic needs of the future should take precedence over the extravagant luxury of the present.

2. *The desirability of growth financed by takeover of habitat is limited by the extinction or reduction in number of sentient subhuman species whose habitat disappears.* Economic growth requires space for growing stocks of artifacts and people and for expanding sources of raw material and sinks for waste material. Other species also require space, their "place in the sun." The instrumental value of other species to us, the life-support services they provide, was touched on in the discussion of biophysical limits above. Another limit derives from the intrinsic value of other species, that is, counting them as sentient, though probably not self-conscious, beings which experience pleasure and pain and whose experienced "utility" should be counted positively in welfare economics, even though it does not give rise to maximizing market behavior.

The intrinsic value of subhuman species should exert some limit on habitat takeover in addition to the limit arising from instrumental value. But it is extremely difficult to say how much (Birch and Cobb 1981). Clarification of this limit is a major philosophical task, but if we wait for a definitive answer before imposing any limits on takeover, then the question will be rendered moot by extinctions which are now occurring at an extremely rapid rate relative to past ages (Ehrlich and Ehrlich 1981).

3. *The desirability of aggregate growth is limited by its self-canceling effects on welfare.* Keynes (1930) argued that absolute wants (those we feel independently of the condition of others) are not insatiable. Relative wants (those we feel only because their satisfaction makes us feel superior to others) are indeed insatiable, for, as Keynes put it, "The higher the general level, the higher still are they." Or, as J. S. Mill expressed it, "Men do not desire to be rich, but to be richer than other men." At the current margin of production in rich countries it is very likely that welfare increments (increments in well-being) are largely a function of changes in relative income (insofar as they depend on income at all). Since the struggle for relative shares is a zero-sum game, it is clear that aggregate growth cannot increase aggregate welfare. To the extent that welfare depends on relative position, growth is unable to increase welfare in the aggregate. It is subject to the same kind of self-canceling trap that we find in the arms race.

Because of this self-canceling effect of relative position, aggregate growth is less productive of human welfare than we heretofore thought. Consequently, other competing goals should rise relative to growth in the scale of social priorities (Abramowitz 1979). Future generations, subhuman species, commnity, and whatever else has been sacrificed in the name of growth should henceforth be sacrificed less simply because growth is less productive of general happiness than used to be the case when marginal income was dedicated mainly to the satisfaction of absolute rather than relative wants.

4. *The desirability of aggregate growth is limited by the corrosive effects on moral standards resulting from the very attitudes that foster growth, such as glorification of self-interest and a scientistic-technocratic worldview.* On the demand side of commodity markets, growth is stimulated by greed and acquisitiveness, intensified beyond the "natural" endowment from original sin by the multibillion-dollar advertising industry. On the supply side, technocratic scientism proclaims the possibility of limitless expansion and preaches a reductionistic, mechanistic philosophy which, in spite of its success as a research program, has serious shortcomings as a worldview. As a research program it very effectively furthers power and control, but as a worldview it leaves no room for purpose, much less for any distinction between good and bad purposes. "Anything goes" is a convenient moral slogan for the growth economy because it implies that anything also sells. To the extent that growth has a well-defined purpose, then it is limited by the satisfaction of that purpose. Expanding power and shrinking purpose lead to uncontrolled growth for its own sake, which is wrecking the moral and social order just as surely as it is wrecking the ecological order (Hirsch 1976).

The situation of economic thought today can be summarized by a somewhat farfetched but apt analogy. Neoclassical economics, like classical physics, is relevant to a special case that assumes that we are far from limits—far from the limiting speed of light or the limiting smallness of an elementary particle in physics—and far from the biophysical limits of the earth's carrying capacity and the ethicosocial limits of satiety in economics. Just as in physics, so in economics: the classical theories do not work well in regions close to limits. A more general theory is needed to embrace both normal and limiting cases. In economics this need becomes greater with time because the ethic of growth itself guarantees that the close-to-the-limits case becomes more and more the norm. The nearer the economy is to limits, the less can we accept the practical judgment most economists make, namely, that "a change in economic welfare implies a change in total welfare in the same direction if not in the same degree" (Abramowitz 1979). Rather, we must learn to define and explicitly count the other component of total welfare that growth inhibits and erodes when it presses against limits.

Moving from Growthmania to the Steady State in Practice:
Failures of Growth as Forced First Steps
Toward a Steady-State Economy

No doubt the biggest growth failure is the continuing arms race, where growth has led to less security rather than more and has raised the stakes from loss of individual lives to loss of life itself in wholesale ecocide. Excessive population growth, toxic wastes, acid rain, climate modification, devastation of rain forests, and the loss of ecosystem services resulting from these aggressions against the environment represent case studies in growth failure. Seeing them as first steps toward a steady-state economy requires the conscious willing of a hopeful attitude.

All the growth failures mentioned above are failures of the growth economy to respect the biophysical limits of its host. I would like also to consider some symptoms of growthmania within the economy itself. Three examples will be considered: money fetishism and the paper economy, faulty national accounts and the treachery of quantified success indexes, and the ambivalent "information economy."

Money Fetishism and the Paper Economy Money fetishism is a particular case of what Alfred North Whitehead called "the fallacy of misplaced concreteness," which consists in reasoning at one level of abstraction but applying the conclusions of that reasoning to a different level of abstraction. It argues that, since abstract exchange value flows in a circle, so do the physical commodities constituting real GNP. Or, since money in the bank can grow forever at compound interest, so can real wealth, and so can welfare. Whatever is true for the abstract symbol of wealth is assumed to hold for concrete wealth itself.

Money fetishism is alive and well in a world in which banks in wealthy countries make loans to poor countries and then, when the debtor countries cannot make the repayment, simply make new loans to enable the payment of interest on old loans, thereby avoiding taking a loss on a bad debt. Using new loans to pay interest on old loans is worse than a Ponzi scheme, but the exponential snowballing of debt is expected to be offset by a snowballing of real growth in debtor countries. The international debt impasse is a clear symptom of the basic disease of growthmania. Too many accumulations of money are seeking ways to grow exponentially in a world in which the physical scale of the economy is already so large relative to the ecosystem that there is not much room left for growth of anything that has a physical dimension.

Marx, and Aristotle before him, pointed out that the danger of money fetishism arises as a society progressively shifts its focus from use value to exchange value, under the pressure of increasingly complex division of labor and exchange. The sequence is sketched below in four steps, using Marx's shorthand notation for labels.

1. *C-C'*. One commodity (*C*) is directly traded for a different commodity (*C'*). The exchange values of the two commodities are by definition equal, but each trader gains an increased use value. This is simple *barter*. No money exists, so there can be no money fetishism.

2. *C-M-C'*. *Simple commodity circulation* begins and ends with a use value embodied in a commodity. Money (*M*) is merely a convenient medium of exchange. The object of exchange remains the acquisition of an increased use value. *C'* represents a greater use value to the trader, but *C'* is still a use value, limited by its specific use or purpose. One has, say, a greater need for a hammer than a knife but has no need for two hammers, much less for fifty. The incentive to accumulate use values is very limited.

3. *M-C-M'*. As simple commodity circulation gave way to *capitalist circulation*, the sequence shifted. It now begins with money capital and ends with money capital. The commodity or use value is now an intermediary step in bringing about the expansion of exchange value by some amount of profit, $\Delta M = M' - M$. Exchange value has no specific use or physical dimension to impose concrete limits. One dollar of exchange value is not as good as two, and fifty dollars is better yet, and a million is much better, etc. Unlike concrete use values, which spoil or deteriorate when hoarded, abstract exchange value can accumulate indefinitely without spoilage or storage costs. In fact, exchange value can grow by itself at compound interest. But as Frederick Soddy (Daly 1980) pointed out, "You cannot permanently pit an absurd human convention [compound interest] against a law of nature [entropic decay]."[1] "Permanently," however, is not the same as "in the meantime," during which we have, at the micro level, bypassed the absurdity of accumulating use values by accumulating exchange value and holding it as a lien against future use values. But unless future use value, or real wealth, has grown as fast as accumulations of exchange value have grown, then at the end of some time period there will be a devaluation of exchange value by inflation or some other form of debt repudiation. At the macro level limits will reassert themselves, even when ignored at the micro level, where the quest for exchange value accumulation has become the driving force.

4. *M-M'*. We can extend Marx's stages one more step to the *paper economy*, in which, for many transactions, concrete commodities "disappear" even as an intermediary step in the expansion of exchange value. Manipulations of symbols according to arbitrary and changing tax rules, accounting conventions, depreciation, mergers, public relations imagery, advertising, litigation, and so on, all result in a positive ΔM for some, but no increase in social wealth, and hence an equal negative ΔM for others. Such "paper entrepreneurialism" and "rent-seeking" activities seem to be absorbing more and more business talent. Echoes of Frederick Soddy are audi-

ble in the statement of Robert Reich (1983, p. 153) that "the set of symbols developed to represent real assets has lost the link with any actual productive activity. Finance has progressively evolved into a sector all its own, only loosely connected to industry." Unlike Soddy, however, Reich does not appreciate the role played by biophysical limits in redirecting efforts from manipulating resistant matter and energy toward manipulating pliant symbols. He thinks that, as more flexible and information-intensive production processes replace traditional mass production, somehow financial symbols and physical realities will again become congruent. But it may be that as physical resources become harder to acquire, as evidenced by falling energy rates of return on investment (Cleveland et al. 1984), the incentive to bypass the physical world by moving from M-C-M' to M-M' becomes ever greater. We may then keep growing on paper, but not in reality. This illusion is fostered by our national accounting conventions. It could be that we are moving toward a nongrowing economy a bit faster than we think. If the cost of toxic waste dumps were subtracted from the value product of the chemical industry, we might discover that we have already attained zero growth in value from that sector of the economy.

Faulty National Accounting and the Treachery
of Quantified Success Indicators
Our national accounts are designed in such a way that they cannot reflect the costs of growth, except by perversely counting the resulting defensive expenditures as further growth. It is by now a commonplace to point out that GNP does not reveal whether we are living off income or capital, off interest or principal. Depletion of fossil fuels, minerals, forests, and soils is capital consumption, yet such unsustainable consumption is treated no differently from sustainable yield production (true income) in GNP. But not only do we decumulate positive capital (wealth), we also accumulate negative capital (illth) in the form of toxic-waste deposits and nuclear dumps. To speak so insouciantly of "economic growth" whenever produced goods accumulate, when at the same time natural wealth is being diminished and man-made illth is increasing represents, to say the least, an enormous prejudgment about the relative size of these changes (Hueting 1980). Only on the assumption that environmental sources and sinks are infinite does such a procedure make sense.

Another problem with national accounts is that they do not reflect the "informal" or "underground" economy. Estimates of the size of the underground economy in the United States range from around 4% to around 30% of GNP, depending on the technique of estimation (Tanzi 1983). The underground economy has apparently grown in recent times, probably as a result of higher taxes, growing unemployment, and frustration with the increasing complexity and arbitrariness of the paper economy. Like household production, of which they are extensions, none of these informal productive activities are registered in GNP. Their growth represents an adaptation to the failure of traditional economic growth to provide employment and security. As an adaptation to growth failure in the GNP sector, the underground economy may represent a forced first step toward an SSE. But not everything about the underground economy is good. Many of its activities (drugs, prostitution) are illegal, and much of its basic motivation is tax evasion, although in today's world there may well be some noble reasons for not paying taxes.

The act of measurement always involves some interaction and interference with the reality being measured. This generalized Heisenberg principle is especially relevant in economics, where the measurement of a success index on which rewards are based, or taxes calculated, nearly always has perverse repercussions on the reality being measured. Consider, for example, the case of management by quantified objectives applied to a tuberculosis hospital, as related to me by a physician. It is well known that TB patients cough less as they get better. So the number of coughs per day was taken as a quantitative measure of the patient's improvement. Small microphones were attached to the patients' beds, and their coughs were duly recorded and tabulated. The staff quickly perceived that they were being evaluated in inverse proportion to the number of times their patients coughed. Coughing steadily declined as doses of codeine were more frequently prescribed. Relaxed patients cough less. Unfortunately the patients got worse, precisely because they were not coughing up and spitting out the congestion. The cough index was abandoned.

The cough index totally subverted the activity it was designed to measure because people served the abstract quantitative index instead of the concrete qualitative goal of health. Perversities induced by quantitative goal setting are pervasive in the literature on Soviet planning: set the production quota for cloth in linear feet, and the bolt gets narrower; set it in square feet, and the cloth gets thinner; set it by weight, and it gets too thick. But one need not go as far away as the Soviet Union to find examples. The phenomenon is ubiquitous. In universities a professor is rewarded according to number of publications. Consequently the length of articles is becoming shorter as we approach the minimum publishable unit of research. At the same time the frequency of coauthors has increased. More and more people are collaborating on shorter and shorter papers. What is being maximized is not discovery and dissemination of coherent knowledge but the number of publications on which one's name appears.

The purpose of these examples of the treachery of quantified success indexes is to suggest that, like them, GNP is not only a passive mismeasure but also an actively distorting influence on the very reality that it aims only to reflect. GNP is an index of throughput, not welfare. Throughput is positively correlated with welfare in a world of infinite sources and sinks, but in a finite world with fully employed carrying capacity, throughput is a *cost*. To design national policies to maximize GNP is just not smart. It is practically equivalent to maximizing depletion and pollution.

The usual reply to these well-known criticisms of GNP is, "So it's not perfect, but it's all we have. What would you put in its place?" It is assumed that we *must* have some numerical index. But why? Might we not be better off without the GNP statistic, even with nothing to "put in its place"? Were not the TB patients better off without the cough index, when physicians and administrators had to rely on "soft" qualitative judgment? The world before 1940 got along well enough without calculating GNP. Perhaps we could come up with a better system of national accounts, but abandoning GNP need not be postponed until then. Politically we are not likely to abandon the GNP statistic any time soon. But in the meantime we can start thinking of it as "gross national cost."

The Ambivalent "Information Economy"   The much-touted "information economy" is often presented as a strategy for escaping biophysical limits. Its modern devotees proclaim that "whereas matter and energy decay according to the laws of entropy . . . information is . . . immortal." And, further, "The universe itself is made of information—matter and energy are only simple forms of it" (Turner 1984). Such half-truths forget that information does not exist apart from physical brains, books, and computers, and, further, that brains require the support of bodies, books require library buildings, computers run on electricity, etc. At worst the information economy is seen as a computer-based explosion of the symbol manipulations of the paper economy. More occult powers are attributed to information and its handler, the computer, by the silicon gnostics of today than any primitive shaman ever dared claim for his favorite talisman. And this in spite of the enormous legitimate importance of the computer, which needs no exaggeration.

Other notions of the information economy are by no means nonsensical. When the term refers to qualitative improvements in products to make them more serviceable, longer-lasting, more repairable, and better-looking (Hawken 1983), then we have what was earlier referred to as "development." To think of qualitative improvement as the embodiment of more information in a product is not unreasonable.

But the best question to ask about the information economy is that posed by T. S. Eliot in "Choruses from 'The Rock' ":

Where is the wisdom we have lost in knowledge?
Where is the knowledge we have lost in information?

Why stop with an information economy? Why not a knowledge economy? Why not a wisdom economy?

Knowledge is structured, organized information rendered intelligible and understandable. It is hard to imagine embodying a bit of isolated information (in the sense of communications theory) in a product. What is required for qualitative improvement of products is knowledge—an understanding of the purpose of the item, the nature of the materials, and the alternative designs that are permitted within the restrictions of purpose and nature of the materials. Probably many writers on the subject use the term "information" synonymously with "knowledge," and what they have in mind is really already a "knowledge economy." The important step is to go to a "wisdom economy."

Wisdom involves a knowledge of techniques plus an understanding of purposes and their relative importance, along with an appreciation of the limits to which technique and purpose are subject. To distinguish a real limit from a temporary bottleneck, and a fundamental purpose from a velleity, requires wise judgment. Growthmania cannot be checked without wise judgment. Since events are forcing us to think in terms of an information economy, it is perhaps not too much to hope that we will follow that thrust all the way to a wisdom economy, one design feature of which, I submit, will be that of a dynamic steady state.

The main characteristics of such a wisdom economy were adumbrated by Earl Cook (1982) in his list of nine "Beliefs of a Neomalthusian," and I will conclude by listing them:

1. "Materials and energy balances constrain production."

2. "Affluence has been a much more fecund mother of invention than has necessity." That is, science and technology require an economic surplus to support them, and a few extra but poor geniuses provided by rapid population growth will not help.

3. "Real wealth is by technology out of nature," or, as William Petty would have said, technology may be the father of wealth, but nature is the mother.

4. "The appropriate human objective is the maximization of psychic income by conversion of natural resources to useful commodities and by the use of those commodities as efficiently as possible," and "the appropriate measure of efficiency in the conversion of resources to psychic income is the human life-hour, with the calculus extended to the yet unborn."

5. "Physical laws are not subject to repeal by men," and of all the laws of economics the law of diminishing returns is closest to a physical law.

6. "The industrial revolution can be defined as that period of human history when basic resources, especially nonhuman energy, grew cheaper and more abundant."

7. "The industrial revolution so defined is ending."

8. "There are compelling reasons to expect natural resources to become more expensive."

43

9. "Resource problems vary so much from country to country that careless geographic and commodity aggregation may confuse rather than clarify." That is, "it serves no useful purpose to combine the biomass of Amazonia with that of the Sahel to calculate a per capita availability of firewood."

Earl Cook would have been the last person to offer these nine points as a complete blueprint for a wisdom economy. But I think that he got us off to a good start.

Chapter 2

Elements of Environmental Macroeconomics

I have argued in Chapter 1 that the growth economy is an unsustainable goal at the present historical moment, and that we need to shift our vision and practice to a different model—the sustainable or steady-state economy. But economists are a stubborn and resourceful lot, and economics as a discipline provides an array of arguments and techniques that can be used to avoid a rethinking of the fundamental model.

In recent years environmental concerns have been taken up by traditional economists, and their general theme of "internalization of externalities" certainly has its place. However, as a general solution to environmental problems it is proving inadequate. The increasing frequency of appeal to externalities is the clearest possible evidence that more and more relevant facts do not fit within the existing theoretical framework. When increasingly vital facts, including the very capacity of the earth to support life, have to be treated as "externalities," then it is past time to change the basic framework of our thinking so that we can treat these critical issues internally and centrally. In this chapter we will take a look at some of the environmentally relevant contributions of traditional economics (mainly from microeconomics), as well as discuss the traditional absence of any environmental contribution from macroeconomics. Steps toward an environmental macroeconomics are suggested.

Environmental economics, as it is taught in universities and practiced in government agencies and development banks, is overwhelmingly *micro*economics. The theoretical focus is on prices, and the big issue is how to internalize external environmental costs to arrive at prices that reflect full social marginal opportunity costs. Once prices are right, the environmental problem is "solved"— there is no macroeconomic dimension. Cost-benefit analysis in its various permutations is the major tool for estimating full-cost prices. So in practice as well as theory we remain within the domain of microeconomics. There are, of course, good reasons for environmental economics to be closely tied to microeconomics and it is not my intention to argue against that connection. Rather, I ask if there is not a neglected connection between the environment and macroeconomics.

A search through the indexes of three leading textbooks in macroeconomics[1] reveals no entries under any of the following subjects: *environment, natural resources, pollution, depletion.* One of the three does have an entry under "resources," but the discussion refers only to labor and capital, which, along with efficiency, are listed as the causes of growth in GNP. Natural resources are not mentioned. Evidently GNP growth is thought to be independent of natural resources. Is it really the case, as prominent textbook writers seem to think, that macroeconomics has nothing to do with the environment? What historically has impeded the development of an environmental macroeconomics? If there is no such thing as environmental macroeconomics, should there be? Do parts of it already exist? What needs to be added? What policy implications are visible?[2]

The reason that environmental macroeconomics is an empty box lies in what Thomas Kuhn calls a paradigm, and what Joseph Schumpeter more descriptively called a preanalytic vision (Schumpeter 1954). As Schumpeter emphasized, analysis has to start somewhere—there has to be something to analyze. That something is given by a preanalytic cognitive act that Schumpeter called "Vision." One might say that such a vision is what the "right brain" supplies to the "left brain" for analysis. Whatever is omitted from the preanalytic vision cannot be recaptured by subsequent analysis. Schumpeter is worth quoting at length on this point:

> In practice we all start our own research from the work of our predecessors, that is, we hardly ever start from scratch. But suppose we did start from scratch, what are the steps we should have to take? Obviously, in order to be able to posit to ourselves any problems at all, we should first have to visualize a distinct set of coherent phenomena as a worthwhile object of our analytic effort. In other words, analytic effort is of necessity preceded by a preanalytic cognitive act that supplies the raw material for the analytic effort. In this book, this preanalytic cognitive act will be called Vision. It is interesting to note that vision of this kind not only must precede historically the emergence of analytic effort in any field, but also may reenter the history of every established science each time somebody teaches us to *see* things in a light of which the source is not to be found in the facts, methods, and results of the pre-existing state of the science. [p. 41]

The vision of modern economics in general, and especially of macroeconomics, is the familiar circular flow diagram (see figure 2). The macroeconomy

Figure 2. *The economy as an isolated system*

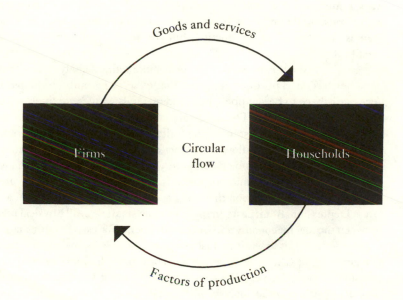
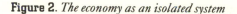

is seen as an isolated system (i.e., as having no exchanges of matter or energy with its environment) in which exchange value circulates between firms and households in a closed loop. What is "flowing in a circle" is variously referred to as production or consumption, but these have physical dimensions. The circular flow does not refer to materials recycling, which in any case could not be a completely closed loop and of course would require energy, which cannot be recycled at all. What is truly flowing in a circle can only be abstract exchange value—exchange value abstracted from the physical dimensions of the goods and factors that are being exchanged. Since an isolated system of abstract exchange value flowing in a circle has no dependence on an environment, there can be no problem of natural resource depletion, nor environmental pollution, nor any dependence of the macroeconomy on natural services, or indeed on anything at all outside itself (Daly 1985). Since analysis cannot supply what the preanalytic vision omits, it is only to be expected that macroeconomics texts would be silent on environment, natural resources, depletion and pollution.

Things are no better when we turn to the advanced chapters at the end of most macroeconomics texts, where the topic is growth theory. True to the preanalytic vision the aggregate production is written as $Y = f(K,L)$, i.e., output is a function of capital and labor stocks. Resource flows (R) do not even enter! Nor is any waste output flow noted. And if occasionally R is stuck in the function along with K and L it makes little difference since the production function is almost always a multiplicative form, such as Cobb-Douglas, in which R can approach zero with Y constant if only we increase K or L in a compensatory fashion. Resources are seen as "necessary" for production, but the amount required can be as little as one likes!

What is needed is not ever more refined analysis of a faulty vision, but a new vision. This does not mean that everything built on the old vision will necessarily have to be scrapped, but fundamental changes are likely when the pre-analytic vision is altered. The necessary change in vision is to picture the macroeconomy as an open subsystem of the finite natural ecosystem (environment), and not as an isolated circular flow of abstract exchange value, unconstrained by mass balance, entropy and finitude (see figure 3). The circular flow of exchange value is a useful abstraction for some purposes. It highlights issues of aggregate demand, unemployment, and inflation that were of interest to Keynes in his analysis of the Great Depression. But it casts an impenetrable shadow on all physical relationships between the macroeconomy and the environment. For Keynes, this shadow was not very important, but for us it is. Just as, for Keynes, Say's law and the impossibility of a general glut cast an impenetrable shadow over the problem of the Great Depression, so now the very Keynesian categories that were revolutionary in their time are obstructing the analysis of the major problem of our time—namely, what is the proper scale of the macroeconomy relative to the ecosystem?

Once the macroeconomy is seen as an open subsystem, rather than an isolated system, the issue of its relation to its parent system (the environment) cannot be avoided. The obvious question is, How big should the subsystem be relative to the overall system?

The Environmental Macroeconomics of Optimal Scale

Just as the micro unit of the economy (firm or household) operates as part of a larger system (the aggregate or macroeconomy), so the aggregate economy is likewise a part of a larger system, the natural ecosystem. The macroeconomy is an open subsystem of the ecosystem and is totally dependent upon it, both as a source for inputs of low-entropy matter / energy and as a sink for outputs of high-entropy matter / energy. *The physical exchanges crossing the boundary between the total ecological system and the economic subsystem constitute the subject matter of environmental macroeconomics.* These flows are considered in terms of their scale or total volume relative to the ecosystem, not in terms of the price of one component of the total flow relative to another. Just as standard macroeconomics focuses on the volume of transactions rather than the relative prices of different items traded, so environmental macroeconomics focuses on the volume of exchanges that cross the boundary between sys-

Figure 3. *The economy as an open subsystem of the ecosystem*

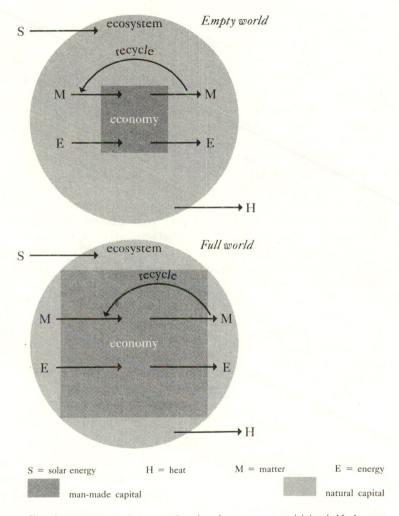

S = solar energy   H = heat   M = matter   E = energy

man-made capital   natural capital

Since the ecosystem remains constant in scale as the economy grows, it is inevitable that over time the economy becomes larger *relative* to the containing ecosystem. This transition from an "empty world" to a "full world" is depicted in figure 3. The point is that the evolution of the human economy has passed from an era in which man-made capital was the limiting factor in economic development to an era in which remaining natural capital is the limiting factor. This theme is developed in Part 2.

tem and subsystem, rather than the pricing and allocation of each part of the total flow within the human economy or even within the nonhuman part of the ecosystem.

The term "scale" is shorthand for "the physical scale or size of the human presence in the ecosystem, as measured by population times per capita resource use." Optimal *allocation* of a given scale of resource flow within the economy is one thing (a microeconomic problem). Optimal *scale* of the whole economy relative to the ecosystem is an entirely different problem (a macro-macro problem). The micro allocation problem is analagous to allocating optimally a given amount of weight in a boat. But once the best relative location of weight has been determined, there is still the question of the absolute amount of weight the boat should carry. This absolute optimal scale of load is recognized in the maritime institution of the Plimsoll line. When the watermark hits the Plimsoll line the boat is full, it has reached its safe *carrying capacity*. Of course, if the weight is badly allocated, the water line will touch the Plimsoll mark sooner. But eventually as the absolute load is increased, the watermark will reach the Plimsoll line even for a boat whose load is optimally allocated. Optimally loaded boats will still sink under too much weight— even though they may sink optimally! It should be clear that optimal allocation and optimal scale are quite distinct problems. The major task of environmental macroeconomics is to design an economic institution analogous to the Plimsoll mark—to keep the weight, the absolute scale, of the economy from sinking our biospheric ark.[3]

The market, of course, functions only within the economic subsystem, where it does only one thing: it solves the allocation problem by providing the necessary information and incentive. It does that one thing very well. What it does not do is solve the problems of optimal scale and of optimal distribution. The market's inability to solve the problem of just distribution is widely recognized, but its similar inability to solve the problem of optimal or even sustainable scale is not as widely appreciated.[4]

An example of the confusion that can result from the nonrecognition of the independence of the scale issue from the question of allocation is provided by the following dilemma.[5] Which puts more pressure on the environment, a high or a low discount rate? The usual answer is that a high discount rate is worse for the environment because it speeds the rate of depletion of nonrenewable resources and shortens the turnover and fallow periods in the exploitation of renewables. It shifts the allocation of capital and labor towards projects that exploit natural resources more intensively but it restricts the total number of projects undertaken. A low discount rate will permit more projects to be undertaken even while encouraging less intensive resource use for each project. The allocation effect of a high discount rate is to increase throughput, but the scale effect is to lower throughput. Which effect is stronger is hard to say, although one suspects that over the long run the scale effect will dominate. The resolution to the dilemma is to recognize that two independent policy goals require two independent policy instruments. We cannot serve both optimal scale and optimal allocation with the single policy instrument of the discount rate (Tinbergen 1952). The discount rate should be allowed to solve the allocation problem, within the confines of a solution to the scale problem provided by a presently nonexistent policy instrument, which we may for now call an "economic Plimsoll line," that limits the scale of the throughput.

Economists have recognized the independence of the goals of efficient allocation and just distribution and are in general agreement that it is better to let prices serve efficiency, and to serve equity with income redistribution policies. Proper scale is a third, independent policy goal and requires a third policy instrument. This latter point has not yet been accepted by economists, but its logic is parallel to the logic underlying the separation of allocation and distribution. In pricing factors of production and distributing profits the market does, of course, influence the distribution of income. Providing incentive requires some ability to alter the distribution of income in the interests of efficiency. The point is that the market's criterion for distributing income is to provide an incentive for efficient allocation, not to attain justice. And in any case, historical conditions of property ownership are major determinants of income distribution and have little to do with either efficiency or justice. These two values can conflict, and the market does not automatically resolve this conflict. The point to be added is that there are not just two, but three, values in conflict: allocation (efficiency), distribution (justice), and scale (sustainability).

Microeconomics has not discovered in the price system any built-in tendency to grow only up to the scale of aggregate resource use that is optimal (or even merely sustainable) in its demands on the biosphere. *Optimal scale, like distributive justice, full employment, or price level stability, is a macroeconomic goal.* And it is a goal that is likely to conflict with the other macroeconomic goals. The traditional solution to unemployment is growth in production, which means a larger scale. Frequently the solution to inflation is also thought to be growth in real output, and a larger scale. And most of all, the issue of distributive justice is "finessed" by the claim that aggregate growth will do more for the poor than redistributive measures. Conventional macroeconomic goals tend to conflict, and certainly optimal scale will conflict with any goal that requires further growth once the optimum has been reached.

Scale has a maximum limit defined either by the regenerative or absorptive capacity of the ecosystem, whichever is less. However, the maximum scale is not likely to be the optimal scale. Two concepts of optimal scale can be distinguished, both formalisms at this stage, but important for clarity.

1. *The anthropocentric optimum.* The rule is to expand scale (i.e., grow) to the point at which the marginal benefit to human beings of additional man-made physical capital is just equal to the marginal cost to human beings of sac-

rificed natural capital. All nonhuman species and their habitats are valued only in-strumentally according to their capacity to satisfy human wants. Their intrinsic value (capacity to enjoy their own lives) is assumed to be zero.

2. *The biocentric optimum.* Other species and their habitats are pre-served beyond the point necessary to avoid ecological collapse or cumulative de-cline, and beyond the point of maximum instrumental convenience, out of a recog-nition that other species have intrinsic value independent of their instrumental value to human beings. The biocentric optimal scale of the human niche would therefore be smaller than the anthropocentric optimum.

The definition of sustainable development does not specify which concept of optimum scale to use. It is consistent with any scale that is not above the maximum. Sustainability is probably the characteristic of optimal scale on which there is most consensus. It is a necessary, but not sufficient, condition for optimal scale.

Policy Outruns Theory:
Tradeable Permits as a Forced Separation
of Allocation, Distribution, and Scale

The tradeable pollution permits scheme, explained below, is a beautiful example of the independence and proper relationship among allocation, distribution, and scale. Consider step by step what this policy requires in practice.

First we must create a limited number of rights to pollute. The ag-gregate or total amount of pollution corresponding to these rights is determined to be within the absorptive capacity of the airshed or watershed in question. That is to say, the scale impact is limited to a level judged to be ecologically sustainable—an economic Plimsoll line must be drawn as the very first step. Far from ignoring scale, this policy requires that the issue of sustainable or optimal scale be settled at the beginning. It may be done on the basis of a carrying capacity estimate, a safe minimum standards estimate, or a cost-benefit study, but some limit to total pollu-tion must be set.

Second, the limited number of rights corresponding to the chosen scale must be distributed initially to different people. Perhaps equally to citizens, or to firms, or perhaps collectively as public property then to be auctioned or sold by the government to individuals. But there must be an initial distribution before there can be any allocation and reallocation by trading.

Only in third place, after having made social decisions regarding an ecologically sustainable scale and an ethically just distribution, are we in a position to allow reallocation among individuals through markets in the interests of efficiency. A separation between allocation and scale requires that the total quantity of permits be fixed, but that the price at which the permits trade be free to vary. If the total quantity were determined by a willingness-to-pay study that also gave a shadow price as well as an aggregate quantity, then the neoclassical economist who wants to avoid separating allocation and scale must insist that trading take place at the calculated shadow price. Otherwise there will be a separation between allocation and scale. In practice, the price is always free to vary, clearly indicating that the pragmatic, operational solution has been to separate allocation and scale.

It is clear that scale is not determined by prices, but by a social decision reflecting ecological limits. Distribution is not determined by prices, but by a social decision reflecting a just distribution of the newly created assets. Subject to these social decisions, individualistic trading in the market is then able to allocate the scarce rights efficiently. For some reason economists have analyzed the tradeable pollution permits scheme almost entirely in relation to the command and control allocative schemes. They have indeed shown it to be superior to command and control in terms of allocative efficiency. But with all the emphasis on allocation the critical role of scale went unnoticed, and the role of distribution, while certainly noticed, was not sufficiently emphasized. Tradeable permits have been considered the individualistic "free market" solution, without emphasizing that this market is free only after having been firmly and collectively fixed within scale and distributive limits.

The greens (environmentalists), too, have shown considerable misunderstanding of this scheme, condemning it as "giving away licenses to pollute." The point is that this scheme limits the total scale of pollution, need not give away anything but can sell the rights for public revenue, yet allows reallocation among individuals in the interest of efficiency. Some greens complain that under this scheme the rich have an advantage. The rich *always* have an advantage, but does this scheme increase or decrease the preexisting advantage of the rich? It could do either, it all depends on the initial distribution of ownership of the new assets, and not on the fact that they are tradeable.

The usual way for economists to deal with the scale issue, when forced to think about it at all, is to try to subsume it under allocation, claiming that if we just get prices right there will be no scale problem. Of course, when the scale of the economy was small, then the right price for nonscarce environmental services was zero. Economists reason that when these services become scarce it is simply necessary to find the right positive price and everything will be efficiently allocated. It is true that pricing newly scarce resources is necessary to solve the allocation problem. The mistake is to assume that it therefore solves the scale problem as well. A small scale with a lot of zero prices for environmental services is quite a different state of the world from a large scale with a lot of positive prices for those previously free environmental services. In both cases "prices are right" and allocation is efficient. But it still makes sense to ask whether people are better off in the first or second case. The difference is a matter of scale.

The neoclassical economist would reply that such a question is easily answered. If the larger scale exists, it was obviously chosen by individuals in numerous micro decisions in which they were willing to pay the marginal environmental costs of growing to the larger scale because they judged them to be less than the marginal benefits. Of course, the individuals' judgment could be biased by "externalities," but "right prices" means that these have all been internalized in prices.

The price of a commodity reflects the value of the next-best alternative commodity to which the factors embodied in the commodity in question could have been allocated. In practice, nature is excluded from the world of commodities whose opportunity costs are measured by market prices. Prices do not balance marginal ecosystem services sacrificed against marginal social benefit of a larger population or greater per capita resource use (i.e., larger scale). This balance requires calculation and imposition of shadow prices that value the *in natura* use of all resources in terms commensurate with the customary pecuniary exchange valuation of commodities. This view requires heroic assumptions about our knowledge of the external costs resulting from ecosystem disruption, and how these costs are imputed to the micro decisions that gave rise to them. The ecosystem is under no obligation to respond to increasing stress by sacrificing its services in order of their increasing importance to us, conveniently giving economists a "well-behaved" marginal cost function. Discontinuities, thresholds, and complex webs of interdependence make a mockery of the idea that we can nicely balance smoothly increasing ecosystem costs with the diminishing marginal utility of production at the macro level. The notion that systemic vital costs of collective behavior (greenhouse effect, ozone depletion) are best dealt with by pretending that every individual could and should, on the basis of assumed perfect knowledge, decide his or her own willingness to pay to avoid the loss of such services, is not an idea that comes easily to the unprejudiced mind. It requires years of indoctrination in "methodological individualism."

The distribution and scale questions, like the allocation question, are *economic* in that they involve costs and benefits. But the dimensions in which costs and benefits are defined are different in the three cases. Allocative prices are not even relevant to estimating the costs and benefits of scale expansion, just as they are not relevant to estimating the costs and benefits of a step towards a more equal distribution of income or wealth. We have three independent optima requiring three independent policy instruments. In each case an optimum is formally defined by the equality of rising costs and falling benefits at the margin. But the definitions and measures of costs and benefits in each of the three cases are different because the problems being solved are different. The relative price of shoes and bicycles is instrumental in allocating resources efficiently between shoes and bicycles, but is clearly not instrumental for deciding the proper range of inequality in wealth or income, nor for deciding how many people consuming how much per capita of natural resources is sustainable.

Distribution and scale involve relationships with the poor, the future, and other species that are fundamentally social in nature rather than individual. *Homo economicus* as the self-contained atom of methodological individualism, or as the pure social being of collectivist theory, are both severe abstractions. Our concrete experience is that of "persons in community." We are individual persons, but our very individual identity is defined by the quality of our social relations. Our relations are not just external, they are also internal, that is, the nature of the related entities (ourselves in this case) changes when relations among them changes. We are related not only by a nexus of individual willingnesses to pay for different things, but also by relations of trusteeship for the poor, the future, and other species. The attempt to abstract from these concrete relations of trusteeship and reduce everything to a question of individual willingness to pay is a distortion of our concrete experience as persons in community, an example of A. N. Whitehead's "fallacy of misplaced concreteness."[6]

The prices that measure the opportunity costs of reallocation are unrelated to measures of the opportunity costs of redistribution or of a change in scale. Any tradeoff among the three goals (e.g., an improvement in distribution in exchange for a worsening in scale or allocation, or more unequal distribution in exchange for sharper incentives seen as instrumental to more efficient allocation) involves an ethical judgment about the quality of our social relations rather than a willingness-to-pay calculation. The contrary view, that this choice among basic social goals and the quality of social relations that help to define us as persons should be made on the basis of individual willingness to pay, just as the tradeoff between chewing gum and shoelaces is made, seems to be dominant in economics today and is part of the retrograde modern reduction of all ethical choice to the level of personal tastes weighted by income.

It is instructive to consider the historical attempt of the Scholastic economists to subsume distribution under allocation (or more likely they were subsuming allocation under distribution—at any rate they did not make the distinction). This was the famous "just price" doctrine of the Middle Ages, which has been totally rejected in economic theory, although it stubbornly survives in the politics of minimum wages, farm price supports, water, and electric power subsidies, and so on. However, we do not as a general rule try to internalize the external cost of distributive injustice into market prices. We reject the attempt to correct market prices for their unwanted effects on income distribution. Economists nowadays keep allocation and distribution quite separate, and argue for letting prices serve only efficiency, while serving justice with the separate policy of transfers of wealth through taxes and social programs. This follows Tinbergen's dictum of equality of policy goals and instruments. The point is that just as we cannot subsume distribution under allocation, neither can we subsume scale under allocation.

Although the usual attempt is to subsume scale under allocation, a few economists have recently implicitly subsumed it under distribution.[7] The argument is that excessive scale erodes carrying capacity and inflicts a cost on future generations. Since future generations are different people, this is a matter of distribution, not allocation. A sustainable scale is nothing other than an intergenerational distribution of the resource base that is fair to the future. This argument is raised against economists who subsume scale under allocation by arguing that intertemporal allocation via discounting the future is the rational (efficient) way to deal with provision for the future. The intergenerational discounting argument is circular because the discount rate, like other prices, is determined on the basis of some given distribution (intergenerational distribution of the resource base in this instance). To then use the discount rate to determine that same distribution between generations is circular. You have to have the distribution to get the discount rate, yet the discounting approach wants to use the discount rate to determine the intergenerational distribution—which is mistakenly called an intergenerational "allocation."

I think that this critique of discounting is correct. But it should not be thought of as a way to subsume the scale problem entirely under the distribution problem. Although justice with respect to the future is certainly an important motivation behind sustainability as a goal, and excessive scale can indeed mean a loss of sustainability, that does not exhaust the question of optimal scale. Scale can become too large from the point of view of the present, even if it remains possible to pass on the too-large economy to the future forever. For example, we could take over the habitat of most other species, driving all nonessential species to extinction, and by careful self-discipline impose on ourselves a rigorous and costly management to compensate for the displaced self-managing natural systems. Scale could be too large even if sustainable. For this reason scale cannot be totally subsumed under distribution, although it must be admitted that scale issues do overlap with one part of distribution, the intergenerational part, to a considerable degree.

Although discussed in terms of pollution, the logic of tradeable permits extends to controlling depletion as well. It can be applied regionally, nationally, and even internationally, as with carbon emission permits to limit the greenhouse effect. It can even be applied to population control as in the tradeable birth quotas suggested by Kenneth Boulding (1964). In fact, to my knowledge, Boulding's was the first clear exposition of the logic of the scheme, although applied to the least likely area of acceptance politically. The tradeable permits idea is truly a paradigm for many sensible policies, as well as by now a fact of experience that should be allowed to alter economic theory. Specifically, theory should recognize scale, along with allocation and distribution, as a fundamental part of the economic problem. If operationality (the congruence of abstract concepts with policy instruments) is a criterion for judging theories, then the theoretical separation of scale and allocation advocated here is superior to the neoclassical approach of lumping them together, because the latter requires nonoperational assumptions to save appearances of methodological individualism, while the former is already being accepted in the practical policy of tradeable permits.

How Big Is the Economy?

As long as the human economy was infinitesimal relative to the natural world, then sources and sinks could be considered infinite, and therefore not scarce. And if they are not scarce then they are safely abstracted from economics. There was no need to consider the larger system since it imposed no scarcities. This was a reasonable view at one time, but no longer. As Kenneth Boulding says, when something grows it gets bigger! The economy has gotten bigger, the ecosystem has not. How big has the economy become relative to the ecosystem?

Probably the best index of the scale of the human economy as a part of the biosphere is the percentage of human appropriation of the total world product of photosynthesis. Net primary production (NPP) is the amount of solar energy captured in photosynthesis by primary producers, less the energy used in their own growth and reproduction. NPP is thus the basic food resource for everything on earth not capable of photosynthesis. Vitousek et al. (1986) calculate that 25% of potential global (terrestrial and aquatic) NPP is now appropriated by human beings.[8] If only terrestrial NPP is considered, the fraction rises to 40%. Taking the 25% figure for the entire world, it is apparent that two more doublings of the human scale will give 100%. Since this would mean zero energy left for all nonhuman and non-domesticated species, and since humans cannot survive without the services of ecosystems (which are made up of other species), it is clear that two more doublings of the human scale is an ecological impossibility, although arithmetically possible. Furthermore, the terrestrial figure of 40% is probably more relevant since we are unlikely to increase our take from the oceans very much. Total appropriation of the terrestrial NPP can occur in only a bit over one doubling time. Perhaps it is theoretically possible to increase the earth's total photosynthetic capacity somewhat, but the actual trend of past economic growth is decidedly in the opposite direction.

Assuming a constant level of per capita resource consumption, the doubling time of the human scale would be equal to the doubling time of population, which is on the order of forty years. Of course, economic growth currently aims to increase the average per capita resource consumption and consequently to reduce the doubling time of the scale of the human presence below that implicit in the demographic rate of growth. The greenhouse effect, ozone layer depletion, and acid rain all constitute evidence that we have already gone beyond a prudent Plimsoll line for the scale of the macroeconomy.

Cowboy, Spaceman, or Bull in the China Shop?

If one starts from the vision of the economic process as an open subsystem of a closed finite total system, then the question of how big the subsystem should be relative to the total system is hard to avoid. How then have we managed to avoid it? In two ways: first, by viewing the economic subsystem as infinitesimally small relative to the total system, so that scale becomes irrelevant because it is negligible; second, by viewing the economy as coextensive with the total system. If the economy includes everything, then the issue of scale relative to a total system simply does not arise. These polar extremes correspond to Boulding's colorful distinction between the "cowboy economy" and the "spaceman economy." The cowboy of the infinite plains lives off of a linear throughput from source to sink, with no need to recycle anything. The spaceman in a small capsule lives off of tight material cycles and immediate feedbacks, all under total control and subservient to his needs. For the cowboy, scale is negligible; for the spaceman, scale is total. There is no material environment relative to which scale must be determined; there is no ecosystem, only economy. In each of these polar cases, the only problem is allocation. Scale is irrelevant.

It is only in the middle ground between the cowboy and the spaceman that the issue of scale does not get conflated with allocation. But, as Boulding realized, the middle ground happens to be where we are. Between the cowboy and spaceman economies is a whole range of larger and smaller "bull-in-the-china-shop economies" where scale is a major concern. We are not cowboys because the existing scale of the economy is far from negligible compared to the environment. But neither are we spacemen, because most of the matter/energy transformations of the ecosystem are not subject to human control either by prices or by central planning. In a finite system subject to the conservation of mass, the more that is brought under our economic control, the less remains under the spontaneous control of nature. As our exactions from and insertions back into the ecosystem increase in scale, the qualitative change induced in the ecosystem must also increase, for two reasons. The first is the first law of thermodynamics (conservation of matter/energy). The taking of matter and energy out of the ecosystem must disrupt the functioning of that system even if nothing is done to the matter and energy so removed. Its mere absence must have an effect. Likewise, the mere insertion of matter and energy into an ecosystem must disrupt the system into which it is newly added. This must be the case even without appealing to any qualitative degradation of the matter and energy thus relocated. The second reason is the second law of thermodynamics, which guarantees that the matter/energy exacted is qualitatively different from the matter/energy inserted. Low-entropy raw materials are taken out, high-entropy wastes are returned. This qualitative degradation of the matter/energy throughput, along with the purely quantitative dislocation of the same, induces changes in the ecosystem which to us are surprising and novel because our information and control system (prices) assumes nonscarcity (nondisruptability) of environmental source and sink functions. Economic calculation is about to be overwhelmed by novel, uncertain, and surprising feedbacks from an ecosystem that is excessively stressed by having to support too large an economic subsystem (Perrings 1987).

How big should the subsystem be relative to the total ecosystem? Certainly this, the question of optimal scale, is the big question for environmental macroeconomics. But since it is such a difficult question, and since we cannot go back to the cowboy economy, we have acquired a tendency to want to jump all the way to the spaceman economy and take total control of the spaceship earth. (The September 1989 special issue of *Scientific American* entitled "Managing Planet Earth" is representative of this thrust.) But, as environmentalist David Orr points out, God, Gaia, or Evolution was doing a nice job of managing the earth until the scale of the human population, economy, and technology got out of control. Planetary management implies that it is the planet that is at fault, not human numbers, greed, arrogance, ignorance, stupidity, and evil. We need to manage ourselves more than the planet, and our self-management should be, in Orr's words, "more akin to child-proofing a day-care center than to piloting spaceship earth." The way to child-proof a room is to build the optimal scale playpen within which the child is both free and protected from the excesses of its own freedom. It can enjoy the light and warmth provided by electrical circuits beyond its ken, without running the risk of shorting out those circuits, or itself, by experimenting with the "planetary management technique" of teething on a lamp cord.

Our manifest inability to centrally plan economies should inspire more humility among the planetary managers who would centrally plan the ecosystem. Humility should argue for the strategy of minimizing the need for planetary management by keeping the human scale sufficiently low so as not to disrupt the automatic functioning of our life-support systems, thereby forcing them into the domain of human management. Those who want to take advantage of the "invisible hand" of self-managing ecosystems have to recognize that the invisible hand of the market, while wonderful for allocation, is unable to set limits to the scale of the macroeconomy. Our limited managerial capacities should be devoted to institutionalizing an economic Plimsoll line that limits the macroeconomy to a scale such that the invisible hand can function in both domains to the maximum extent. It is ironic that many free marketeers, by opposing any limit to the scale of the market economy (and therefore to the increase in externalities), are making more and more inevitable the very central planning that they oppose. Even worse is their celebration of the increase in GNP that results as formerly free goods become scarce and receive a price. For allocation it is necessary that newly scarce goods not continue to have a zero price—no one disputes that. The issue is that, for all we know, we might have been better off to remain at the smaller scale at which the newly scarce goods were free and their proper allocative price was still zero. The increase in measured national income and wealth resulting as formerly free goods are turned into scarce goods is more an index of cost than of benefit, as was recognized by the classical economist Lauderdale back in 1819 (Lauderdale 1819; Foy 1989).

A Glittering Anomaly

Optimal scale of a single activity is not a strange concept to economists. Indeed, microeconomics is about little else. An activity is identified, be it producing shoes or consuming ice cream, and a cost function and a benefit function for the activity in question are defined. Good reasons are given for believing that marginal costs increase and marginal benefits decline as the scale of the activity grows. The message of microeconomics is to expand the scale of the activity in question up to the point where marginal costs equal marginal benefits, a condition which defines the optimal scale. All of microeconomics is an extended variation on this theme.

When we move to macroeconomics, however, we never again hear about optimal scale. There is apparently no optimal scale for the macroeconomy. There are no cost and benefit functions defined for growth in scale of the economy as a whole. It just doesn't matter how many people there are, or how much they each consume, as long as the proportions and relative prices are right. But if every micro activity has an optimal scale, then why does not the aggregate of all micro activities have an optimal scale? If I am told in reply that the reason is that the constraint on any one activity is the fixity of all the others and that when all economic activities increase proportionally the restraints cancel out, then I will invite the economist to increase the scale of the carbon cycle and the hydrologic cycle in proportion to the growth of industry and agriculture. I will admit that if the ecosystem can grow indefinitely then so can the aggregate economy. But until the surface of the earth begins to grow at a rate equal to the rate of interest, one should not take this answer too seriously.

The total absence in macroeconomics of the most basic concept of microeconomics is a glittering anomaly, and it is not resolved by appeals to the fallacy of composition. What is true of a part is not necessarily true for the whole, but it can be and usually is unless there is some aggregate identity or self-canceling feedback at work. (As in the classic example of all spectators standing on tiptoe to get a better view and each canceling out the better view of the other, or in the observation that while any single country's exports can be greater than its imports, nevertheless the aggregate of all exports cannot be different than the aggregate of all imports.) But what analogous feedback or identity is there that allows every economic activity to have an optimal scale while the aggregate economy remains indifferent to scale? The indifference to scale of the macroeconomy is due to the preanalytic vision of the economy as an isolated system—the inappropriateness of which has already been discussed.

Chapter 3

Consumption:
Value Added, Physical
Transformation, and Welfare

At the heart of the current crisis in economic theory and practice is the fact that we are consuming the earth's resource beyond its sustainable capacities of renewal, thus running down that capacity over time—that is, we are consuming natural capital while calling it income. So it is natural that we turn our attention to another set of key topics in economic theory: consumption, value added, and welfare. What insights can we gain from traditional economics? What mistakes must we correct?

While all countries must worry about both population and per capita resource consumption, it is evident that the South needs to focus more on population, and the North more on per capita resource consumption. This fact will likely play a major role in North/South treaties and discussions. Why should the South control its population if the resources saved thereby are merely gobbled up by Northern overconsumption? Why should the North control its overconsumption if the saved resources will merely allow a larger number of poor people to subsist at the same level of misery? Without for a minute minimizing the necessity of population control, it is nevertheless incumbent on the North to get serious about consumption control. These considerations lend a sense of urgency to the reconsideration of the meaning of consumption.

Consumption and Value Added

When we speak of consumption what is it that we think of as being consumed? Alfred Marshall reminded us of the laws of conservation of matter/energy and the consequent impossibility of consuming the material building blocks of which commodities are made:

> Man cannot create material things—his efforts and sacrifices result in changing the form or arrangement of matter to adapt it better for the satisfaction of his wants—as his production of material products is really nothing more than a rearrangement of matter which gives it new utilities, so his consumption of them is nothing more than a disarrangement of matter which destroys its utilities. [Marshall 1961, pp. 63–64]

What we destroy or consume in consumption is the improbable arrangement of those building blocks, arrangements that give utility for humans, arrangements that were, according to Marshall, made by humans for human purposes. This utility added to matter/energy by human action is not production in the sense of being the creation of matter/energy, which is just as impossible as its destruction by consumption. Useful structure is added to matter/energy (natural resource flows) by the agency of labor and capital stocks. The value of this useful structure imparted by labor and capital is called "value added" by economists. This value added is what is "consumed," that is, used up in consumption. New value needs to be added again by the agency of labor and capital before it can be consumed again. That to which value is being added is the flow of natural resources, conceived ultimately as the indestructible building blocks of nature. The value consumed by humans is, in this view, no greater than the value added by humans— consumption plus savings equals national income—which in turn is equal to the sum of all value added. In the standard economist's vision we consume only that value which we added in the first place. And then we add it again, and consume it again, etc. This vision is formalized in the famous diagram of the isolated circular flow of value between firms (production) and households (consumption), found in the initial pages of every economics textbook.

For all the focus on value added, one would think that there would be some discussion of *that to which value is being added*. But modern economists say no more about it than Marshall. It is just "matter," and its properties are not very interesting. In fact they are becoming ever less interesting to economists as science uncovers their basic uniformity. As Barnett and Morse (1963) put it,

> Advances in fundamental science have made it possible to take advantage of the uniformity of matter/energy—a uniformity that makes it feasible, without preassignable limit, to escape the quantitative constraints imposed by the character of the earth's crust. [p. 11]

That to which value is being added consists of merely homogeneous, indestructible building blocks—atoms in the original sense—of which there is no

conceivable scarcity. That to which value is added is therefore inert, undifferentiated, interchangeable, and superabundant—very dull stuff indeed, compared to the value-adding agents of labor, with all its human capacities, and capital, which embodies the marvels of human knowledge. It is not surprising that value added is the centerpiece of economic accounting, and that the presumably passive stuff to which value is added has received minimal attention (Daly and Cobb 1994, chap. 10).

Three examples will show how little attention is given to "that to which value is added," which for brevity I will refer to below as "resources."

Some supposed philistines ("non-economists" as they have been called, with even greater condescension) have questioned whether there are enough resources in the world for everyone to use them at the rate Americans do. This "ignorant" fear is put to rest by Lester Thurow (1980, p. 118), who points out that the question assumes that the "rest of the world is going to achieve the consumption standards of the average American without at the same time achieving the productivity standards of the average American. This of course is algebraically impossible. The world can consume only what it can produce."

In this view, you can only disarrange matter (consume) if you have previously arranged it (produced), and resources are totally passive recipients of form (value) added by labor and capital. Value added is everything, and it is impossible to subtract value that was never added. So if you are consuming something you must have produced it, either recently or in the past. More and more high-consuming people just means more and more value was added. Where else could the arrangements of matter have come from? It is "algebraically impossible" for consumption to exceed value added, at least in the economist's tight little abstract world in which value added by labor and capital is by definition the source of all value produced, and consequently of all value consumed.

In the passage from Marshall quoted earlier, he refers to "new utilities" added by human beings, thus leaving open the possibility that matter might have some preexisting utility. But subsequent economists, in emphasizing *new* utilities or value *added*, have neglected to consider any value that nature has already provided. In the standard economic-textbook view, we consume *only* that value which we have added to natural resource flows. And then we add it again to the same indestructible building blocks, and consume it again, add it again, etc., in the celebrated circular flow.

A second example comes from William Nordhaus, who said that global warming would have only a small effect on the U.S. economy because basically only agriculture is sensitive to climate, and agriculture is only 3% of total value added, of gross national product. Evidently it is the value added to seeds, soil, sunlight, and rainfall by labor and capital that keeps us alive, not the seeds, soil, and sunlight themselves. Older economists might have asked about what happens to marginal utility, price, and the percentage of GNP going to food, when food becomes very scarce—say, due to a drought? Could not the 3% of GNP accounted for by agriculture easily rise to 90% during a famine, in view of the price inelasticity of the demand for food? But these considerations give "mere stuff" a more than passive role in value, and diminish the dogmatic monopoly of value added by human agents of labor and capital.

The importance of mere stuff is frequently downplayed by pointing out that the entire extractive sector (mines, wells, quarries, and so on) accounts for a mere 5 or 6% of GNP. But if the 95% of value added is not independent of the 5% in the extractive sector, but rather depends upon it—is *based* on it—then the impression of relative unimportance is false. The image this conjures in my mind is that of an inverted pyramid balanced on its point. The 5 or 6% of the volume of the pyramid near the point on which it is resting represents the GNP from the extractive sector. The rest of the pyramid is value added to extracted resources. That 5% is the base upon which the other 95% rests—that to which its value is added. Value cannot be added to nothing. Adding value is more like multiplication than addition—we multiply the value of "stuff" by labor and capital. But multiplying a zero always gives zero. Indeed, since the value of the extracted resources themselves (the 5 or 6% of GNP) represents mostly value added by labor and capital in extraction of the resource, practically the entire pyramid of value added is resting on a tiny point of near zero dimension representing the in situ value of the resources (user cost). This image of a growing and tottering pyramid makes me want to stop thinking exclusively about value added and think some more about that to which value is being added. What, exactly, is holding up this pyramid of value added? The size of the pyramid tells us nothing about the size of the resource base upon which it rests.

A third example comes from the theory of production and involves the customary use of a multiplicative form for the production function, the most popular being the Cobb-Douglas. Frequently production is treated as a function of capital and labor alone—resources are omitted entirely. Recently economists have taken to including resources. However, the welcome step toward realism thus taken is very small because, although resources are now recognized as necessary for production, the amount of resources needed for any given level of output can become arbitrarily small, approaching zero, as long as capital or labor are substituted in sufficient quantities. And it is implicitly assumed that the extra capital and labor can be produced without extra resources! Georgescu-Roegen (1979, p. 98) referred to this "paper and pencil exercise" as Solow's and Stiglitz's "conjuring trick."[1]

These three examples have in common a tendency to downplay the dependence of economic activity on resources and on the natural system that generates them, and to exaggerate the relative importance and independence of the human contribution.

Consumption and Physical Transformation

The vision sketched above, found in all textbooks based on the circular flow of value added, is entirely consistent with the first law of thermodynamics. Matter/energy is not produced or consumed, only transformed. But this vision embodies an astonishing oversight—it completely ignores the second law of thermodynamics (Georgescu-Roegen 1971; Soddy 1922).[2] Matter is arranged in production, disarranged in consumption, rearranged in production, etc. The second law tells us that all this rearranging and recycling of material building blocks takes energy, that energy itself is not recycled, and that on each cycle some of the material building blocks are dissipated beyond recall. It remains true that we do not consume matter/energy, but we do consume (irrevocably use up) the *capacity to rearrange* matter/energy.

Contrary to the implication of Barnett and Morse, matter/energy is not at all uniform in the quality most relevant to economics—namely its capacity to receive and hold the rearrangements dictated by human purpose, the capacity to receive the imprint of human knowledge, the capacity to embody value added. The capacity of matter/energy to embody value added is not uniform, and it wears out and must be replenished. Matter/energy is not totally passive. If the economic system is to keep going it cannot be an isolated circular flow. It must be an open system, receiving matter and energy from outside to make up for that which is dissipated to the outside. What is outside? The environment. What is the environment? It is a complex ecosystem that is finite, non-growing, and materially closed, while open to a non-growing, finite flow of solar energy.

Seeing the economy as an open subsystem forces us to realize that consumption is not only disarrangement within the subsystem, but involves disarrangements in the rest of the larger system that contains it, the environment (Perrings 1987). Taking matter/energy from the larger system, adding value to it, using up the added value, and returning the waste clearly alters the environment. The matter/energy we return is not the same as the matter/energy we take in. If it were, we could simply use it again and again in a closed circular flow. Common observation tells us, and the law of entropy confirms, that waste matter/energy is qualitatively different from raw materials. Low-entropy matter/energy comes in, high-entropy matter/energy goes out, just as in an organism's metabolism. We irrevocably use up not only the value we added by rearrangement, but also the preexisting arrangement originally imparted by nature, as well as the very energetic capacity to further arrange, also provided by nature. We not only consume the value we add to matter, *but also the value that was added by nature before we imported it into the economic subsystem* and that was necessary for it to be considered a resource in the first place. The capacity to rearrange that is used up within the subsystem can be restored by importing low-entropy matter/energy from the larger system and exporting high-entropy matter/energy back to it. But the rates of import and export, determined largely by the scale of the subsystem, must be consistent with the complex workings of the parent system, the ecosystem. The scale of the subsystem matters.

From this perspective value is still being added to resources by the agents of labor and capital. But that to which value is added is not composed of inert, indifferent, uniform building blocks or atoms. Value is added to that matter/energy which is most capable of receiving and embodying the value being added to it by human economic activity. That receptivity might be thought of as "value added by nature." Carbon atoms scattered in the atmosphere can receive value added only with the enormous expenditure of energy and other materials. Carbon atoms structured in a tree can be rearranged much more easily. Concentrated copper ore can hold value added, atoms of copper at average crustal abundance cannot. Energy concentrated in a lump of coal can help us add value to matter; energy at equilibrium temperature in the ocean or atmosphere cannot. The more work done by nature, the more concentrated and receptive the resource is to having value added to it, the less capital and labor will have to be expended in rearranging it to better suit our purposes.

From a utility or demand perspective, value added by nature ought to be valued equally with value added by labor and capital. But from the supply or cost side it is not, because value added by humans has a real cost of disutility of labor and an opportunity cost of both labor and capital use. We tend to treat natural value added as a subsidy, a free gift of nature. The greater the natural subsidy, the less the cost of labor and capital (value added) needed for further arrangement. The less the humanly added value, the lower the price, and the more rapid the use. Oil from East Texas was a much greater net energy subsidy from nature to the economy than is offshore Alaskan oil. But its price was much lower precisely because it required less value added by labor and capital.[3] The larger the natural subsidy, the lower its price and the faster we use it up!

Thanks in part to this natural subsidy, the economy has grown relative to the total ecosystem to such an extent that the basic pattern of scarcity has changed. It used to be that adding value was limited by the supply of agents of transformation, labor and capital. Today adding value is limited more by the availability of resources that have been subsidized by nature to the point that they can receive value added. Mere knowledge means nothing to the economy until it becomes incarnate in physical structures. Low-entropy matter/energy is the restricted gate through which knowledge is incorporated in matter and becomes man-made capital. No low-entropy matter/energy, no capital—regardless of knowledge. Of course, new knowledge may include discovery of new low-entropy resources, and new methods of transforming them to better serve human needs (e.g., atomic energy). But new knowledge may also discover new limits and new costs (radiation associated with atomic energy causes cancer). New knowledge always entails surprises. To assume that they will always be pleasant surprises is unwarranted.

The physical growth of the subsystem is the transformation of natural capital into man-made capital. A tree is cut and turned into a table. We gain the service of the table; we lose the service of the tree. In a relatively empty world (small economic subsystem, ecosystem relatively empty of human beings and their artifacts) the service lost from fewer trees was nil, and the service gained from more tables was significant. In today's relatively full world, fewer trees mean loss of significant services, and more tables are not so important if most households already have several tables, as in much of the world they do. Of course continued population growth will keep the demand for tables up, and we will incur ever greater sacrifices of natural services by cutting more and more trees, as long as population keeps growing. The size or scale of the economic subsystem is best thought of as per capita resource consumption times population (which of course is the same as total resource consumption). The point is that there is both a cost and a benefit to increasing the scale of the subsystem (total consumption). The benefit is economic services gained (more tables); the cost is ecosystem services sacrificed (fewer trees to sequester CO_2, provide wildlife habitat, erosion control, local cooling, etc.). As scale increases, marginal costs tend to rise, marginal benefits tend to fall.[4] Equality of marginal costs and benefits define the optimal scale, beyond which further growth in scale (total consumption) would be antieconomic.

As we come to an optimal, or mature scale, production is no longer for growth but for maintenance. A mature economy, like a mature ecosystem (E. P. Odum 1969), shifts from a regime of growth efficiency (maximize P/B, or production per unit of biomass stock) to a regime of maintenance efficiency (maximize the reciprocal, B/P, or the amount of biomass stock maintained per unit of new production). Production is the maintenance cost of the stock and should be minimized. As Kenneth Boulding (1945) argued almost fifty years ago,

> Any discovery which renders consumption less necessary to the pursuit of living is as much an economic gain as a discovery which improves our skills of production. Production—by which we mean the exact opposite of consumption, namely the creation of valuable things—is only necessary in order to replace the stock pile into which consumption continually gnaws. [p. 2]

Consumption and Welfare

Welfare is the service of want satisfaction rendered by stocks of capital, both man-made and natural. The proper economic object is to transform natural into man-made capital to the optimal extent—that is, to the point where total service (the sum of services from natural and man-made capital) is a maximum. As discussed in the previous section, this occurs where the marginal benefit of services of more man-made capital is just equal to the marginal cost of natural services sacrificed when the natural capital that had been yielding those services is transformed into man-made capital. The theoretical existence of an optimal scale of the economic subsystem is clear in principle. What remains vague are the measures of the value of services, especially of natural capital, but also of man-made capital. But if economic policy is anything it is the art of dialectically reasoning with vague quantities in the support of prudent actions. We can have reasons for believing that an optimum scale exists—and that we are either above it or below it—without knowing exactly where it is. For policy purposes a judgment about which side of the optimum we are on is what is critical. Reasons were offered in Chapters 1 and 2 for believing that we (both the United States and the world as a whole) have overshot the optimal scale. To those reasons a few more considerations are added below.

Human welfare is not a function of consumption flows, but of capital stocks. We cannot ride to town on the maintenance costs, the depletion and replacement flow of an automobile, but only in the complete automobile, a member of the current stock of automobiles. Once again, Boulding (1949) got it right fifty years ago:

> I shall argue that it is the capital stock from which we derive satisfactions, not from the additions to it (production) or the subtractions from it (consumption): that consumption, far from being a desideratum, is a deplorable property of the capital stock which necessitates the equally deplorable activities of production: and that the objective of economic policy should not be to maximize consumption or production, but rather to minimize it, i.e., to enable us to maintain our capital stock with as little consumption or production as possible. [p. 79]

This shift from maximizing production efficiency toward maximizing maintenance efficiency is the exact economic analog of the shift in ecosystems mentioned earlier, as they reach maturity—that is, from maximizing P/B to maximizing the reciprocal, B/P. As a mature scale is reached, production is seen more and more as a cost of maintaining what already exists rather than as the source of additional services from added stock. The larger something has grown, the greater, *ceteris paribus*, are its maintenance costs. More new production, more throughput, is required just to keep the larger stock constant against the entropic ravages of rot, rust, and randomization.

Boulding's and Odum's insights can be expressed in a simple identity (Daly 1991)[5]:

$$\frac{\text{Service}}{\text{Throughput}} = \frac{\text{Service}}{\text{Stock}} \times \frac{\text{Stock}}{\text{Throughput}}$$

Stocks of man-made capital are at the center of analysis. On the one hand it is the stock that yields service; on the other it is the stock that is regrettably consumed and consequently requires maintenance by new production, which in turn requires new throughput and new sacrifices of natural capital with consequent reductions of the service of natural capital. We can define *growth* as increase in throughput, holding the two right-hand ratios constant. Service thus increases in proportion to throughput as a result of growth. *Development* can be defined as an increase in service from increases in the two right-hand efficiency ratios, holding throughput constant. "Economic growth," growth in GNP, is a conflation of these two processes: (1) growth (physical increase) and (2) development (qualitative improvements that allow more stock maintenance per unit of throughput, and more service per unit of stock). Since physical growth is limited by physical laws, while qualitative development is not, or at least not in the same way, it is imperative to separate these two very different things. Failure to make this distinction is what has made "sustainable development" so hard to define. With the distinction, it is easy to define sustainable development as "development without growth—without growth in throughput beyond environmental regenerative and absorptive capacities."[6] So far the politicians and economists are so wedded to growth that they insist that economic growth is itself the main characteristic of sustainable development, and therefore speak in muddled terms like "sustainable growth" (as, for example, the President's Council on Environmental Quality has done).

If we accept that it is the stock of capital that yields service (capital in Irving Fisher's sense, including the stock of consumer goods as well as producer goods), then we still must ask, How much extra welfare do we get from extra man-made capital stock, say in the United States at the present time? How much extra cost in terms of sacrificed service of natural capital is required by the transformation of more natural capital into man-made capital? We do not have good measures of costs and benefits of aggregate growth, so we must rely on common sense plus those preliminary measures that we do have, such as the Index of Sustainable Economic Welfare (ISEW), which certainly suggests that growth in GNP in the United States has passed the optimum in terms of welfare (Daly and Cobb 1994; Cobb and Cobb, 1994). A similar conclusion was reached by Jackson and Marks (1994), who constructed an ISEW for England.

Conclusion

What are the policy consequences of the issues discussed in this chapter for North/South cooperation in economic development and in sharing the "global economic pie"? Consider two views.

1. The traditional value-added view of income would lead one to reject the very notion of a "global pie" of income to be divided justly or unjustly among nations and people. There is no given pie—there are only a lot of separate tarts, which some statistician has stupidly aggregated into an abstract pie. The tarts are the product of value added by the labor and capital of the nations that produced them, and nothing more. If nation A is asked to share some of its large tart with nation B, which baked a small tart, the appeal should be made to nation A's generosity and not to any notion of distributive justice, much less exploitation.

If you believe that all value comes from labor and capital, and that nature contributes only a material substratum, nondestructible and superabundant, and hence valueless, then this is a reasonable view. Are you poor? Just add more value by your own labor and capital. You have your own labor, and you can accumulate your own capital, or borrow it at interest from abroad. There are no limits from nature. Stop whining, get busy, and shut up about this imaginary pie. This view is common among neoclassical economists. In fact, it is a corollary to John Locke's justification of private property—to claim something as one's property requires that one has mixed one's labor with the materials of which it is made—i.e., added value to it.

2. The alternative view that nature adds value would look carefully at the tarts that different peoples have baked. Is the tart only the product of the baker's labor and the kitchen's capital, which alone add value to substitutable and superabundant atoms? No: to bake a tart you need flour, sugar, butter, and apples. Before that you need wheat, sugar cane, milk, and apple trees. And before that you need gene pools for wheat, sugar cane, cows, and apples, with some minimal degree of diversity, as well as soil whose fertility is maintained by worms, microbes, and minerals, and sunlight without too much ultraviolet radiation, rainfall that is not too acidic, catchment areas to keep that rain from eroding topsoil, and predictable seasonal temperatures regulated by the mix of gasses in the atmosphere. In other words, we need natural capital and the flow of resources and services that it renders—a whole lot more than indestructible building blocks! Our dowry of natural capital is more or less given, and is not the product of human labor and capital. Parts of that dowry are highly systemic and indivisible among nations. And the part that is divisible was divided by geologic, not economic, processes.

I want to shift attention from traditional value added to "that to which value is added." While one may argue that value added by labor and capital rightly belongs to the laborer and the capitalist (let them fight over how to divide it), one cannot distribute nature's value added so easily, especially the systemic life support services of global natural capital that transcend national boundaries. In this latter sense there really is a global pie, and the demands for justice regarding its division and stewardship cannot be subsumed under the traditional notion that value belongs to whoever adds it.

Operational Policy and Sustainable Development

Introduction

In the chapters in Part 2, I seek to develop operational principles for sustainable development. They were written while I was at the World Bank, and grew out of my major preoccupation while there, namely to get the criteria of sustainable development out of the realm of pious generalities and into the realm of policy and investment criteria. The resistance of higher Bank management at that time (discussed above, in the introduction to this book) was reinforced by academic economists, some calling themselves "environmental" or even "ecological" economists, who were also unwilling to see business as usual in their discipline fundamentally altered by a new point of view. This resistance was to me particularly annoying and hard to understand, since when sustainable development is correctly understood many of the tools of traditional economics will still be essential in elaborating policies for sustainability.[1] Devotion to growthmania dies hard.

In spite of resistances, I do believe that both World Bank and academic economists are beginning to change their minds. The challenge from environmentalists has played a large role in effecting this incipient awakening. The emerging "transdiscipline" of "ecological economics," with its society and journal of that title, are providing a bridge to unite economics and ecology in the furtherance of sustainable development. Similar efforts have come from the Beijer Institute for Ecological Economics in Stockholm, the University of London Environmental Economics Centre, and many other organizations throughout the world.[2]

The first chapter in this section begins with a recap of points established in Part 1, and then pushes to some policy conclusions, followed by a consideration of ways to operationalize the policies. This chapter, especially its last sections, is probably the most technical discussion in the book. The following chapter, written as a farewell address to the World Bank, is less technical, seeking to integrate broad areas of policy into a coherent program—aiming especially at coherence between national (internal) and international (external) policies, an issue that will be further explored in Part 5.

Chapter 4

Operationalizing Sustainable Development by Investing in Natural Capital

The preanalytic vision at the foundation of standard economics is that of an isolated circular flow of exchange value between firms and households. Nothing enters from the environment nor exits to it. The physical environment is completely abstracted from (see figure 2, Chapter 2).

By contrast, the preanalytic vision of ecological economics is that the economy, in its physical dimensions, is an open subsystem of a finite, non-growing, and materially closed ecosystem (see figure 3, Chapter 2).

The economic subsystem has grown relative to the containing ecosystem to the extent that remaining natural capital has become scarce relative to man-made capital, reversing the previous pattern of scarcity. This forces into practical attention three neglected macroeconomic questions: How big *is* the economic subsystem relative to the containing ecosystem? How big *can* it be without destroying the larger sustaining system? and, How big *should* it be in order to optimize life enjoyment? Life enjoyment can be interpreted in an anthropocentric way (for human beings, recognizing only instrumental value of other species), or in a biocentric way (recognizing intrinsic as well as instrumental value of other species).

Although the environment has been abstracted from by standard economics, the concept of sustainability has been recognized and incorporated into the very definition of income as "the maximum amount that a community can consume over some time period and still be as well off at the end of the period as at the beginning" (Hicks 1946). Being as well off means having the same capacity to produce the same income in the next year—i.e., *maintaining capital intact*.[1] The criterion of sustainability is thus explicit in this Hicksian definition of income. But the condition of maintaining capital intact has applied only to man-made capital, since in the past natural capital was abstracted from because it was not scarce. The Hicksian definition of income must in the future apply to total scarce capital, which now includes natural capital as well as man-made.

Shifting Investment toward Natural Capital

We now begin to move from principles to policy. There are two ways to maintain total capital intact: (1) the *sum* of man-made and natural capital can be maintained constant in some aggregate value sense, or (2) *each* component can be maintained intact separately, again in some aggregate value sense, but this time there is aggregation only within the two categories and not across them. The first way is reasonable if one believes that man-made and natural capital are substitutes. This view holds that it is totally acceptable to divest natural capital as long as one creates by investment an equivalent value in man-made capital. The second way is reasonable if one believes that man-made and natural capital are complements. The complements must each be maintained intact (separately or jointly in fixed proportion), because the productivity of one depends on the availability of the other. The first case is called *weak sustainability*, and the second case is called *strong sustainability*.

Man-made and natural capital are fundamentally complements and only marginally substitutes. Therefore, strong sustainability is ultimately the relevant concept, although even weak sustainability would be an improvement over current practice. Since this proposition will likely be contested, it is worth taking time to consider the three basic reasons behind it.

One way to make an argument is to assume the opposite and show that it is absurd. If man-made capital were a near perfect substitute for natural capital, then natural capital would be a near perfect substitute for man-made capital. But if so, there would have been no reason to accumulate man-made capital in the first place, since we were endowed by nature with a near perfect substitute. But historically we did accumulate man-made capital—precisely because it is complementary to natural capital.

Man-made capital is itself a physical transformation of natural resources which come from natural capital. Therefore, producing more of the alleged substitute (man-made capital), physically requires more of the very thing being substituted for (natural capital)—the defining condition of complementarity!

Man-made capital (along with labor) is an agent of transformation of the resource flow from raw material inputs into product outputs. The natural resource flow (and the natural capital stock that generates it) are the *material cause* of production; the capital stock that transforms raw material inputs into product output is the *efficient cause* of production. One cannot substitute efficient cause for material cause—one cannot build the same wooden house with half the timber no matter how many saws and carpenters one tries to substitute. Also, to process more timber into more wooden houses in the same time period requires more saws and carpenters. Clearly the basic relation of man-made and natural capital is one of complementarity, not substitutability. Of course, one could substitute bricks for timber, but that is the substitution of one resource input for another, not the substitution of capital for resources.[2] In making a brick house one would face the analogous inability of trowels and masons to substitute for bricks.

The complementarity of man-made and natural capital is made obvious at a concrete and commonsense level by asking, What good is a saw-mill without a forest, a fishing boat without populations of fish, a refinery without petroleum deposits, an irrigated farm without an aquifer or river? We have long recognized the complementarity between public infrastructure and private capital—what good is a car or truck without roads to drive on? Following Lotka and Georgescu-Roegen, we can take the concept of natural capital even further and distinguish between *endosomatic* (within-skin) and *exosomatic* (outside-skin) natural capital. We can then ask, What good is the private endosomatic capital of our lungs and respiratory system without the public exosomatic capital of green plants that take up our carbon dioxide in the short run, while in the long run replenishing the enormous atmospheric stock of oxygen and keeping the atmosphere at the proper mix of gases— that is, the mix to which our respiratory system is adapted and therefore complementary.

If natural and man-made capital are obviously complements, how is it that economists have overwhelmingly treated them as substitutes? First, not all economists have—Leontief's input-output economics, with its assumption of fixed factor proportions, treats all factors as complements. Second, the formal, mathematical definitions of complementarity and substitutability are such that in the two-factor case, the factors must be substitutes.[3] Since most textbooks are written on two-dimensional paper, this case receives most attention. Third, mathematical convenience continues to dominate reality in the general reliance on Cobb-Douglas and other constant elasticity of substitution production functions, in which there is nearly infinite substitutability of factors, in particular of capital for resources. Thankfully, some economists have begun to constrain this substitution by the law of conservation of mass! Fourth, exclusive attention to the margin results in marginal substitution obscuring overall relations of complementarity. For example, private expenditure on extra car maintenance may substitute for reduced public expenditure on roads. But this marginal element of substitution should not obscure the fact that private cars and roads are basically complementary forms of capital.[4] Fifth, there may well be substitution of capital for resources in aggregate production functions reflecting a change in product mix from resource-intensive to capital-intensive products. But this is an artifact of changing product aggregation, not factor substitution along a given product isoquant. Also, a new product may be designed that gives the same service with less resource use—for example, light bulbs that give more lumens per watt. This is technical progress—a qualitative improvement in the state of the art—not the substitution of a quantity of capital for a quantity of resources in the production of a given quantity of a specific product.

No one denies the reality of technical progress, but to call such changes the substitution of capital for resources (or of man-made for natural capital) is confusing. It seems that some economists are counting all improvements in knowledge, technology, and managerial skills—in short, anything that would increase the efficiency with which resources are used—as "capital." If this is the usage, then "capital" and resources would by definition be substitutes in the same sense that more efficient use of a resource is a good substitute for having more of the resource. But to formally define capital as efficiency would make a mockery of the neoclassical theory of production, where efficiency is a ratio of output to input, and capital is a quantity of input.

If we accept that natural and man-made capital are complements rather than substitutes, then what follows? *If factors are complements, then the one in shortest supply will be the limiting factor.* If factors are substitutes, then neither can be a limiting factor since the productivity of one does not depend much on availability of the other. The notion of a limiting factor is familiar to ecologists in Leibig's law of the minimum. The idea that either natural or man-made capital could be a limiting factor simply cannot arise if the factors are thought to be substitutes. Once we see that they are complements, then we must ask which one is the limiting factor—that is, which is in shortest supply?

This proposition gives rise to the following thesis: *that the world is moving from an era in which man-made capital was the limiting factor into an era in which remaining natural capital is the limiting factor.* The production of caught fish is currently limited by remaining fish populations, not by number of fishing boats; timber production is limited by remaining forests, not by sawmills; barrels of pumped crude oil is limited by petroleum deposits (or perhaps more stringently by the capacity of the atmosphere to absorb CO_2), not by pumping capacity; and agricultural production is frequently limited by water availability, not by tractors, harvesters, or even land area. We have moved from a world relatively full of natural capital and empty of man-made capital (and people) to a world relatively full of the latter and empty of the former (see figure 3, Chapter 2).

Economic logic requires that we maximize the productivity of the limiting factor in the short run, and invest in increasing its supply in the long run. When the limiting factor changes, then behavior that used to be economic becomes uneconomic. Economic logic remains the same, but the pattern of scarcity in the world changes, with the result that behavior must change if it is to remain economic. Instead of maximizing returns to and investing in man-made capital (as was appropriate in an empty world), we must now maximize returns to and invest in natural capital (as is appropriate in a full world). *This is not "new economics," but new behavior consistent with "old economics" in a world with a new pattern of scarcity.*

In conclusion, since natural capital has replaced man-made capital as the limiting factor, we should adopt policies that maximize its present productivity and increase its future supply. This conclusion is far from being trivial or irrelevant, because it means that current policies of maximizing the productivity and accumulation of man-made capital are no longer "economic," even in the most traditional sense. In addition, the Hicksian definition of income imposes the condition that capital be maintained intact. If natural capital is the limiting factor, then the proper measurement of income requires that natural capital maintenance take priority.

But how could the pattern of scarcity have changed so dramatically without economists noticing it? Several factors account for this development. First, exponential growth is deceptive. The bottle goes from half-full to totally full in the same time it took to go from 1% to 2% full. Second, economists have considered man-made and natural capital to be substitutes, when they are basically complements. If factors are substitutes, then a shortage of one does not limit the productivity of the other. Neither factor can be limiting if they are good substitutes. So even as the world moves from 40% to 80% full in the next roughly forty-year doubling time (Vitousek et al. 1986),[5] economists are counting on man-made capital to restore the conditions of relative emptiness by substituting for natural capital. Third, if we subconsciously realize that production growth cannot continue, then the only way to cure poverty is to confront both sharing and population control. Since these are considered impossible by political "realists," it is gratuitously concluded that whatever argument gave rise to this conclusion must be wrong. These three biases may have kept us from seeing the obvious—namely, that man-made and natural capital are complements, and that natural capital has become the limiting factor. More man-made capital, far from substituting for natural capital, just puts greater complementary demands on it, running it down faster to temporarily support the value of man-made capital, making it all the more limiting in the future.

A related reason for the denial of the new limiting role of natural capital is that raising its relative price in response to its new scarcity would be politically inconvenient. The price paid for natural capital is simultaneously income to the owner—the landlord, who, as Adam Smith told us, loves to reap where he has not sown. A higher relative price of resources implies a redistribution from laborers and capitalists to landlords. Even if the government takes over the function of the landlord, as it in effect has by becoming the largest resource owner, there is still a conflict between government as landlord and labor/capital as resource users. There is, of course, also a more celebrated conflict between labor and capital in industrial society. One of the government's main problems is to maintain industrial peace between labor and capital. This has historically been accomplished by taking from the landlord and giving to labor and capital. Nobody loves a landlord, but to the extent that government has become the landlord, its strategy of buying industrial peace by a policy of cheap resources is no longer at the expense of the erstwhile landlord class. Instead it represents an abdication of the government's role as trustee for both the public interest and the interest of future generations.[6] Taking this trustee role more seriously will require higher resource prices, and a higher risk of sharpening the labor-capital conflict. Environmentalism does not usually engage these larger issues of political economy. The challenge to environmentalists in the twenty-first century will be to confront these fundamental questions.

How to Invest in Natural Capital

Even if one is convinced by the previous argument that the focus of investment should shift from man-made to natural capital, a problem remains. Since natural capital is by definition not man-made, it is not immediately obvious what is meant by "investing" in it. Yet the term "investment" applies because the concept involves the classical notion of "waiting" or refraining from current consumption as the way to invest in natural capital. Before investigating further the meaning of investment in natural capital, we should examine the concept of natural capital itself.

Natural capital is the stock that yields the flow of natural resources— the population of fish in the ocean that regenerates the flow of caught fish that go to market; the standing forest that regenerates the flow of cut timber; the petroleum deposits in the ground whose liquidation yields the flow of pumped crude oil. The natural income yielded by natural capital consists of natural services as well as natural resources. Natural capital is divided into two kinds, as represented in the examples given: renewable (fish, trees), and non-renewable (petroleum). Man-made capital is used here in Irving Fisher's sense to include stocks of both producer and consumer goods.

Several difficulties with these definitions should be noticed. First, capital has traditionally been defined as "produced (man-made) means of production," yet natural capital was not and cannot be produced by man. A more functional definition of capital is "a stock that yields a flow of useful goods or services into the future," and natural capital fits this concept very well, as do durable consumer goods. And, of course, renewable resources can be exploited to extinction and rendered nonrenewable—while nonrenewable resources can be renewed if we are prepared to wait indefinitely. Subject to these caveats, the terms are well defined and are in current use (Costanza and Daly 1992).

Also, there is an important category that overlaps those of natural and man-made capital—such things as plantation forests, fish ponds, herds of cattle bred for certain characteristics, etc., are not really man-made, but are significantly modified from their natural state by human action. We will refer to these things as "cultivated natural capital." This is a broad category, including agriculture, aquaculture, and plantation forestry. How does it affect our distinction between natural and man-made capital, and the claim that they are complements? One can analyze cultivated natural capital into its components of man-made and natural capital proper. For example, a plantation forest has a natural capital component of sunlight, rainfall, and soil nutrients plus a man-made capital component of management services such as planting, spacing, culling, and control of diseases. In general, there seems to be a strong complementary relation between the natural and man-made components of cultivated natural capital. Nevertheless, cultivated natural capital does substitute for natural capital proper in certain functions—those for which it is cultivated, such as timber production—but not wildlife habitat or biodiversity in the case of a plantation forest.[7]

For renewable resource management, "waiting" investment simply means constraining the annual offtake. Keeping the annual offtake equal to the annual growth increment (sustainable yield) is equivalent to maintenance investment—that is, the avoidance of running down the productive stock, equivalent to the Hicksian condition that capital remain intact. Net investment in renewables requires additional waiting—allowing all or a part of the growth increment to be added to the productive stock each year rather than be consumed. Investment in natural capital, both maintenance and net investment, is fundamentally passive with respect to natural capital which is simply left alone and allowed to regenerate. Cultivated natural capital investment also involves waiting, except that it is never really left alone; even during the waiting period, some tending and supervision is required.

By definition, investment in renewable natural capital must be only passive. But more active investment is possible in cultivated natural capital. How far can we go with this type of investment? Can we cultivate an entire biosphere? Does Biosphere II in Arizona stand a chance of working? Beyond its undoubted experimental value on a small scale, is a larger version of such active investment in cultivated natural capital at the ecosystem and biospheric scale likely to be a good bet in the future? Can the whole ocean become a catfish pond? Even if it could, would there not still be complementarity with the more basic natural capital of sunlight, chlorophyll, and decomposers?

No one knows how far we can rely on cultivated natural capital. However, we are currently so far away from the requisite understanding of ecosystems that their large scale redesign should be ruled out as at best quantitatively insignificant, and at worst qualitatively dangerous. As Paul Ehrlich has reminded us, ecological economics is a discipline with a time limit. We do not have time to learn how to create a cultivated "Biosphere II." We must save the remnants of Biosphere I and allow them to regenerate by the passive investment of waiting. The term laissez-faire thus acquires a new and deeper meaning for ecological economists.

Nonrenewable natural capital cannot be increased either actively or passively. It can only be diminished. We can only divest nonrenewable natural capital itself, even though we invest in the man-made capital equipment that hastens its rate of extraction and divestment. Nonrenewable natural capital is like an inventory of already produced goods, rather than a productive machine or a reproducing population. For nonrenewable natural capital the question is not how to invest, but how to best liquidate the inventory, and what to do with the net wealth realized from that liquidation. Currently, we are counting this liquidated wealth as income (included in both gross national product, and net national product), which is clearly wrong, because it is not a permanent or sustainable source of consumption.

A better alternative would be to dedicate all or part of the net receipts of nonrenewable resource liquidation to finance waiting investments in renewable natural capital—that is, to allow reduction of the offtake of renewables in order to build up renewable stocks to larger levels producing larger sustainable yields which represent true income. The basic idea is to convert nonrenewable natural capital into a renewable substitute, to the extent possible. The general rule would be to deplete nonrenewables at a rate equal to the rate of development of renewable substitutes. Thus, extractive projects based on nonrenewables must be paired in some way with a project that develops the renewable substitute. Net receipts of nonrenewable exploitation are divided into two components (an income component and a capital set-aside), such that the capital set-aside, when invested in a renewable substitute each year, will, by the time the nonrenewable is depleted, have grown to a stock size whose sustainable yield is equal to the income component that was being consumed all along. The capital set-aside will be greater the lower the growth rate of the renewable substitute and the shorter the lifetime of the nonrenewable reserves (i.e., the reserve stock divided by annual depletion). The logic and calculations have been worked out by El Serafy (1988) in the context of national income accounting, but they apply with equal relevance to accounting at the project level. The true rate of return on the project pair would be calculated on the basis of the income component only as net revenue. This differs from the usual cost-benefit evaluation of projects in explicitly costing sustainability by using income (sustainable by definition) rather than cash flow, and by requiring actual rather than hypothetical replacement investment. It does *not* require that the project itself be immortal, nor that nonrenewables should forever remain in the ground, never to benefit anyone (see Hartwick and Hageman 1993).

Difficulties remain in the question of defining "substitute"—whether narrowly or broadly. Probably a broad definition would be indicated initially—at least broad enough to encompass improvements in energy efficiency as a renewable substitute for petroleum depletion, and improvements in recycling as a renewable substitute for copper depletion.

In the case of divestment of a *renewable* resource stock, capital consumption is treated as depreciation of a productive asset (the sacrificed base population that was producing a permanent yield). Depreciation should be deducted from gross income to get net income. In the case of nonrenewables, the reduction of stocks is treated as a liquidation of existing inventories rather than as depletion of capacity for future production, and consequently, should not even be a part of gross income, as El Serafy rightly insists.

A difficulty in the application of the rule can easily be imagined. Suppose alcohol is the nearest renewable substitute for gasoline. If one tried to invest all of the capital component of current petroleum net revenues in natural capital or cultivated natural capital (wood or sugarcane alcohol), the price of alcohol would have to rise enormously to allow large amounts of land to be bid away from food to plant sugarcane. (This is an indication of how far away we are from sustainability.) The solution would be to begin pricing current petroleum energy at the cost of sugarcane energy—that is, at the cost of its long-run renewable substitute. Then, as the prices of both petroleum and alcohol energy increase, the rate of depletion of petroleum will be slowed. As depletion is slowed, the life expectancy of petroleum reserves will increase, and the percentage of net petroleum rents representing the capital set-aside will diminish. At some higher price, the amount of petroleum rents to be invested in alcohol will fall. In effect, the difficulty of investing the petroleum capital component in a renewable substitute will provide the effective limit on the rate of depletion of petroleum. This remains true even if fusion energy rather than alcohol is used as the long-run permanent substitute.

This rule is similar to that of economist John Ise (1925), who argued that nonrenewables should be priced at the cost of their nearest renewable substitute. In the previous example, alcohol was treated as the nearest renewable substitute, but other renewable near substitutes may be cheaper (e.g., technical improvements in energy efficiency) and should be the effective near substitute as long as they remain the cheaper alternative. This last point can be generalized: *Although we cannot invest in nonrenewables, we can manage their liquidation in such a way as to increase direct passive investment in renewables and indirect active investment in measures to increase throughput productivity that make waiting (throughput reduction) easier.*

Any investment that enables us to reduce the volume of throughput needed to maintain a given level of welfare can be considered an indirect investment in natural capital. There are two classes of investment for reducing the need for throughput. The most obvious is investment in reducing population growth—first stopping growth and then gradually reducing numbers of people by reducing birth rates. Investments in female literacy and social security systems, along with contraceptives and their delivery systems, offer investment opportunities of this kind. The second class of investment (and the focus of the remainder of this discussion) is in increasing the efficiency of throughput use. More generally, this means increasing the efficiency with which capital, both natural and man-made, is used to provide life-support and life-enhancing services.

Think of the world initially consisting of only natural capital—our initial dowry. We convert some of it into man-made capital in order better to serve our wants. The extent to which we should continue this conversion is economically limited. The efficiency with which we use the world to satisfy our wants depends on two things: the amount of service we get per unit of man-made capital, and the amount of service we sacrifice per unit of natural capital lost as a result of its conversion into man-made capital. This overall ecological economic efficiency can be stated as the ratio

$$\frac{\text{MMK services gained}}{\text{NK services sacrificed}}$$

where *MMK* is man-made capital and *NK* is natural capital. In an empty world (or locality), there would be no noticeable sacrifice of NK services required by increases in MMK, so the denominator would be irrelevant. In a full world any increase in MMK would come at a noticeable reduction in NK and its services.

This efficiency ratio can be "unfolded" into four components by means of the following identity (Daly 1991):

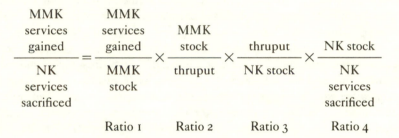

$$\underbrace{\frac{\substack{\text{MMK} \\ \text{services} \\ \text{gained}}}{\substack{\text{NK} \\ \text{services} \\ \text{sacrificed}}}}_{} = \underbrace{\frac{\substack{\text{MMK} \\ \text{services} \\ \text{gained}}}{\substack{\text{MMK} \\ \text{stock}}}}_{\text{Ratio 1}} \times \underbrace{\frac{\substack{\text{MMK} \\ \text{stock}}}{\text{thruput}}}_{\text{Ratio 2}} \times \underbrace{\frac{\text{thruput}}{\text{NK stock}}}_{\text{Ratio 3}} \times \underbrace{\frac{\text{NK stock}}{\substack{\text{NK} \\ \text{services} \\ \text{sacrificed}}}}_{\text{Ratio 4}}$$

Each term of the identity represents a dimension of efficiency that might be improved by increased investment in knowledge or technique. Ratio 1 represents service efficiency; Ratio 2, maintenance efficiency; Ratio 3, growth efficiency; and Ratio 4, ecosystem efficiency.

Ratio 1 is the *service efficiency* of the man-made capital stock. It depends on (1) the technical design efficiency of the product itself, (2) the economic efficiency of resource allocation among the different product uses in conformity with individual preferences and ability to pay, and (3) the distributive efficiency among individuals. The first two are straightforward and conform with standard economics, but the third requires explanation. Usually distribution is carefully separated from efficiency by the Pareto condition that utility cannot be compared across individuals. Of course, in practice we do compare utility across individuals, and it does make sense to believe that total social utility is increased when resources are redistributed from the low marginal utility uses of the rich to the high marginal utility uses of the poor. One can reject the total egalitarianism implicit in carrying this idea to its logical extreme, while at the same time agreeing with Joan Robinson that it is possible to allow too much of the good juice of utility to evaporate from commodities by allowing them to be too unequally distributed. Investments in distributive efficiency might reasonably be ruled out-of-bounds in an empty world that offered the easier alternative of growth. In a full world, growth is limited, and all improvement must come from efficiency improvement, so we can no longer neglect the possibility of efficiency increase through redistribution. Economists have studied these aspects of service efficiency, especially allocative efficiency via the price mechanism, in great detail. Further refinements from deeper study of Ratio 1 will probably be less productive than the study of the other three ratios, except for the redistributive possibility.

Ratio 2 reflects the *maintenance efficiency* or durability of the man-made capital stock. While Ratio 1 measures the service intensity per unit of time of the man-made stock, Ratio 2 measures the number of units of time over which the stock yields that service. Ratio 2 is the durability of the stock, or the "residence time" of a unit of resource throughput as a part of the man-made capital stock. A slower rate of throughput means reduced depletion and pollution. Maintenance efficiency is increased by designing commodities to be durable, repairable, and recyclable, or by designing patterns of living that make certain commodities less necessary to begin with.

Ratio 3 is the *growth efficiency* of natural capital in yielding an increment available for offtake as throughput. Basically, it is determined by the intrinsic biological growth rate of the exploited population in its supporting ecosystem. For example, pine trees grow faster than mahogany, so in uses where either will do, pine is more efficient. Nature generally presents a menu of different species growing at different rates. To the extent that we are able to design our technologies and consumption patterns to depend on the faster-growing species, that will be more efficient, *ceteris paribus*.

With the advent of genetic engineering, there will be more attempts to speed up growth rates of exploited species (e.g., the bovine growth hormone). The "green revolution" involves an attempt to speed up growth rates of wheat and rice—or at least the consumable portions of these plants. Since an increase in biological growth rate frequently comes at the expense of stability, resilience, and resistance to disease or predators, it may be that attempts to speed up any such "reproductive" rates will usually end up costing more than they are worth. It is for now certainly better for us to slow down our own biological growth rate than to attempt to speed up the growth rates of all the species we depend upon. Nevertheless, we can to some degree adapt our pattern of consumption to depend more on naturally faster-growing species, where possible.

For sustained-yield exploitation, Ratio 3 will vary with the size of the population maintained, according to the familiar inverted U-shaped function. For any chosen combination of population size and yield, the ratio would remain constant over time under sustained yield management. Maximum sustained yield would, of course, maximize this dimension of efficiency over the long run (if harvesting costs are constant). In the short run, this ratio can be driven very high by the nonsustainable practice of exceeding renewable rates of harvest and thereby converting permanent stock into one-time throughput. There is a strong tendency to cheat on this dimension.

Ratio 4 measures the amount of natural capital stock that can be exploited for throughput (either as source or sink) per unit of other natural services sacrificed. For example, if we exploit a forest to get maximum sustainable yield of timber (or maximum absorption of CO_2), then we will, to some degree, sacrifice other natural services of the forest such as wildlife habitat, erosion control, and water catchment. We want to minimize the loss of other ecosystem services per unit of natural capital managed with the objective of yielding a single service—usually that of generating raw material throughput. Ratio 4 might be called *ecosystem service efficiency*, reflecting the minimization of loss of other ecosystem services when a population or ecosystem is exploited primarily for throughput.

The world is complex, and no simple identity can capture everything. But these four dimensions of ecological economic efficiency may be helpful to ecological economists in devising ways to invest indirectly in natural capital. As NK is converted into MMK—as we go from an "empty world" to a "full world" in both vision and reality—we want at each step to maximize the service from the increment of MMK and to minimize the loss of ecosystem service from the decrement of NK. But at some point, even if carried out efficiently, this process of conversion of NK into MMK will itself reach an economic limit, an optimal scale of the economic subsystem beyond which further expansion would increase costs faster than benefits. This optimal scale is defined by the usual economic criterion of equating marginal costs and benefits. This criterion assumes that marginal benefits decline and that marginal costs increase, both in a continuous fashion. It is reasonable to think that marginal benefits decline because humans are sufficiently rational to satisfy their most pressing wants first. But the assumption that marginal costs (sacrificed ecosystem services) will increase in a continuous fashion is problematic. As the human niche has expanded, the stresses on the ecosystem have increased, but there has been no rational ordering by human or providential intelligence to ensure that the least important ecosystem services are always sacrificed first. We appear to be sacrificing some vital services rather early. This is another way of saying that Ratio 4, ecological service efficiency, has been ignored. If we begin to pay attention to that dimension of efficiency, then we may expect human rationality to begin to order ecosystem service sacrifices from least to worst, and thus justify the economist's usual assumption of gradually rising marginal costs. That would make the optimal scale of the human niche more definable.

The present lack of rational sequencing of ecosystem costs is due both to nonrecognition of the problem and to ignorance of ecosystem functioning. Prudence in the face of large uncertainties about ecosystem costs should lead us to be very conservative about risking any further expansion. But even with complete certainty and a least-cost sequence of environmental costs, there is still an optimal scale beyond which it is antieconomic to grow. And of course this notion of optimal scale is purely anthropocentric, counting all other species only for their instrumental value to human welfare. If we attribute intrinsic value in some degree to other sentient creatures, then the optimal scale of the human niche would be smaller than if only human sentience counted. Investment in natural capital would then have the additional benefit of increasing life-support services to nonhuman species whose enjoyment of life would no longer be counted as zero, though it certainly should not be counted as equal to human life enjoyment. To recognize that a sparrow's intrinsic value is greater than zero does not negate the fact that a human is worth many sparrows. But not even theology, much less economics, can say how many sparrows are worth a human.

Chapter 5

Fostering Environmentally Sustainable Development: Four Parting Suggestions for the World Bank

I have four suggestions for better serving the goal of environmentally sustainable development through World Bank policy and action. These four prescriptions are presented in order of increasing generality and radicalism. That is, the first two are fairly specific and should, I think, be relatively noncontroversial. The third will be debated by many, and the fourth will be considered outrageous by most Bank economists. I cannot omit the fourth, however, because it is required by the first three; it provides an external policy that is coherent with the internal policies contained in the first three recommendations.

1. *Stop counting the consumption of natural capital as income.* Income is by definition the maximum amount that a society can consume this year and still be able to consume the same amount next year. That is, consumption this year, if it is to be called income, must leave intact the capacity to produce and consume the same amount next year. Thus sustainability is built into the very definition of income. But the productive capacity that must be maintained intact has traditionally been thought of as man-made capital only, excluding natural capital. We have habitually counted natural capital as a free good. This might have been justified in yesterday's empty world, but in today's full world it is antieconomic. The error of implicitly counting natural capital consumption as income is customary in three areas: the UN's System of National Accounts, the evaluation of projects that deplete natural capital, and international balance-of-payments accounting.

With regard to the first area—the System of National Accounts—the error is well recognized and efforts are underway to correct it. Indeed, the World Bank played a pioneering role in this important initiative, and I hope it will continue to contribute to "greening the GNP."

The second area of concern, project evaluation, is well recognized by standard economics, which has long taught the need to count "user cost" (depletion charges) as part of the opportunity cost of projects that deplete natural capital. Bank *best* practice counts user costs, but *average* Bank practice ignores them. Uncounted user costs show up in inflated net benefits and an overstated rate of return for depleting projects. This biases investment allocation toward projects that deplete natural capital and away from more sustainable projects. Correcting this bias is the logical first step toward a policy of sustainable development. User cost must be counted not only for depletion of nonrenewables, but also for projects that divest renewable natural capital by exploiting it beyond sustainable yield. The "sink," or absorptive, services of natural capital, as well as its "source," or regenerative, services, can also be depleted if used beyond sustainable capacity. Therefore a user cost must be charged to projects that deplete sink capacity, such as the atmosphere's ability to absorb CO_2 or the capacity of a river to carry off wastes. It is admittedly difficult to measure user cost, but attempting to avoid the issue simply means that we assign to depleted natural capital the precise default value of zero, which is frequently not the best estimate. Even when zero is the best estimate, it should be arrived at not by default but by reasoned calculation based on explicit assumptions about backstop technologies, discount rates, and reserve lifetimes.[1]

In the third area, balance-of-payments accounting, the export of depleted natural capital—whether petroleum or timber cut beyond sustainable yield—is entered in the current account, and thus treated entirely as income. This is an accounting error. Some portion of those nonsustainable exports should be treated as the sale of a capital asset, and entered on capital account. If this were properly done, some countries would see their apparent balance-of-trade surplus converted into a true deficit, one that is being financed by drawdown and transfer abroad of their stock of natural capital. Reclassifying transactions in a way that converts a country's balance of trade from a surplus to a deficit would trigger a whole different set of International Monetary Fund recommendations and actions. This reform of balance-of-payments accounting should be the initial focus of the IMF's new interest in environmentally sustainable development. The World Bank should warmly encourage the managers and staff of its sister institution to get busy on this—it does not come naturally to them.

2. *Tax labor and income less, and tax resource throughput more.* In the past it has been customary for governments to subsidize resource throughput to stimulate growth. Thus energy, water, fertilizer, and even deforestation, are even now frequently subsidized. To its credit, the World Bank has generally opposed these subsidies. But it is necessary to go beyond the removal of explicit financial subsidies to the removal of implicit environmental subsidies as well. By "implicit

environmental subsidies" I mean external costs to the community that are not charged to the commodities whose production generates them.

Economists have long advocated internalizing external costs either by calculating and charging Pigouvian taxes (taxes which when added to marginal private costs make them equal to marginal social costs), or by Coasian redefinition of property rights (such that resources that used to be public property, and not valued in markets, become private property whose values are protected by their new owners). These solutions are elegant in theory, but often quite difficult in practice. A blunter but much more operational instrument would be simply to shift our tax base away from labor and income onto throughput. We have to raise public revenue somehow, and the present system is highly distortionary in that by taxing labor and income in the face of high unemployment in nearly all countries, we are discouraging exactly what we want more of. The present signal to firms is to shed labor and substitute more capital and resource throughput, to the extent feasible. It would be better to economize on throughput because of the high external costs of its associated depletion and pollution, and at the same time to use more labor because of the high social benefits associated with reducing unemployment.

Shifting the tax base to throughput induces greater throughput efficiency, and internalizes, in a blunt manner, the externalities from depletion and pollution. True, the exact external costs will not have been precisely calculated or exactly attributed to those activities that caused them, as with a Pigouvian tax that aims to equate marginal social costs and benefits for each activity. But those calculations and attributions are so difficult and uncertain that insisting on them at the outset would be equivalent to a full-employment act for econometricians and prolonged unemployment and environmental degradation for everyone else.

Politically, this shift in the tax base, increasingly referred to as "ecological tax reform," could be sold under the banner of revenue neutrality. However, the income tax structure should be maintained so as to keep progressivity in the overall tax structure by taxing very high incomes and subsidizing very low incomes (negative income tax). But the bulk of public revenue would be raised from taxes on throughput, at either the depletion or the pollution end. The income tax would be mainly for redistribution rather than revenue. The throughput taxes would be both for revenue and to encourage throughput minimization. Some people worry that our tax base would disappear as throughput was minimized. But throughput cannot approach zero, and when it is minimized then taxes on it will still raise revenue, and tax rates can be raised to meet any revenue needs. It is value added that can be taxed out of existence, not throughput! Furthermore, taxing something that has become inelastic in demand is allocatively efficient.

The shift could be carried out gradually by a preannounced schedule to minimize disruption.[3] This shift should be a key part of structural adjustment, but should be pioneered in the North. Indeed, sustainable development itself must be achieved in the North first. It is absurd to expect any sacrifice for sustainability in the South if similar measures have not first been taken in the North. The major weakness in the World Bank's ability to foster environmentally sustainable development is that it only has leverage over the South, not the North. Some way must be found to push the North also. The World Bank must serve as an honest broker and represent the South in its legitimate expectations of the North— and not just vice versa. The Nordic countries and the Netherlands have already begun to do this.

3. *Maximize the productivity of natural capital in the short run, and invest in increasing its supply in the long run.* Economic logic requires that we behave in these two ways toward the *limiting factor* of production—that is, maximize its productivity and invest in its increase. Those principles are not in dispute. Disagreements do exist about whether natural capital is really the limiting factor. Some argue that man-made and natural capital are such good substitutes that the very idea of a limiting factor, which requires that the factors be complementary, is irrelevant.[4] It is true that without complementarity there is no limiting factor. So the question is, Are man-made capital and natural capital basically complements or substitutes? Here again we can provide perpetual full employment for econometricians, and I would welcome more empirical work on this, even though I think it is sufficiently clear to common sense that natural and man-made capital are fundamentally complements and only marginally substitutable.[5]

In the past natural capital has been treated as superabundant and priced at zero, so it did not really matter whether it was seen as a complement or a substitute for man-made capital. Now remaining natural capital appears to be both scarce and complementary, and therefore limiting. For example, cut timber is limited not by the number of sawmills, but by the remaining standing forests. Pumped crude oil is limited not by man-made pumping capacity, but by the remaining stocks of petroleum in the ground, and the natural capital of the atmosphere's capacity to serve as a sink for CO_2 is likely to be even more limiting to the rate at which petroleum can be burned than is the source limit of remaining oil in the ground.

In the short run, raising the price of natural capital by taxing throughput, as advocated above, will give the incentive to maximize natural capital productivity. Investment in natural capital over the long run is also needed. But how do we invest in something which by definition we cannot make? If we could make it, it would be man-made capital! For renewable resources we have the possibility of fallowing investments, or more generally "waiting" in the Marshallian sense—allowing this year's growth increment to be added to next year's growing stock rather than consuming it.[6] For nonrenewables we do not have this option. We can only liquidate them. So the question is, How fast do we liquidate, and how much of the proceeds can we count as income if we invest the rest in the best available renewable substitute? And, of course, How much of the correctly counted income do we then consume and how much do we invest?

One renewable substitute for natural capital is the mixture of natural and man-made capital represented by plantations, fish farms, and the like, which we may call "cultivated natural capital." But even within this important hybrid category we have a complementary combination of natural and man-made capital components—a plantation forest may use man-made capital to plant trees, control pests, and choose the proper rotation, for example—but the complementary natural capital services of rainfall, sunlight, soil, and so on are still there, and eventually still become limiting. Also, cultivated natural capital usually requires a reduction in biodiversity relative to natural capital proper, which must be counted as a cost.

For both renewable and nonrenewable resources, investments in enhancing throughput productivity are needed. Increasing resource productivity is indeed a good substitute for finding more of the resource. But the main point is that investment should be in the limiting factor, and to the extent that natural capital has replaced man-made capital as the limiting factor, the Bank's investment focus should shift correspondingly. I do not believe that it has. In fact, the failure to charge user cost on natural capital depletion, noted earlier, surely biases investment away from replenishing projects.

4. *Move away from the ideology of global economic integration by free trade, free capital mobility, and export-led growth—and toward a more nationalist orientation that seeks to develop domestic production for internal markets as the first option, having recourse to international trade only when clearly much more efficient.* At the present time global interdependence is celebrated as a self-evident good. The royal road to development, peace, and harmony is thought to be the unrelenting conquest of each nation's market by all other nations. The word "globalist" has politically correct connotations, while the word "nationalist" has come to be pejorative. This is so much the case that it is necessary to remind ourselves that the World Bank exists to serve the interests of its members, *which are nation states, national communities*—not individuals, not corporations, not even NGOs (nongovernmental organizations). It has no charter to serve the one-world-without-borders cosmopolitan vision of global integration—of converting many relatively independent national economies, loosely dependent on international trade, into one tightly integrated world economic network upon which the weakened nations depend for even basic survival.

The model of international community upon which the Bretton Woods institutions rest is that of a "community of communities," an international federation of *national* communities cooperating to solve global problems under the principle of subsidiarity. The model is not the cosmopolitan one of direct global citizenship in a single integrated world community without intermediation by nation states.

To globalize the economy by erasure of national economic boundaries through free trade, free capital mobility, and free, or at least uncontrolled, migration is to wound fatally the major unit of community capable of carrying out any policies for the common good. That includes not only national policies for purely domestic ends, but also international agreements required to deal with those environmental problems that are irreducibly global (CO_2, ozone depletion). International agreements presuppose the ability of national governments to carry out policies in their support. If nations have no control over their borders they are in a poor position to enforce national laws, including those necessary to secure compliance with international treaties that they have signed.

Cosmopolitan globalism weakens national boundaries and the power of national and subnational communities, while strengthening the relative power of transnational corporations. Since there is no world government capable of regulating global capital in the global interest, and since both the desirability and the possibility of a world government are highly doubtful, it will be necessary to make capital less global and more national. I know that this is an unthinkable thought right now, but take it as a prediction—ten years from now the buzz words and hot concepts will be "renationalization of capital" and the "community rooting of capital for the development of national and local economies," not the current shibboleths of export-led growth stimulated by whatever adjustments are necessary to increase global competitiveness. "Global competitiveness" (frequently a thought-substituting slogan) usually reflects not so much a real increase in resource productivity as a standards-lowering competition to reduce wages, externalize environmental and social costs, and export natural capital at low prices while calling it income.[7]

The World Bank should use the occasion of its fiftieth birthday to reflect deeply on the forgotten words of one of its founders, John Maynard Keynes:

> I sympathize therefore, with those who would minimize, rather than those who would maximize, economic entanglement between nations. Ideas, knowledge, art, hospitality, travel—these are the things which should of their nature be international. But let goods be homespun whenever it is reasonably and conveniently possible; and, above all, let finance be primarily national.[8]

National Accounts and Sustainable Development

Introduction

As mentioned in the introduction to Part 1, it is necessary to know exactly what is supposed to be growing in "economic growth" before we can discuss whether it should be slowed down or speeded up. This focuses attention on the procedures and principles underlying our system of national accounts, more commonly known as GNP accounts. Chapter 6 in this section makes a conservative case, written for the World Bank, for changing our national accounts. Chapter 7 makes some much more radical suggestions, drawing on the ideas of Irving Fisher.

In our book *For the Common Good*,[1] John B. Cobb, Jr., and I, with major help from Clifford Cobb, developed an Index of Sustainable Economic Welfare (ISEW) for the United States. We began with personal consumption and made a number of adjustments in order to convert that figure into a better index of economic welfare. We made adjustments for changes in the degree of equality of income distribution, depletion of natural capital, increases in foreign debt, and many other things designed to give a better measure of economic welfare and its sustainability. Of course we had to make many arbitrary judgments, but in our opinion no more arbitrary than those made in standard GNP accounting—in fact less so.

Between 1950 and 1970 (roughly) the GNP and the ISEW rose together. From the early 1970s the ISEW remained flat, actually declining somewhat in the early 1980s, while the GNP continued to rise throughout that period. In sum, we found that empirical evidence that GNP growth has increased economic welfare in the United States since about 1970 is nonexistent. This conclusion is conservative, because we did not subtract the cost of harmful products such as tobacco or alcohol, nor did we make any adjustment for the declining marginal utility of income as aggregate income grows. We have no illusions that our index is really an accurate measure of sustainable economic welfare, but we do think that it is more defensible than GNP in this regard. Since over the last several decades the general welfare of the population, as we conservatively measured it, has ceased to increase with GNP, we feel that it is unwarranted to continue to justify policies on the basis of their contribution to GNP growth.[2]

We did not offer the ISEW as the proper goal of economic policy—it too has flaws. If GNP were a cigarette, then the ISEW would be that cigarette with a charcoal filter. If you are addicted to cigarettes it's better to smoke one with a charcoal filter; if you are addicted to numerical measures of welfare, it's better to use the ISEW. The fact is that we are so addicted, and addictions call for satisfaction. But we should not rest content with this addiction, and should begin to think about breaking it. After all, GNP, an invention of the 1930s, has been with us for far less time than has tobacco. That passions for growth have become attached to such arbitrary measures of welfare sometimes makes me think that we would be better off without any such measures at all. The mere existence of any numerical index of welfare is a standing invitation to the fallacy of misplaced concreteness—to serving the inevitably distorted reflection of reality represented in the index instead of directly serving the reality itself. There is a limit to what one can do with numbers—just as there is a limit to what one can do without them. Finding the right balance is not easy.

The goal of the chapters in this section, unlike that of the ISEW, is not to measure welfare but to do a better job of measuring income. The latter task is easier, but the two efforts face a number of problems in common. Chapter 6 offers a simple adjustment to make our net national income a better measure of true (Hicksian) income. Chapter 7 represents a way to relate national accounting as a policy guide to sustainable development as a goal—that is, an effort to imagine how national accounts might be structured so as to measure not only the benefits of growth but also its costs, in a manner that might permit comparison at the margin and thereby help in finding the optimal scale of the macroeconomy.

Chapter 6

Toward a Measure of Sustainable Net National Product

Sustainable Income

The central criterion for defining the concept of income has been well stated by Sir John Hicks:

> The purpose of income calculations in practical affairs is to give people an indication of the amount which they can consume without impoverishing themselves. Following out this idea, it would seem that we ought to define a man's income as the maximum value which he can consume during a week, and still expect to be as well off at the end of the week as he was at the beginning. Thus when a person saves he plans to be better off in the future; when he lives beyond his income he plans to be worse off. Remembering that the practical purpose of income is to serve as a guide for prudent conduct, I think it is fairly clear that this is what the central meaning must be. [1946, p. 172]

The same basic idea of income holds at the national level. Income is not a precise theoretical concept but rather a practical guide to the maximum amount that can be consumed by a nation without eventual impoverishment. We know that we cannot consume the entire gross national product without eventually impoverishing ourselves.

If we did consume the entire GNP there would be no fund out of which to replace depreciating machines, buildings, roads, etc. Therefore, we subtract depreciation and get net national product (NNP), which is usually taken as income in Hicks's sense. The central defining characteristic of income is *sustainability*. The term "sustainable income" ought therefore to be considered a redundancy. The fact that it is not is a measure of how far we have strayed from the central meaning of income and, consequently, of the need for correction.

But could we really consume even NNP year after year without impoverishing ourselves? No, we could not, because the production of NNP requires supporting activities that are not biophysically sustainable, and the measurement of NNP overestimates the maximum net product available for consumption. NNP fails to account for the depreciation of reproducible natural capital (forests, fisheries) and for the liquidation of nonreproducible natural inventories (oil, gas). Consequently, NNP increasingly fails as a guide to prudent conduct by nations.

Two adjustments to NNP are needed to make it a closer approximation to Hicks's concept of income and a better guide to prudent behavior. One adjustment is simply to extend the principle of depreciation to cover consumption of natural capital stocks depleted through production. The other is to subtract defensive expenditures, or regrettable expenditures necessary to defend ourselves from the unwanted side effects of our aggregate production and consumption. Regrettable defensive expenditures are in the nature of intermediate goods, costs of production rather than final product available for consumption. To correct for having counted defensive expenditures in NNP (e.g., the cleaning up of oil spills), their size must be estimated and subtracted to arrive at an estimate of maximum sustainable consumption, or true income.

Let us then define the corrected income concept, "sustainable social net national product" (SSNNP), as net national product (NNP) minus both defensive expenditures (DE) and depreciation of natural capital (DNC). Thus,

$$SSNP = NNP - DE - DNC.$$

This definition entails no interference whatsoever with the current structure of the UN's System of National Accounts (SNA). There is no loss of historical continuity or comparability. Two additional accounts are introduced, not for frivolous or trendy reasons, but simply to gain a closer approximation of the central and well-established meaning of income. No attempt is made to deal with the controversial issues of national income accounting, such as inclusion of leisure, disutility of labor, household production, and services of long-lived consumer durables. The relation of income to welfare is not addressed.

Since NNP is a familiar concept, it remains only to discuss briefly the new accounts: defensive expenditures (DE) and depletion of natural capital (DNC), which are by no means novel ideas, but are not yet included as part of an extended SNA.

Defensive Expenditures

The explosion of the populations of human bodies, of artifacts of all kinds, and of the populations of plants and animals exploited for human use that has happened in the past fifty years might better be called an implosion, since it has occurred in a finite environment. The term "implosion" suggests a compressing together rather than an expanding apart, a process of congestion, mutual interference, and self-canceling collision. Defensive expenditures reflect this increasingly prevalent phenomenon of mutually interfering, self-canceling activities.

The category of defensive expenditures can be large or small depending on where the boundaries are drawn. Christian Leipert of the International Institute for Environment and Society in Berlin has suggested five broad categories of defensive expenditures (Leipert 1986).

1. Defensive expenditures induced by the overexploitation of environmental resources in the general course of economic growth, such as the costs of all environmental protection activities and expenditures for environmental damage compensation.

2. Defensive expenditures induced by spatial concentration, centralization of production, and associated urbanization, such as increased commuting costs, housing, and recreation costs.

3. Defensive expenditures induced by the increased risks generated by the maturation of the industrial system, such as increased expenditures for protection against crime, accident, sabotage, and technical failure.

4. Defensive expenditures induced by the negative side effects of car transport, such as traffic accidents with associated repair and medical expenses.

5. Defensive expenditures arising from unhealthy consumption and behavioral patterns and from poor working and living conditions, such as costs generated by drug addiction, smoking (both active and passive), and alcohol.

These categories are neither exhaustive nor mutually exclusive and are naturally somewhat arbitrary. Category 1 might, in our classification, fit better under DNC. But it represents a start at subtracting expenditures that do not reflect any increase in the net product available for consumption without eventual impoverishment.

Depletion of Natural Capital

This is entirely analogous to the depreciation of man-made capital. In fact, Keynes justified the concept of user cost for man-made capital by analogy with the more self-evident case for charging user cost for natural resources. The obvious categories of natural capital are geological (nonrenewable) and biological (renewable). Both, of course, are depletable. Depletion of geological capital is necessary for industrial and agroindustrial production. New geological discoveries do not reverse the process of depletion, but they do extend the time span over which the depletion can continue.

Depletion of renewable natural capital is in some ways a more serious matter because reduced stocks or populations of plants and animals will lead to a reduction in sustainable flow of resource inputs and ecosystem services. Only by a future investment (reduction in consumption) could the larger sustainable flow be reestablished, and even that is often not possible. Even in commercially exploited populations that are above the level of maximum sustainable yield and therefore would yield more with a smaller stock, the consumption of the stock diminution is not a sustainable source of income, but rather capital consumption.

Geological and ecological information on depletion comes in physical units and must be priced or evaluated in some way before it can be subtracted from NNP. This will no doubt involve some arbitrary conventions. Valuation might be based either on the principle of replacement cost or on willingness to pay, whichever is less, in order to be "conservative." It is not clear that any greater arbitrariness would be involved than already exists in current estimates of depreciation of man-made capital, especially if one counts obsolescence or "moral" depreciation as well as physical.

Income, as Hicks emphasized, is not a theoretically precise concept, but rather a practical guide to prudent behavior. Surely some reasonable allowances, however imprecise, for depletion of natural capital and some correction for the double counting of defensive (intermediate) expenditures are required if the income concept is to remain a guide to prudent behavior by nations, which is its fundamental reason to be. The two adjustments are in keeping with the central idea of income and involve no disruption of the existing SNA. The need for such adjustments has already led independent scholars to begin work on measuring defensive expenditures and the depletion of natural capital. What remains is to give official status and formal recognition to these adjustments aimed at keeping the income concept as a reliable guide to prudent behavior in a world that has changed significantly since national income accounting was first institutionalized.

Chapter 7

On Sustainable Development and National Accounts

There is an anomaly that confronts current views on economic development: namely, that economic development as currently understood and measured is neither sustainable for a long future nor generalizable to all presently living people. I present here a preliminary proposal for changes in national accounting and valuation procedures necessary to correct this fundamental anomaly in GNP-based theories of growth and development.

The Anomaly: An Impossibility Hypothesis

In the days of mercantilism, economists urged nations to accumulate treasure through a favorable (surplus) balance of international trade. The policy implications of mercantilist (bullionist) orthodoxy were that nations with gold mines should invest much capital and labor in digging up metals with only minimal use value, and that all nations, especially those without mines, should strive to trade products of great use value for relatively useless yellow metal which represented the wealth and power of the state. Since trade was competitive, costs had to be kept low, and since labor was the major cost, wages had to be low. The way to keep wages low is to have an excess supply of laborers, either through population growth or technological unemployment. For a country to be rich, therefore, the majority of the citizens had to be poor, and to dedicate themselves to producing, either directly in mines or indirectly through trade, something which was of no use to them as individuals. Furthermore, the policy advice to strive for a surplus balance of payments was clearly not a goal that could be attained by all countries, since one country's surplus is some other country's deficit. The policy goal of a balance-of-payments surplus, even if it was really beneficial to the surplus country, is not a generalizable goal, and today is used in textbooks as a classic example of the "fallacy of composition."

We smile and shake our heads at the mercantilist view, so full of contradictions and impossibilities which are easy to see from our historical vantage point. It is not so easy to see the anomalies in our own development theories, but I want to suggest that some might exist—that we may be advocating something that is impossible, somewhat analogous to urging all countries to run a surplus balance of payments, and which will only lead to conflict and disappointment. The case of mercantilism shows that such an error is not without historical precedent. Maximizing GNP probably makes more sense than maximizing gold stocks, but serious anomalies remain. I am not referring here to the problem of distribution, which has been widely recognized and on which economists have contributed much useful work. I refer instead to the fact that GNP, however distributed, may be more an index of cost than of benefit—a point to be developed later. The first question to be raised concerns the impossibility of generalizing "development" as it is currently understood (real GNP per capita and associated resource flows similar to U.S. levels) to all countries in the world.

Most basic laws of science are impossibility statements: it is impossible to create or destroy matter energy, it is impossible to travel faster than the speed of light, it is impossible to make a perpetual motion machine, and so on. In today's world, however, impossibility is not a popular concept. Yet if we know that something is impossible then we can save an infinite amount of time and money by not trying to do it. Economists therefore should be very interested in impossibility theorems, and I would like to suggest one—namely, that a U.S.-style resource consumption standard for a world of 4.8 billion people is impossible, and even if it could be attained it would be very short-lived. Even less possible, then, would be the dream of an ever-growing standard of resource consumption for an ever-growing world population.

This impossibility hypothesis is not a straightforward logical impossibility like that of all countries simultaneously having a surplus balance of payments. It suggests a factual rather than a logical impossibility. What evidence is there to support it? There are all sorts of studies, including Meadows et al. (1972), the Leontief UN study (1977), Lester Brown et al. (1971), and the *Global 2000 Report to the President* (1980). The latter's major finding was that "if present trends continue the world in 2000 will be more crowded, more polluted, less stable ecologically, and more vulnerable to disruption than the world we live in now. . . . Despite greater material output the world's people will be poorer in many ways than they are today." To what extent are these trends driven by our goals of growth and development as currently defined? Can we say that the cost of being "poorer in many ways" is greater or less than the benefit of greater material output? The second question takes us into the problem of national accounts. For now, let us focus on the prior question of the feasibility of economic growth and development when generalized to all people in the world.

Sometimes simple back-of-an-envelope calculations are more instructive than voluminous studies. Consider that it requires about one-third of the current annual world extraction of nonrenewable resources to support that 6% (or less) of the world's population in the United States at a per capita level to which it is thought that the rest of the world should aspire. This means that even if U.S. levels of capitalization and technology could be instantaneously extended worldwide, current resource flows could at most support 18% of the world's population at the U.S. resource consumption standard, with nothing left over for the other 82%. Without the labor services of the bottom 82%, the top 18% would of course not be so well off as this simple calculation suggests.

It may be objected that the obvious solution is to expand total world resource flows by whatever factor is necessary to generalize the U.S. per capita standard of resource consumption. How much would that be? Returning to the back of the envelope, let M be the required factor and R be the current world annual resource extraction. For world per capita resource usage to equal U.S. per capita resource usage requires that

$$\frac{M \cdot R}{4.8 \times 10^9} = \frac{R/3}{2.3 \times 10^8},$$

where $4.8 \times 10^9 =$ world population and $2.3 \times 10^8 =$ U.S. population. From this,

$$M = 7$$

Thus the annual resource flows would have to increase by roughly a factor of seven. It is interesting that this factor of seven estimate is rather neatly bracketed by the Brundtland Commission's call for a five- to tenfold expansion of the world economy. Current rates of material and energy use are already doing serious damage to the life-support capacity of our globe. Could we really get away with a sevenfold increase? And if so, for how long?

But even the sevenfold increase is a gross underestimate, because we have neglected the differences in accumulated capital stock that would be required to process and transform that larger annual flow. This capital stock would have to be accumulated out of a still larger flow in the initial years. Harrison Brown (1970) estimates that to supply the rest of the world with the average per capita "standing crop" of the industrial metals already embodied in the existing artifacts of the ten richest nations would require more than sixty years' production of these metals at 1970 rates. But even assuming for the sake of argument instantaneous capital accumulation *ex nihilo*, the problem is still understated because of increasing costs due to depletion of mines and wells. A sevenfold increase in net, usable minerals will require a much greater than sevenfold increase in gross resource flows, since more energy and materials will be required in the extraction of energy and material from ever less accessible sources. And it is the gross flow rather than the net that produces environmental impact. The monetary and environmental costs of attempting the impossible are the more demonstrable, but the cost of instability and social conflict engendered by repeated failure to meet impossible expectations could be even more disruptive politically.

Technological optimists counter the above argument by claiming that technology can increase resource productivity without limit, and that therefore all nations can become richer. Even if true, such a claim does not counter the argument, which has been in terms of per capita resource use, not per capita product or welfare. Even if technology could increase resource productivity without limit, so that the same physical resource flow would yield an ever greater value flow, we would still face the problem of keeping physical flows within ecological limits, and still could not generalize the current U.S. industrial economy to the whole world. We might generalize some new, as yet unknown system that made much more efficient use of resources, but that is more a concession to the impossibility hypothesis than a refutation of it. If the technological optimist really believes in unlimited increase in resource productivity, then limitations on the volume and distribution of the physical resource flow would be seen as desirable, since this would force technological effort into increasing resource productivity (unlimited possibility) and away from the path of increasing intensity of resource usage (strictly limited possibility). In any case, the impossibility hypothesis is unaffected, since even if "development" in some sense continues indefinitely, the currently underdeveloped countries still cannot all pass through the window of the high-resource-consuming industrial stage of the developed countries of today. Therefore a major question becomes how high a resource consumption level should less developed countries aim at?

These considerations also suggest a concept of "overdevelopment" as correlative to "underdevelopment": an overdeveloped country might be defined as one whose level of per capita resource consumption is such that if generalized to all countries could not be sustained indefinitely; correspondingly an underdeveloped country would be one whose per capita resource consumption is less than what could be sustained indefinitely if all the world consumed at that level. Instead of "indefinitely" one might substitute an arbitrary time period, say one hundred or five hundred years, to lend greater specificity. A serious shortcoming of these definitions is that since they are in per capita terms they do not take account of the absolute size of population and its distribution among countries. This means, for example, that a currently underdeveloped country might be reclassified as an overdeveloped country solely as a result of population growth in *other* countries.

What is generalizable to all depends on how many is "all"! In any event, population growth must be stopped as soon as humanely possible.

Some economists have begun to express doubts about the traditional notion of economic development. Economic historian Richard Wilkinson writes, "Predictions on when the resources which modern industrial technology depends on will run out are usually within the same time scale as the predictions of when many underdeveloped countries may reach maturity" (1973). Disturbing coincidence!

A similar view was expressed by John M. Culbertson (1971): "But elevating the present population of India to the present-day standard of living of upper-class Americans is unthinkable because of its implications for environmental destruction."

The usual attitude, however, is that expressed by Paul W. McCracken (1975), former economic advisor to the president of the United States: "The action most urgently needed in the world economy is for the stronger economies to be willing to accept higher levels of living. Their reluctance to do so seems to be of Calvinistic proportions." Unless the abstemious rich make the "sacrifice" of consuming more, the poor will not be able to sell their resources, and hence will not be able to develop. The only problem is insufficiency of aggregate demand. Keynesian pump-priming is the paradigm within which world development is viewed. McCracken and the many economists for whom he is the distinguished spokesman obviously do not believe in any "impossibility hypothesis." Even many "third-world" economists share this view, which is surprising only until one remembers that these third-world economists usually get their degrees in U.S. and British universities, studying under people who think like McCracken. Nor is the situation much different in Western Europe.

It may be that the coincidence of interests seen by McCracken and others is a short-run affair. Taking a longer view, it is possible that by exporting their resources the less developed countries will increase their dependence on the developed countries. The less developed would remain dependent on the developed as export markets. In addition, as the richest and most easily available resources are extracted first, only the leaner and less accessible deposits are available for later development. The latter require more capital-intensive technologies, for which the less developed nations must again depend on the developed. To make the point clearer, consider a thought experiment suggested by Harrison Brown (1970). Suppose all the physical capital stock of the United States were annihilated, with everything else (knowledge, natural resources, and so on) remaining intact. Could we replace the lost physical capital, given time and effort? The answer is no, because that equipment was built with concentrated and easily available resources which are now depleted. The reconstruction could not start again with East Texas oil, but would have to start with offshore Alaskan oil to be exploited without the further natural subsidy of Mesabi range iron ore. Third-world countries that export their prime geological capital in exchange for luxury consumer goods for their elite class could end up in exactly the same fix. Are there any categories in our national accounts that would alert us to such a possibility? Kuwait, for example, has a very high GNP per capita, but is this income or capital consumption? Common sense suggests mainly the latter, but GNP accounts treat it simply as current income.

Enough has been said to indicate the seriousness of the anomalies of current economic development theory. Could it be that, like the mercantilists, we are seeking to maximize something which does not merit maximization? Real GNP may not bear much closer relation to welfare than does gold, yet our national accounts are wedded to the concept, and our investment criteria generally are designed to increase GNP. Development may have to be reconceived in terms other than GNP if the anomalies discussed are to be avoided. It may be that our adherence to GNP has led us to a concept of development that is impossible of general attainment by all countries. To the extent that this is true it becomes imperative to redefine development in such a way that it is attainable by all (or else admit the impossibility and accept the consequences). A reformulation of the meaning of development requires a reformulation of the national accounts in terms in which development is defined. A possible alternative basis for national accounts is adumbrated below.

Cost, Benefit, and Capital Accounts: An Alternative to GNP

It is worth inquiring whether our difficulty with GNP had its origin in A. C. Pigou's decision not to follow Irving Fisher's definition of the "national dividend." Pigou (1970) reasoned as follows:

> Professor Fisher himself takes the position that the national dividend, or income, consists solely of *services* as received by ultimate consumers whether from their material or from their human environment. Thus a piano or an overcoat made for me this year is not a part of this year's income, but an addition to capital. Only the services rendered to me during this year by these things are income. . . . This way of looking at the matter is obviously very attractive from a mathematical point of view.

Fisher's view is attractive mathematically because it does not add up unlike things: only the values of current services (psychic income) are added. We do not conflate income with capital; we do not add up the value of the service itself with the value of the item that renders the service. In his concept of capital, Fisher included the material and human environment. Human beings render services to other human beings, but we count only those services; we do not add in the capital value of the human being in the year he was born or graduated. For the material environment, Fisher had in mind artifacts mainly, not the natural material environment. Conceptually it would be easy to extend his view to cover natural ecosystem services as well, although problems of valuation are great. But in both cases we should treat services from the material environment consistently with services from the human environment. We should always count only service as income, and that which renders service as capital. In so doing we recognize that physical capital always depreciates (due to entropy) and that its continual maintenance and replacement is a cost. The cost of maintaining capital intact must not be counted as a part of the "net national dividend"; and all physical production (except net investment) is a cost of keeping capital intact.

But national income accounting did not develop along the lines outlined above. Pigou (1970) rejected Fisher's approach because "the wide departure which it makes from the ordinary use of language involves disadvantages which seem to outweigh the gain in logical clarity." Although Pigou's position was quite defensible in his own time, it may be that subsequent economic evolution has been less kind to his concepts than to Fisher's, and that if Pigou could have foreseen the extent to which GNP would be relied on as the *summum bonum* of economic policy, he might have opted for logical clarity as did Fisher. Had national accounts developed in accordance with Fisher's concepts, their extension to cover environmental services and ecological and geological capital depletion would have been obvious and easy, except for valuation problems for services without markets. As it is now, incorporation of ecological services and natural capital must be very ad hoc, and in fact it may ultimately be necessary to adopt Fisher's approach.[1]

Why has the traditional national accounting approach of Pigou and others become so inappropriate? At least a part of the answer lies in the fact that the world has changed since 1920, and that change has been qualitative as well as quantitative. It has changed in a way that Fisher's view could have accommodated, but Pigou's could not. The qualitative change I have in mind is that from a relatively empty world to a relatively full world, from a world of "unemployed carrying capacity" to a world of "fully employed carrying capacity." When the world was empty, throughput could be considered a flow from an infinite source to an infinite sink, and not regarded as a cost because not scarce. The fact that a larger stock required a larger throughput meant that throughput was an index of capital stock, and consequently an indirect index of service rendered by the capital stock. And throughput had the irresistible advantage of being more measurable than service. But in a full, finite world where throughput is itself a cost, it is no longer legitimate to make it do double duty as an index of benefit. A certain sacrifice of logic for the sake of measurability and conformity to common language may have been justifiable in Pigou's time, before the cost nature of throughput had become so apparent. But in a full world, throughput is cost, and current "empty-world" accounting concepts such as GNP became inappropriate.

From 1949, when he was still very much an orthodox economist, Kenneth Boulding (1969) argued the logic of Fisher's view:

> I shall argue that it is the capital stock from which we derive satisfactions, not from the additions to it (production) or the subtractions from it (consumption): that consumption, far from being a desideratum, is a deplorable property of the capital stock which necessitates the equally deplorable activities of production: and that the objective of economic policy should not be to maximize consumption or production, but rather to minimize it, i.e., to enable us to maintain our capital stock with as little consumption or production as possible.

Of course GNP is a flow measure of production or consumption. As such it is largely the maintenance cost of the capital stock, a measure of the regrettably necessary activities of depletion, pollution, and labor that are required to maintain the capital stock against physical depreciation that inevitably occurs as the capital is used to satisfy wants. Remember that "capital" is used in the broad sense of Fisher, so that it includes umbrellas, shoes, pencils, and so on. Wants are satisfied by the existing capital stock, not by the unavoidable but regrettable characteristic of the stock to become worn out or used up.

This issue can be clarified with some careful definitions of terms:

1. *Accumulation* (or "capital" in Irving Fisher's sense) is the total inventory of consumers' goods, producers' goods, and human bodies. Accumulation takes two forms: a *fund* or a *stock*. A *stock* is an unstructured inventory of like things or of a homogeneous substance, which gets used a little at a time—that is, some gets totally used up before the rest is affected at all (for example, gasoline). A *fund* is a structured organic whole, all parts of which must participate together, and which depreciates as a whole (for example, an automobile). Stocks get "used up," funds get "worn out." Both require replacement.

2. *Service* is the satisfaction experienced when wants are satisfied (psychic income in Irving Fisher's sense). Service is yielded by accumulations (stocks and funds). The quantity and quality of the stocks and funds determine the intensity of service. Service is yielded over a period of time, and thus appears to be a flow magnitude, but unlike true flows it cannot be accumulated.

3. *Throughput* is the entropic physical flow of matter and energy from nature's sources, through the human economy and back to nature's sinks; it is the flow that is accumulated into stocks and funds and out of which stocks and funds are replaced and maintained.

The basic relationship between these three fundamental magnitudes can be seen by an identity. Let A equal accumulations (both stocks and funds), S equal service, and T equal throughput. Then

$$\frac{S}{T} = \frac{S}{A} \times \frac{A}{T}$$

Service is the final benefit. Throughput is final cost. Accumulation is throughput "frozen" in structured forms and inventories in shapes and amounts appropriate to our purposes and to the duration required for their satisfaction. Eventually this frozen throughput is "melted" by entropy (either through wearing out or using up) and flows back to the environment as waste. Replacement of stocks and funds requires the accumulation of more throughput. The throughput flow begins with depletion of environmental low-entropy resources and ends with the pollution of the environment with high-entropy wastes, facts which underline the cost nature of the throughput. Accumulation cancels out in the identity just as it ultimately wears out in the real world. Nevertheless, accumulation must be the central concept because it is the accumulation that on the one hand yields benefits, and on the other hand imposes costs. For any given accumulation we clearly want maximum service and minimum throughput. Alternatively, for a given ecologically sustainable throughput we would want maximum stock and maximum service per unit of stock.[2]

What is the relation of these concepts to GNP? The relationship is given in the following equation:

GNP = value of some services + value of throughput + value of change in accumulated stocks and funds

GNP adds up parts of each of the three basic magnitudes. GNP counts the value of service of all assets rented during the accounting period, but not the value of services of owner-used assets, with the exception of owner-occupied houses for which a rental value is imputed and counted. Nor does it count natural ecosystem services. The value of the throughput is reflected in the production-consumption flow—the value of production required for maintenance and replacement of people and of stocks and funds, including consumer goods. The last term, value of net change in accumulated stocks and funds, represents net investment. However, it does not include changes in natural stocks and funds, such as depletion of geological stocks, or disruptions of environmental functions, or depletions of ecological funds of other species upon which we depend. The depletion of minerals and the depreciation of ecological life-support "capital" accumulated over millennia is not subtracted in calculating change in stocks and funds,[3] nor is the loss of current service of environmental functions subtracted from the value of current services supplied by produced goods. Indeed, efforts to defend ourselves against the effects of pollution lead to new demands for commodities and services and so lead to an increase in GNP.

How much sense does GNP make when translated into these more basic magnitudes? Consider that service is benefit, throughput is a cost, and net accumulation is a change in stocks and funds. What sense does it make to add these incongruous magnitudes? Is it not as if a merchant's bookkeeper added up receipts plus expenditures plus the change in inventory? Of what analytic interest could such a conflation of numbers possibly be? Should economic development be defined in terms of the increase of such a dubious sum, even when corrected for inflation, population size, and maldistribution?

Clearly such questions must be of prime concern to all development economists. Economics requires the *comparison* of costs and benefits, *not their addition*. The whole thrust of microeconomics is to compare costs and benefits at the margin so as to be able to limit the activity under consideration to its optimum extent. But the macroeconomic activity of national economic growth is not conceived of as having an optimum extent. If quantitative growth in real GNP is considered a permanent norm that must never cease, then it is convenient not to compare costs and benefits lest they become equal at the margin (which is the usual tendency). One way to avoid comparing costs and benefits is to add them together and treat the sum as if it were the most unique of all good things, that for which more is always better than less. But GNP is a conflation of costs, benefits, and changes in accumulation, and is no better a guide to determine the optimum level of economic activity than is the stock of gold bullion.

Some economists would object to the above argument on the grounds that every entry into GNP is based on a transaction, and for that transaction to have occurred each party had to decide that the benefits to him or her of making the deal were greater than the costs to him or her. Therefore any increase in GNP is already based on a micro-level comparison of costs and benefits and an additional macro-level comparison would be redundant at best, and at worst destructive of individual freedom.

But the macro-level comparison is not redundant for two related reasons. First, costs and benefits to the individuals making the transaction do not exhaust all costs and benefits. Private costs and benefits do not fully reflect social costs and benefits. Externalities are pervasive, and become more so as we move from a relatively empty to a relatively full world. Second, arguing from the part to the whole commits the fallacy of composition. Micro rationality often leads to macro irrationality, as evidenced by the paradox of thrift, the tragedy of the commons, the prisoner's dilemma, the tyranny of small decisions, and the arms race. Macro-level comparison of costs and benefits is necessary. Furthermore, this point is accepted by standard economists when they argue in favor of stimulating aggregate growth beyond the individualistically market-determined level. Public policy to stimulate aggregate growth must be based on an implicit comparison of costs and benefits at the macro level and the perception that the social benefits of growth are greater than the social cost. The issue is whether that perception is right or wrong, not the legitimacy of the macro cost-benefit comparison. The three-accounts approach would provide more relevant information and increase the accuracy of our perceptions of social costs and benefits.

Instead of one account, GNP, we should keep three accounts, one for each basic magnitude. We need the following:

1. A *benefit account* which would seek to measure the value of the services yielded by all accumulations (not just those rented during the accounting period, and not just those used by consumers, but also those used in production that is enjoyable and self-fulfilling).

2. A *cost account* which would seek to measure the value of depletion, pollution, and disutility of those kinds of labor that are irksome (and of "waiting" in Alfred Marshall's sense). With separate accounts for costs and benefits we could occasionally ask if the extra benefits of further accumulation were worth the extra costs.

3. A *capital account*, an inventory of the accumulation of stocks and funds and their ownership distribution. Included in the capital account would be not only produced stocks and funds, but also natural capital such as mines, wells, and ecosystem infrastructure.

Currently we count present consumption financed by geological and ecological decapitalization no differently from present consumption financed by sustainable production. Kuwait, for example, has a per capita GNP of some $17,000, of which a significant fraction is royalties based on geological decapitalization. The three-accounts approach would make this decapitalization obvious. It would invite the question of the extent to which petroleum earnings should be tied to compensating capital investments and the extent to which they should be used to finance current consumption.

Ideally, one could argue that accumulation should continue up to the point where the marginal benefit of services rendered by the extra stocks and funds is equal to the marginal cost of the extra throughput required to maintain the extra stocks and funds. Once the optimal accumulation was reached further growth would cease, at least until such time as the underlying conditions of taste and technology changed.

Such optimization is an ideal case. In the real world we are likely to resort to "satisficing" rather than optimizing, that is, seeking a sufficient or satisfactory level of accumulation rather than the optimum level. A separate behavior mode would be associated with each of the three basic magnitudes:

1. The accumulation of stocks and funds would be *satsificed*.

2. Service would be *maximized*, given the sufficient accumulation.

3. Throughput would be *minimized*, given the sufficient accumulation.

Behavior modes 1 and 3 are in direct conflict with the current goal of maximizing GNP. Indeed, optimizing as well as satisficing would be in conflict with fostering growth in GNP.

The problem with an optimizing approach lies not only in the requirement for accurate measures of cost and benefits of further stock accumulation, but also in the requirement that marginal cost and benefit functions be "well-behaved." This means that the marginal benefit curve should be monotonically decreasing and the marginal cost curve monotonically increasing. The former would not be unreasonable to expect since rational people satisfy their most pressing wants first. Thus each additional stock or fund would on average be devoted to a less pressing need. But the marginal cost curve reflects depletion of geological capital and loss of current environmental service functions. There is no reason to expect that loss of environmental function will be incurred in an ordered sequence from less to more important under the pressure of increasing throughput. The wisest course may be to try to set the level of accumulation at an ecologically sustainable amount. Population times per capita resource consumption would be set equal to or, for safety's sake, less than carrying capacity. Sufficiency and sustainability would be the criteria for choosing a level of accumulation. Efficiency would be achieved by maximizing service yielded per unit of accumulated stocks and funds, and by minimizing throughput per unit of stock or fund required for maintenance and replacement. In terms of the identity, maximizing S/A means maximizing S with A given. The ratio S/A reflects the intensity of service yielded per unit of time by the accumulated stocks and funds. That intensity in turn depends on the allocation and distribution of the total accumulation among alternative artifact uses and among different people. Maximizing A/T means, in effect, minimizing T given A.

The ratio A/T reflects the durability of stocks and funds, the number of units of time over which they continue to render service.

It seems to me that Irving Fisher's way of looking at things is eminently sensible, coherent, and logical.[4] It has the advantage of clearly separating costs and benefits and of measuring each more inclusively. Benefits include not only the service of rented assets, but also the service of owner-used assets which are currently omitted. Costs include depletion of natural capital, loss of current environmental service, and disutility of labor, all currently neglected in GNP, or, worse, implicitly treated as benefits. Might this not be a more sensible approach than maximizing GNP, which is nearly equivalent to maximizing throughput and consequently maximizing the costs of depletion and pollution?

Even if it is admitted that the three-accounts approach is theoretically much superior to GNP, there remains the admittedly enormous problem of making these accounts operational. But is not even the poorest approximation to the correct concept always better than an accurate approximation to an irrelevant or erroneous concept? Indeed, it could be reasonably argued that we might be better off to abandon GNP as a criterion even if we had nothing better to put in its place.

G.K. Chesterton tells the story of the English pub that served poisoned beer. People were dropping dead. Some alert citizens had the beer analyzed, discovered it was poisonous, and petitioned the local magistrate to close the pub forthwith. The magistrate said, "The house you mention is one in which people are systematically murdered by means of poison. But before you demand so drastic a course as that of pulling it down or even shutting it up, you have to consider a problem of no little difficulty. Have you considered precisely what building you would Put In Its Place, whether a . . ." The point is, of course, that when something is found bad enough you do not have to put anything in its place, just remove it and be glad to be rid of it. It is admittedly an exaggeration to say that GNP is worse than nothing, but I suspect that the world could get along well enough without it, as it did before 1940. We must face the question of what to Put In Its Place, but without letting its operational difficulty be converted into an argument for staying with the "poisoned beer" of GNP.

Population
and
Sustainable
Development

Introduction

The eventual necessity of a steady-state population has been evident to many for a long time. What holds for the population of human bodies must also hold for the populations of cars, buildings, livestock, and each and every form of physical wealth that humans accumulate. In an empty world the population of people is complementary with the various populations of wealth. But in a full world they tend to become substitutes because they compete for the same space and maintenance throughput of low-entropy resources. It is the total resource flow (the product of population times per capita resource use) that is limited. In a world operating at full resource capacity, more of one factor (human population) means less of the other (artifacts).

Even before this point is reached, more people means more consumption, less investment, and slower growth, thus making it more difficult for poor countries to increase per capita wealth. Also, what most attracted my attention while living in Northeast Brazil in the late 1960s was the effect of class differentials in fertility upon the distribution of income. Fertility in the lower class was over twice that of the upper class—a condition that still obtains in many parts of the world today. The possibility of wages ever rising in the face of a virtually unlimited and rapidly growing supply of labor was nil. The rich got richer while the poor got children. An effective upper-class monopoly on the means of limiting reproduction was added to the traditional monopoly on ownership of the means of production to give an additional dimension of class dominance. It seemed to me that the social factors generating poverty were two: nonownership of the means of production (Marx); and nonownership of the means of limiting reproduction (Malthus). Although Marxists and Malthusians are traditional enemies, it seems to me that their respective understandings of the causes of poverty are logically consistent, however psychologically and ideologically at odds they may be. I wrote two papers on this theme.[1] Chapter 9, below, is a sequel. Chapter 8, on carrying capacity, grew out of my work at the World Bank, in response to intensely practical but scrupulously avoided policy questions in Paraguay and Ecuador. These two chapters are in the nature of case studies, and therefore they are a bit more empirical than the rest of this book.

It is frankly discouraging to see how little the population discussion has advanced during the last thirty years. The Chinese have finally gotten serious about population, at least for a while, but only after having grown well beyond a billion people. Instead of receiving applause and understanding from other countries for facing up to the problem, they mainly get unmeasured criticism for a few reported human rights violations related to population control. Certainly they should be criticized for any violations of human rights (most of which are unrelated to reproduction), but too often the issue of human rights is used to avoid the necessity of population control itself. There is apparently no human right to be born into a country that is not already overpopulated. Were such a right to be recognized, it would imply a correlative responsibility not to overpopulate the country. Heightened sensitivity to reproductive rights seems to have dulled our sensitivity to reproductive responsibilities.

National populations grow by immigration as well as by births. Some Chinese are now claiming refugee immigrant status in the United States on the grounds that a basic human right, reproduction freedom, has been denied them in China. They now want to practice reproductive freedom here. And many U.S. libertarians, as well as authoritarians of both the Catholic and the Protestant right wings, are quite eager for them to do so!

At the same time, both setting immigration policy and enforcement of existing laws to stop illegal immigration are becoming hot political issues, especially in California and Florida. Recent welfare cutbacks have made poor citizens of this country increasingly unwilling to share these benefits with illegal aliens, the very same people who are competing for their jobs and thus lowering their wages. This has created both an understandable resentment toward lack of government enforcement of our immigration laws and an unfortunate hostility toward some immigrants.

Failure of the U.S. federal government to adequately enforce its own immigration laws is increasingly, and correctly, seen as an implicit cheap-labor policy —a way to undercut union power and to increase global competitiveness by lowering domestic wages. It is politically difficult to openly defend a low-wage policy. It is much easier to attain the same result indirectly, by turning a blind eye toward illegal immigration (or, in the case of Brazil, toward the rapid natural increase of the laboring class). In addition to lower wages, other sacrifices made on the altar of global competitiveness include social insurance, workplace safety standards, and environmental protection standards. The problem of a global standards-lowering competition is discussed in Part 5, but for now the causative role of both differential fertility and net immigration in supporting an implicit cheap-labor strategy needs to be noted.

Chapter 8

Carrying Capacity as a Tool of Development Policy: The Ecuadoran Amazon and the Paraguayan Chaco

The remaining sparsely inhabited portions of the world (polar regions, deserts, tropical rainforests) have been "saved for last" for good reason. They are difficult to inhabit and have low average carrying capacity for human activities. Sparse populations are all that have ever been sustainably supported by the ecosystems of such areas. The concept of carrying capacity is an indispensable tool for planning the rational use of these areas, as has been demonstrated by Phillip M. Fearnside in his *Human Carrying Capacity and the Brazilian Rainforest* (1986) and earlier by G. Ledec, R. Goodland, J. Kirchner, and J. Drake, in their paper "Carrying Capacity, Population Growth, and Sustainable Development" (1985). Here I will supplement these two works by showing how in two specific cases even very simple and crude estimates of carrying capacity can have significant policy implications.

For humans the calculation of carrying capacity is far more complex than for other species. Other species have "standards of living" that are constant over time (animals and plants do not experience economic growth, although consumption may vary over the life cycle). Also they have relatively uniform "standards of living" (i.e., per capita resource consumption levels) throughout their populations at a given point in time (no class inequality, with a few exceptions such as social insects whose class structure is genetic rather than social). And the technologies of other species are also relatively constant—genetically given endosomatic technologies that have coevolved with the environment and are consequently well adapted to it. Furthermore, the level of "international" or inter-ecosystem "trade" among animals is relatively constant and limited. For humans these four constants become variables. The calculation of human carrying capacity requires, therefore, some assumptions about (1) living standards, (2) degree of equality of distribution, (3) technology, and (4) extent of trade. As these four variables change, carrying capacity will change. But the concept remains useful because these four variables do not change discontinuously, unpredictably, or beyond all limits. There is inertia and there are ultimate limits.

One need not and should not try to prove that the Ecuadoran Amazon or the Paraguayan Chaco will never support more than x number of people. Never is a long time. It is sufficient for policy purposes to argue that it is very unlikely that within the next generation (twenty-five years) Amazonia could support more than x people living at the average Ecuadoran standard, using known technologies available to Ecuador, assuming Ecuadoran patterns of wealth distribution, and paying for all imports to the region with current exports from the region. A similar statement holds for the Paraguayan Chaco.

Is it possible to make a back-of-the-envelope, order-of-magnitude calculation of x as specified in the preceding paragraph? It is argued below that this is indeed possible, and that for the two regions under consideration very important conclusions for development policy follow from a simple comparison of carrying capacity with population projected over a generational time frame. Ecuador will be considered first, then Paraguay.

The Ecuadoran Amazon

A simple approximation to an extreme upper bound of carrying capacity for the Amazonian region can be gotten by assuming that all of Amazonia could have the same population density as Ecuador as a whole. Amazonia has about 132,000 km² and Ecuador as a whole has a population density of 30 persons per km². This gives 3,960,000, or roughly 4 million, people as an estimate (overestimate) of x in the preceding paragraph.

How many people might the Amazon be required to support in the next generation? At the current 2.8% growth rate, the population of Ecuador will double from 10 million to 20 million in twenty-five years (one generation). The rural areas of the *sierra* and the *costa* are already experiencing net emigration due to demographic pressure, ecological deterioration, and droughts. Aside from the cities this leaves only the Amazon as the area of net immigration. Five provinces in the *sierra* and *costa* (Bolivar, Chimborazo, Loja, Manabi, and Carchi) have actually experienced population decline (net emigration greater than natural increase) between 1972 and 1982 (Landázuri and Jijón 1988). Just the additional 10 million natural increase represents 2.5 times the extreme upper limit of Amazonian carrying capacity! Even if one were to count nonrenewable petroleum reserves as a part of Amazonian carrying capacity, it would make no difference in the fundamental dilemma since these reserves will be thoroughly depleted over the next twenty-five years. Proven reserves will be depleted in less than ten years, and proven plus probable reserves in less than twenty years, assuming 1988 annual extraction rates (World Bank 1988).

In the face of such a population increase any policy of protecting the Amazon by limiting colonization is doomed to failure. How can any government tell millions of poor people that their survival is less important than the survival of trees and birds and undiscovered species? Even if one believes that ethically it is better to save carrying capacity than individual lives, it would still be politically impossible to resist such colonization pressures. And the poor might well reason that if conservation is worth more than their lives then it is also worth more than the wealth of the rich. Demands for redistribution would increase. The rich, knowing their own interests, will also urge opening of the Amazon to temporarily postpone the pressure for redistribution. With 10 million extra people in the next twenty-five years there is no hope for saving the Ecuadorian Amazon from destruction, or of avoiding a great deal of misery.

The above is the foreseeable outcome of present trends projected one generation. This outcome is well within the expected lifetime of the average Ecuadoran now living. What policies might avoid such an impasse?

Consider the following outline of an alternative scenario.

1. Serious and radical birth control policy, beginning with family planning incentives, but eventually moving to real population control. Perhaps it would be possible to cut the increase from 10 to 5 million in the next twenty-five years, and then down to zero growth in the following generation. Even with strong efforts this will take time.

2. To buy time to bring about population control, and to absorb the unavoidable increment of at least 5 million, strive to increase carrying capacity by the following means.

a. Land reform. Use best agricultural land for food crops rather than cattle. Human carrying capacity can be increased by eating lower on the food chain, and by using the best valley land for agriculture and the hillsides for grazing—the opposite of the present pattern. Intensification of agriculture (irrigation) may offer some scope for raising carrying capacity as well.

b. Redistribution. Redirect resources to vital consumption and away from luxury. High sumptuary taxes with revenues invested in production of basic goods would be one way of doing this.

c. Reinvest petroleum rents and other nonrenewable surpluses in renewable resource development: reforestation, land reclamation, fisheries, etc. In general seek to balance the rate of depletion of nonrenewables with the rate of creation of renewable substitutes.

d. Exploit that part of Amazonia that is suited for sustainable agriculture, and keep the rest in its natural state, allowing only sustainable hunting, fishing, gathering, ecotourism, and scientific research.

Such a radical program could only be carried out by a nation that clearly perceived its alternatives as national survival versus national liquidation. That is clearly not the perception of the government of Ecuador, or of the majority of its citizens. Even the leading environmental organizations in Ecuador, dedicated to preserving biodiversity in the Amazon, have evaded taking any serious stand on the population issue. Yet in twenty-five years Ecuador will be another Haiti if present trends are allowed to continue. Not only does the Ecuadoran government not realize this, neither do the multilateral development banks. A nation in the process of environmental liquidation will not be able to pay back loans at interest—it is simply not *creditworthy*. Ecuador needs some writing down of past debt, not new debt, unless the new debt is invested much more sustainably and productively than hitherto. But reduction of past debt cannot be expected as long as any part of petroleum rents are used for consumption rather than investment in renewable alternatives. Unless Ecuador sees its situation as drastic and takes radical action on its own it cannot expect radical action by others in its behalf, no matter how much the facts may justify the need to write down its international debt. Those same dire facts also justify drastic actions by Ecuador to assure its own survival. Unless economic development and finance agencies inject urgency and more vision than at present, then Ecuador is unlikely to take serious action.

Perhaps one reason Ecuador does not perceive its situation as drastic is that the development banks are eager to lend it more money. The obvious conclusion for Ecuador to draw is that since it is creditworthy in the eyes of the development banks, things could not really be so bad. The development banks think things must not be so bad because Ecuador is willing to borrow at interest and obviously considers itself creditworthy without drastic policies. Each party takes comfort from the other's optimism. Neither party has yet faced the facts.

In order to avoid facing the facts a number of thought-stopping myths and slogans are sometimes invoked. One is that the Amazon is a vast inexhaustible source of wealth and fertility—a latter-day version of El Dorado. This is simply wrong. Another is that technology will save the day. But what specific technologies (in the next twenty-five years) are envisioned? Nuclear power and the "green revolution" have proved disappointing. Biotechnology and nontraditional export bonanzas are the currently advocated technical fixes. But specifically what kinds of biotechnology could contribute specifically what kinds of products in the next twenty-five years? And what nontraditional exports, other than cocaine, could make a difference over this time period? Cut flowers and kiwi fruits flown to the U.S. market will not even make a dent in the problem.

A policy of birth control is often dismissed on the grounds that Ecuador is a Catholic country. But so is Italy, and it has a low birthrate. The Catholic church, although clearly an obstacle, nevertheless urges responsible parenthood, and does not deny arithmetic. Some demographic transition enthusiasts believe that birthrates fall only after industrialization has occurred. But this is contradicted by the demographic history of France and other countries. Certain economists (Julian Simon) even believe that demographic pressure is a positive force in development and therefore that population growth should be encouraged. Such myths find a ready market among policy makers unwilling to deal with the twin taboos of population control and income redistribution. But if Ecuador does not dispell these taboos it will not be a viable country, it will not be creditworthy, and loans from the development banks will not be repayable. Even the transfer represented by unpaid loans will likely do more harm than good by extending the illusion a bit longer.

Since population control is the sine qua non of sustainable development, for Ecuador it is important to look at current fertility patterns to get some idea of how much scope there is for fertility reduction by voluntary means. The most salient fact about this pattern is that for women with no education average completed fertility is 6.4 births, while for women with university education it is 2.3 births. In other words, the fertility of the lowest social class is almost *triple* that of the highest class (CEPAR 1988). This class difference is much greater than the rural-urban difference (4.1 births for urban women, 6.1 for rural), although the latter is also significant. The point of these comparisons is to show that birth control is already practiced by the upper and urban classes, and that what is lacking is a democratization of birth control—both attitudes and techniques. The democratization of attitudes will require a real democratization of opportunities as well—especially education and job opportunities for women, as emphasized at the Cairo Population Conference.

The relatively high rate of reproduction of the lower class insures an "unlimited" supply of labor at low wages which promotes inequality in the distribution of income. Far from being a repressive policy, birth control serves to spread to the lower classes the attitudes and practices of the upper class. A lower birth rate tends to equalize the distribution of per capita income, in two ways; (1) it reduces the number of heads among which a wage must be shared in the short run, and (2) it permits the wage to rise by moving away from an unlimited supply of labor in the long run.

Of women having two children only 38% desired to have more; of women having three children only 20% desired to have more; and of women who have four children only 8.5% desired to have more. For all women on average the desired number of children is three (CEPAR 1988, pp. 74, 89). Yet completed fertility for all women in Ecuador averages 4.3. Some 35% of all births in Ecuador in the last five years were either not wanted or not wanted at that time (ibid., p. 89).

Clearly the first step in population control is the voluntary elimination of unwanted fertility, which would have a significant demographic effect as well as providing a basic human right to the lower class—one that is already enjoyed by the upper class. Birth control is therefore not politically unrealistic, in spite of dogmatic opposition from both the Catholic right and the Marxist left.

The Paraguayan Chaco

Paraguay's greatest environmental advantage has been its small population (some 3 million in 1982, and close to 4 million today). At the current 2.5% annual rate of population growth (doubling time of twenty-eight years, or slightly more than one generation) this advantage is rapidly disappearing. Furthermore, this environmental advantage has historically been considered as an economic disadvantage. Demographic factors are exacerbated by the fact that all public lands available for colonization have been distributed. In the future land cannot be made available to some without taking it away from others. Also, the fractionating of landholdings into uneconomic minifundia is driven by population growth and the practice of equal inheritance.

There is very little concern about population growth. Traditionally the goal has been to increase the population by bringing in colonists to settle the land. After the disastrous War of the Triple Alliance, Paraguay was left, in 1875, with only about 220,000 people. It is therefore understandable that pro-natalist views should still be dominant. The question for the next generation, however, is, Where will the 4 million additional Paraguayans live and work? Since 98% of the population lives in the eastern half of the country, that leaves the western half (the Chaco) as the obvious place. As just mentioned, land is becoming scarce in the east, and land conflicts have already become violent. Furthermore, an FAO study concluded that "the agricultural frontier has already exceeded the limits of desirable development in most of the Eastern Region," and that continued expansion would be profoundly destructive of the ecosystem (PNUD 1979). In 1979, when this statement was written, Paraguay had about 3 million people, and now has close to 4 million, all but 2% of whom still live in the east.

There are no official estimates of human carrying capacity of the Chaco, or of the east either. Government officials speak of 5 million or 20 million people in the Chaco of the future, and at the same time state that the agricultural future of the country is in the Chaco. They have not thought in terms of carrying capacity over the next generation. What, then, is a reasonable estimate of carrying capacity for the next generation?

An upper bound estimate can be gotten, as in the case of Ecuador, by assuming the Chaco could be populated to the same density as the east. The population density of the east is 18.6 persons per km^2, and the area of the Chaco is

247,000 km², giving a product of 4,594,000 people. Most people agree that this is an extreme overestimate for any foreseeable future. But it serves to rule out of court any talk of absorbing more than 5 million people in the Chaco, and that is an advance over the current level of discussion.

It is possible, however, to get a much better estimate using the actual experience of colonists in the Chaco. This would have been desirable in the case of the Ecuadoran Amazon also, and would probably have led to a much lower estimate, but such information was not available. The Mennonites have the most successful colony in the Chaco. We can take the Mennonite population density and generalize that to the entire Chaco. In 1987 there were 6,650 Mennonites living on 420,000 hectares, giving a density of 0.0158 persons per hectare. Multiplying that by 100, the umber of hectares in 1 km², gives 1.58 persons per km². That density times the total area of 247,000 km² gives 390,260, or roughly 400,000 persons, not even half a million!

Although still crude, it is obvious that the second estimate is more realistic. But the Mennonites themselves have unused land and estimate that they could support twice their present numbers if they used all their land, which they will have to do in thirty-five years if they maintain their 2% growth rate. So perhaps our estimate should be 800,000. Also, the Mennonite standard of living, though hardly luxurious, is above the average for Paraguay, so a few more thousands could be supported by lowering per capita consumption levels to the national average, even though this goes against the basic notion of development.

On the other hand, our calculation implicitly assumed that the Mennonites have average Chaco land, when in fact it is better than average. The calculation also assumes that other settlers during the next generation could do as well as the Mennonites. This is doubtful for several reasons. First, the Mennonites brought with them the peasant traditions of Europe, which are absent among Paraguayan *colonos*. They also had a strong community of mutual aid and support, as well as outside help from European and American Mennonites. Furthermore, it took them over two generations (sixty years) of hard work and sacrifice to reach their present level. All things considered, even half a million may be an overestimate, especially if ranching rather than agriculture turns out to be the best use of most Chaco land, as seems likely.

Since water rather than soil quality seems to be the limitative factor, one naturally thinks of large irrigation projects as a way of increasing carrying capacity. However, the Mennonites are extremely skeptical of irrigation in the Chaco because they are convinced that it would lead to salinization of the soil (raising the level of existing salt closer to the surface and within reach of plant roots).

The low population density of the Chaco makes it the "obvious" place to put the 4 million new people. Putting them in the east would sharpen land conflicts and require redistribution. The stage is set for an expensive settlement program of the type witnessed in the Brazilian Amazon. The likelihood of failure due to ecological reasons is very high. Politically the colonization of the Chaco will probably be seen as the way to minimize already serious land conflicts in the east, postpone dealing with population control, and maintain temporarily the mirage of progress and optimism, as well as offer a great national project to galvanize public support. Against such political advantages the sobering calculation of carrying capacity may not be very persuasive. Elements of a realistic policy for Paraguay would not be very different form those listed for Ecuador.

Conclusions

In both cases, the simple estimate of carrying capacity has served to clarify the gravity of the situation. Although the calculations are simple and crude, the inferences made from them are quite robust because the conscious tendency was to err on the high side in estimating carrying capacity. For policy purposes refined econometric models would add little to what is already obvious. What is lacking is not more exact information, but the political will to respect the ecological reasons for the historically low population density, whether in the Ecuadoran Amazon or the Paraguayan Chaco, and to limit human populations accordingly. The fact that human carrying capacity is not constant in no way removes the serious rate and magnitude contradictions over the next generation in the two cases here considered. Nor does the "Hong Kong solution" of importing food for a dense population by exporting manufactured goods and financial services seem realistic for either the Ecuadoran Amazon or the Paraguayan Chaco. For one thing, the regions are remote. Also, the limited niche for food importers in the world economy is rapidly filling up.

Attempting the impossible will waste unlimited amounts of resources and cause much conflict. The first rule of development policy therefore should be, "Do not attempt the impossible." The first operational corollary of this rule is, "Respect carrying capacity."

None of this is meant to imply that carrying capacity is only relevant to developing countries. If the United States of America had worried about carrying capacity, it would not have become so dangerously dependent on depleting petroleum reserves belonging to other nations. If the United States cannot even pass a reasonable gasoline tax to discipline unsustainable consumption, is it realistic to expect Paraguay and Ecuador to control population? Both actions may appear politically unrealistic in the short run, but not taking such actions is biophysically unrealistic in the long run, even where "long run" means only twenty-five years.

Chapter 9

Marx and Malthus in Northeast Brazil: A Note on the World's Largest Class Difference in Fertility and Its Recent Trends

During the early 1970s I published several articles dealing with differential fertility and distribution of income per head in Northeast Brazil.[1] The central thesis of the study was that even though aggregate gross national product per head for Northeast Brazil (the largest poor region in the Western Hemisphere) had grown very rapidly over the previous decade, this growth represented "swelling" rather than development, because the income per head of the poorer 80% of the population was at best constant, while that of the richer 20% was growing very rapidly. One very important reason for this disparity, and for the absence of any net "trickle down" effect, was the more rapid population growth of the lower class, due to much higher fertility which more than compensated for the higher mortality of the poor. To the Marxist notion of exploitation based on class monopoly of the means of production there must be added a notion of Malthusian or "Roman" exploitation based on class monopoly of the means of limiting reproduction. In ancient Rome (as in Northeast Brazil) the role of the proletariat was to procreate a plentiful supply of laborers and servants for the republic (i.e., the patricians).

In policy discussions of the 1960s the demographic problem was commonly dismissed by pointing to the fact that total GNP was growing at over 6% while population was growing at around 3%. The consequent growth in GNP per head of around 3% was considered more than adequate. Add to that statistics showing the sparse density of population per square kilometer in Amazonia, and the demographic problem, it was thought, could be dismissed as an exaggeration at best, or neo-Malthusian apologetics at worst. This dismissal, of course, was as statistically inept as the famous recipe for "fifty percent rabbit stew" (one rabbit, one horse). As will be seen later, this error is still prevalent in high circles.

The estimate of total fertility that I made for the late 1960s was eight surviving children for the poorer 80 to 90% of the population and four surviving children for the richer 10 to 20%. This class difference in net reproduction ratio of the order of 100% strongly affects the distribution of income per head. The effects may be summarized under three headings.

1. *The denominator effect.* A given family income divided among more people results in a lower family income per head. Since families with lower incomes have about twice as many children as those with higher incomes, the effect of differential fertility on the distribution of income per head is very large and very regressive.

2. *The numerator or wage effect.* The rapid reproduction of the lower class results in an unlimited supply of cheap labor. Lower wages (smaller numerator for the lower class) mean higher profits, more reinvestment, and faster growth in aggregate income (higher numerator for the upper class). But growth was never fast enough to offset the effect of differential reproduction, and did not, therefore, exert an upward pressure on wages leading to the expected "trickle down." Also, the abundant supply of cheap labor allows the educated wives of members of the upper classes to employ domestic servants, thus freeing themselves for relatively high-paying jobs, thereby reinforcing class inequality in the numerator (total family income). In Northeast Brazil, poorer families have fewer breadwinners than richer families, even though they have more members. In 1970, 65.1% of the families with income per head less than half the minimum wage had only a single breadwinner, while the corresponding figure for those with incomes more than twice the minimum wage was only 54.5%.[2]

3. *The age of structure effect.* More rapid population growth in the lower class results in a younger average age than in the upper class and in a higher dependency ratio. This makes it more difficult for members of the lower class to save, and also tends to keep wives out of the labor force. The opposite is the case for the upper class. More speculatively, the lower average age of the lower class enhances the dominance of the upper for the simple reason that, up to a limit not yet reached, older people find their greater knowledge and experience of life to be an advantage in the political and economic domination of a younger group. In 1970, for Brazil as a whole, the percentage of the population younger than fifteen years in the lowest income class (less than half minimum wage) was 47.8%. For the next lowest category (between 50 and 100% of minimum wage) the figure was 28.7%, while for the highest category (more than two minimum wages) it was only 21.1%.[3] Since we would expect people under fifteen to have lower incomes on average than those over fifteen, it stands to reason that in a class with 48% of its members less than fifteen years old, other things equal, income per head would be lower than in a class

with 21% of its members under fifteen. Since differential fertility directly determines age structure it also indirectly determines distribution of income per head to a significant degree.

My basic conclusion in 1970 was that a family planning program aimed at the democratization of birth control was a necessary (but obviously not sufficient) condition for economic development, understood as improving the lot of the bottom 80% of the population of Northeast Brazil. Such a thesis did not, and still does not, enjoy official acceptance, even though it is widely debated.[4] The opposition to family planning during the 1960s was quite intense and came from the conservative wing of the Catholic church, the nationalists, the military, the leftists, and the oligarchy. With such an alliance of enemies it was not to be expected that population control would become official policy soon, and it has not. The common opposition of the leftists and the oligarchy to population control is especially interesting since they hold opposite expectations about the political consequences of rapid population growth in the lower class. The leftists think (or thought?) that it would hasten the revolution by building up the pressure of misery, while the oligarchy apparently believes that it will increase stability by absorbing any surplus above subsistence that the proletariat might use on its own behalf. The nationalists and the military want an abundant proletariat to serve in the army and colonize the Amazon to secure it against foreign penetration. The leftists want a growing proletariat to fight for the revolution, and the oligarchy wants a growing proletariat to work in its factories, farms, and households at low wages. Everyone wants someone else to do their dirty work, and the larger the exploited population the better for those who want to keep their hands clean. Both leftists and oligarchs seemed to believe that "foxes should not advocate birth control for rabbits!"

What are things like now, some fifteen years later? What new information has become available? To what extent does it support or contradict the picture presented in my article of 1970 and summarized above? What changes have occurred in official attitudes and policy?

Two new sources of information are relevant. First, the census of 1970 gives new information on fertility and mortality differentials by income in 1970. As will be seen below, this information strongly supports the basic thesis. Secondly, in the PNAD-1977[5] comparable information is given for that year, indicating a rather significant lowering of total fertility, along with a narrowing of the extreme class differences. Information from both sources was elaborated in a joint project by UNICEF and IBGE published in 1982.[6] Table 1 is reproduced from that study.

The most striking feature of table 1 is the enormous drop in total fertility[7] between the adjacent income categories of "below half minimum wage" and "half to 1 minimum wage." For the Northeast (1970) the fall is from 9.26 to 2.38—a reduction of nearly seven births between the lowest class (comprising 84.6% of the population of women between the ages of fifteen and forty-nine), and the adjacent

Table 1. *Total fertility of women 15 to 49 years old, for Brazil as a whole, the Northeast region and São Paulo state, by rural and urban households, according to family income per head for 1970 and 1977*

Family income per head (in relation to minimum wage)	Total fertility for women between the ages of 15 and 49									
	1970							1977		
	Brazil			Northeast Region			State of São Paulo	Brazil	North-east region	State of São Paulo
	Total	*Urban*	*Rural*	*Total*	*Urban*	*Rural*	*Total*	*Total*	*Total*	*Total*
Total*	6.35	5.06	8.31	8.36	7.00	9.44	4.38	4.35	6.22	2.87
Below half	8.19	7.60	8.74	9.26	8.62	9.67	7.08	7.13	7.73	6.31
Half to 1	2.66	2.62	2.90	2.38	2.39	2.36	2.85	3.17	3.37	3.16
1 to 2	2.22	2.25	2.10	2.83	2.79	3.59	2.17	2.27	2.43	2.10
Over 2	1.83	1.82	—	2.83	2.83	—	1.79	1.88	2.91	1.93

Note: Estimated using Brass's method on the basis of a one per cent sample of the 1970 Population Census and data from PNAD-77.
*Women from the class with no income are included in the general total.
Source: Perfil Estatístico de Crinças e Mães no Brasil (Rio de Janeiro, IBGE, 1982), p. 38.

"lower middle class" (containing 5.6% of the same population). For the two highest categories, together accounting for about 3% of the population, total fertility is a little higher at 2.83. Using the latter figure as a basis of comparison gives a class differential of 6.43. We can say with some confidence that the class differential in total fertility lies between 6.4 and 7.0.

My estimate in 1970 of eight and four for the lower and upper classes, respectively, referred to surviving children rather than live births. Given the infant mortality rates in the Northeast of around 15 to 20%,[8] a total fertility of 9.26 is roughly consistent with an average of eight surviving children, so in retrospect that estimate still looks good. However, for the upper class I evidently overestimated fertility. Apparently it was around 2.38 rather than 4 (correction for infant mortality in the upper class would be minor, but would lower the 2.38 figure, thus making my estimate of four surviving children an even greater overestimate). My implicit estimate of the class differential was, therefore, about 5(= 9 − 4), while the real differential was apparently close to 7(= 9.26 − 2.38). Consequently the effect of differential fertility on income distribution was actually underestimated in my paper of 1970 because the differential itself was underestimated. The new data strengthen the main argument of that paper, for 1970. However, Merrick and Berquo in their very thorough and recent study report a total fertility for the lower class of 8.55, and for the upper class of 3.95 for the Northeast in 1970.[9] These figures, cited from a study by Carvalho and Paiva, reflect different statistical definitions of social class, based on total household income in absolute cruzeiros rather than fam-

ily income per head in multiples of a minimum wage. A significant difference in total fertility is apparent regardless of the exact definition of lower and upper class.

There are, of course, limitations in the use of either total family income or family income per head. As Wood and Carvalho remark, "Larger households tend to have larger total incomes because of the greater number of earners,
but smaller incomes per household member."[10] When households are grouped by
income per head differential fertility and income inequality are greater than when
households are grouped according to total household income. Neither category is
"biased." They are simply different concepts, each useful and reasonable as long as
we remember the definitions and avoid mixing them in comparisons.

Between 1970 and 1977, however, there was a substantial drop in to-
tal fertility for all classes together in all regions of the country. In the Northeast it
fell by about 2 (from 8.36 to 6.22). Moreover, the gap between the groups "below
half minimum wage" and "half to one minimum wage" narrowed from around 7 to
around 4.4 (7.73–3.37). Part of this narrowing was due to a very surprising increase
in the fertility of the "half to one minimum wage" category (from 2.38 to 3.37), an
increase of over 40% in seven years. Why this strong movement against the trend
for this particular class which was previously the least fertile? There are good reasons to believe that this reflects a statistical reclassification rather than a real change
in behavior. Since monetary correction for inflation lagged behind the rate of inflation between 1970 and 1977, the real purchasing power of the minimum wage was
eroded, and although some people from the lowest category nominally passed into
the next income category there was no change in either their real incomes or their
reproductive behavior. Consequently, these people raised the fertility of the nomi-
nal income class into which inflation moved them. Clearly the real class differential
in fertility in 1977 was greater than 4.4, although still significantly lower than the
difference of 7 recorded in 1970—probably around 5.4 on the reasonable assumption that the entire increase in fertility in the "half to one minimum wage" class
was spurious.

Between 1970 and 1977 there has been a clear narrowing of extreme
class differences in fertility, and a consequent weakening of the effect on distribution of income per head compared to 1970. However, lower-class total fertility was
still over twice that of the upper class, so the effect remains highly significant.
Moreover, since total income growth has now slowed drastically, the pressure of
high fertility on income per head in the lower class may now be even greater in absolute terms.

The differential of nearly 7 recorded in 1970 was probably the great-
est class difference in fertility in the world, and perhaps in all history. A cursory review of the literature yields a few benchmark comparisons which do not prove that
Northeast Brazil has had the highest class difference in fertility in the world but,
nevertheless, do render that conjecture very plausible.

1. For Peru in 1960, Stycos[11] defined five socioeconomic classes and found the difference in total fertility between the lowest (7.6) and the highest class (3.8) to be 3.8.

2. For Mexico City in 1970, Zambrano Lupi[12] found that total fertility of mothers with less than three years of education was 7.85 and that of mothers with university education 4.53, a difference of 3.32.

3. In Calcutta, Pakrasi and Halder[13] found that total fertility in the class with the lowest monthly expenditure was 7.95 against 4.52 in the class with the highest monthly expenditure, giving a class differential of 3.43.

4. For the United States in 1910, Petersen[14] reports a difference between the total fertility of "rural workers and farmers" (5.6) and "urban professionals" (1.8) of 3.8.

5. For Brazil as a whole in 1970, Wood and Carvalho[15] discovered that total fertility for the lowest of four household income classes was 7.6 while that of the highest class was 3.3, giving a difference of 4.3.

In all of these cases the comparisons are between a top class and a bottom class, with a substantial excluded middle, while in Northeast Brazil there is no excluded middle since our bottom category alone contains 80% of the population and we are comparing it with the adjacent category. Even so, the differences cited above fall far short of the figure of nearly 7 for Northeast Brazil in 1970, and are also well below the 1977 figure of 5.4. I doubt whether any other society in the world has such a large fertility difference between classes of comparable inclusivity.

Furthermore, the difference is not between indigenous peoples and colonizers, nor between religious or linguistic subcultures. The fertility difference in Northeast Brazil is one of economic class. Both classes speak the same language, belong to the same church, are of the same racial background, watch the same TV *novelas*, go to the same *futbol* games, and vote (or are forbidden to vote) in the same elections. A class difference in total fertility of almost 7 children seems so extreme that it should have attracted a great deal of attention. It did not. Nor is much attention now paid to the current difference of about 5.4, which must also be among the very highest in the world. Why have these striking facts been so little noticed?

One possibility, of course, is that the figures are wrong. The majority (but by no means unanimous) reaction of my economist colleagues at the Federal University of Ceará, when presented with table 1, was one of disbelief. The fertility differences, they said, were too large and occurred too abruptly between adjacent classes, which were not as different as all that on the social scale. They may be right.

On the other hand, the source (IBGE) is the best available, and two independent data sets were used, both giving the same general picture. Furthermore, the two adjacent classes between which the big change occurred are less close than might appear because the first category (below half minimum wage) is open-ended downward and contains around 80% of the total number of families and 92% of the total number of individuals in 1970. The family incomes per head of most people in this populous category are actually less than one-quarter of the minimum wage. In 1970, 67% of the families and 76% of the individuals were in the group "below one-quarter minimum wage. Thus, the median for the open-ended category, "below half minimum wage" is going to be well below one-quarter of the minimum wage. The median of the next category (half to one minimum wage) can be approximated by the mid-point of 75% of minimum wage. Viewing it in this way, we see that the median income per head of the second category is *three times* that of the first, even though they are adjacent.

The fact that these figures provoke disbelief as a first reaction among many *nordestinos* may be more an indication of customary blindness to the social reality they reflect, than a reason to doubt the numbers. That at least was the interpretation of some of the people at IBGE in Rio de Janeiro who carried out the study, when informed of the disbelief prevalent among my colleagues in Ceará. In any event, the subject deserves more study by believers and doubters alike.

A broader question that also deserves more study was raised years ago by João Lyra Madeira.[17] Why has the whole subject of fertility been tainted with a virtual taboo in Brazilian demography and economics? Nowadays "taboo" is perhaps too strong a word—yet there remains a certain "disinclination" to study fertility in its socioeconomic context. When a subject is taboo it usually reveals an injustice too blatant to defend openly, but too important to the interests of the status quo to challenge openly. I am reminded of the segregated Southern United States of my childhood. It was obvious to an unexceptional child that, by and large, the blacks did the dirty work and were poor, while the whites did the more interesting work and were better paid. And segregation laws were intended to keep it that way. It was acceptable to take explicit notice of this fact as long as one did not dwell on it, or pursue it too deeply. Very few whites in the South of the 1940s really hated blacks (or "colored people" as was then the polite term). In fact, most whites liked blacks on a personal level and "in their place," as the cliché went. Similarly, I suggest that upper-class Brazilians in the Northeast have a genuine affection for their lower-class countrymen on a personal level and "in their place," which means working in the factories, farms, and households of the upper class. Northeast Brazil is much less racist than the United States, but economic class divisions are stronger.

In a class society it is natural that there should be class differences in everything, including fertility. The fact that differential fertility *reinforces* the basic class structure of the society is what makes it inconvenient to study the issue in depth. It is inconvenient to the oligarchy because it exposes another dimension of class exploitation. One might think, therefore, that Marxists would be eager to expose the facts. However, they are unwilling to admit any cause for poverty other than monopoly ownership of the means of production. Neo-Malthusian policies are especially distasteful to Marxists because they hold out the possibility of improvement by individual action, thereby weakening class solidarity and taking some wind out of the sails of their single cure for all ills, the class revolution. Consequently, the subject is neglected.

Because of this neglect the exceptionally large fertility differentials in Northeast Brazil are still awaiting adequate "explanation." As I have indicated, I believe the basic explanation lies in the class nature of the society. As I argued in my studies of 1970 and 1971, the literal role of a proletariat is to proliferate.[18] The literal meaning of the word "proletariat" in ancient Rome was those with many children, the poorest class of society whose members were exempt from taxes and whose service to the republic was mainly in the procreation of children. Implicit in this literal meaning and explicitly developed in Malthusian and neo-Malthusian thought is the association of poverty with rapid proliferation. By Marx's time the word had largely lost its Latin meaning, and Marx severed any remaining etymological connection with proliferation by redefining the word to mean nonowners of the means of production who must sell their labor to the capitalists in order to survive. A theory of poverty is also implicit in Marx's definition, specifically that poverty is a consequence of the monopoly ownership of the means of production by a few and the consequent nonownership of the means of production by many. Ideologically, in the sense of providing a single cause and a single cure for poverty, the two traditions conflict. But logically the Marxian and Malthusian theories do not conflict. It is quite possible for one class to have a monopoly of both the means of production and the means of limiting reproduction. In fact, Marx himself tells us that mere possession of land and capital is not sufficient to make a man a landlord or a capitalist if there be lacking the requisite social correlative, the proletarian with no alternative but to sell his labor to the capitalist.[19] Rapid reproduction of "correlatives" supports and reinforces the unequal distribution of productive wealth that is the dominant feature of social life in Northeast Brazil.

Further demographic evidence of the class nature of the society, and partial explanation of the extreme fertility differences, is provided by the statistics on class differences in mortality found in table 2.

For the Northeast as a whole in 1970 there was a difference in life expectancy at birth of 17.5 years between the lowest category (below half minimum wage) containing over 80% of the population, and the highest category (more than twice the minimum wage) containing about 1% of the population. In the urban Northeast the difference was nearly 20 years! A species, or class, facing high death rates (low life expectancy) must have high birthrates to survive. Although highly

Table 2. *Life expectancy at birth obtained on the basis of mortality among children under five years of age, according to regional and rural or urban location of household, and family income per head for 1970 and 1977*

Rural or urban location of household and family income per head (in relation to minimum wage)	Brazil		Northeast Region		State of São Paulo		Metropolitan region of São Paulo	
	1970	1977	1970	1977	1970	1977	1970	1977
Total	53.27	58.20	44.64	49.77	59.08	64.81	59.51	63.51
Below half	52.53	55.43	44.66	48.63	57.77	62.89	58.25	59.91
From half to 1	58.04	62.13	48.01	54.46	60.45	64.12	60.75	63.57
From 1 to 2	64.36	65.83	58.70	60.28	67.54	67.99	66.29	67.57
Over 2	66.58	68.97	62.12	64.68	69.53	69.64	69.32	70.37
Urban	53.89	—	42.66	—	59.87	—	—	—
Below half	52.46	—	62.48	—	58.46	—	—	—
From half to 1	58.41	—	48.30	—	61.02	—	—	—
From 1 to 2	64.58	—	58.23	—	67.64	—	—	—
Over 2	67.76	—	62.21	—	69.49	—	—	—
Rural	52.57	—	45.97	—	56.50	—	—	—
Below half	52.58	—	45.95	—	56.50	—	—	—
From half to 1	57.53	—	50.23	—	—	—	—	—
From 1 to 2	60.99	—	—	—	—	—	—	—
Over 2	—	—	—	—	—	—	—	—

Note: Estimated using Sullivan's method on the basis of a one per cent sample of the Population Census of 1970 and data from PNAD-77.
Source. Perfil Estatístico de Crianças e Mães no Brasil (Rio de Janeiro, IBGE, 1982), p. 61.

significant, the class differences in mortality are less dramatic than those in fertility. That is, higher fertility in the lower class much more than compensates for higher mortality.

By 1977 the corresponding class difference in life expectancy in the Northeast had fallen to about 15 years. The biggest change, almost 11 years, occurred between the categories "half to one minimum wage" and "one to two minimum wages," whereas the big change in fertility over the same period was between the previous two categories of "below half minimum wage" and "half to one minimum wage." The fall in the birthrate thus occurred before that of the death rate as we move up the scale of family income per head—a fact which seems to weaken the hypothesis that birthrates fall as a lagged response to falling death rates. In sum, class differences in mortality are not as extreme as the fertility differences, nor is the dividing line so dramatic, nor at the same income level. Nevertheless, mortality differences add significantly to the total picture of the real dimensions of a class society. The demographic dimensions of class in Northeast Brazil may be summarized as follows.

1. In 1970 there was a class difference in total fertility of almost 7 births and a difference in life expectancy at birth of around eighteen years.

2. In 1977 there was a class difference in total fertility of around 5.4 and a difference in life expectancy at birth of around fifteen years.

There has been a dramatic improvement over the seven years, even though there is still a long way to go. The change in mortality was an objective of public policy. The change in fertility was not sought directly by policy, but was a consequence of other factors. What other factors?

One cannot appeal to the usual "demographic transition thesis" because the economic condition of the lower 80% did not improve, yet that is where the bulk of the reduction in fertility occurred. Furthermore, as we have noted, the big fall in fertility occurred at lower levels of income per head than did the big fall in mortality. In fact it could be argued for the Northeast, as Merrick and Berquo have done for Brazil as a whole,[20] that the deteriorating real income of the lower class led them to reduce their fertility in order to maintain their rising consumer expectations. Alternatively, and perhaps more relevant to the Northeast, they suggest that the increase in the misery of the lower class may have lowered fecundity and the will to reproduce. The fall in fertility was not a consequence of improved economic conditions for the masses. Rather, it seems to have been the result of a certain democratization of birth control in terms both of attitudes and access to devices. This incipient spread of habits from the upper to the lower class was not a policy objective of the government—far from it. It seems to have happened in response to a latent desire on the part of the proletariat to control reproduction, once the practice received a certain legitimacy.

This increased legitimacy came from several sources. First, urbanization helped spread information. Secondly, the liberal wing of the Catholic church gave more emphasis to "responsible parenthood" than to the relative acceptability of alternative birth control methods. Thirdly, the practice of birth control by the upper class has a natural diffusion from *donas de casa* to *empregadas*, and from doctors to patients, because caring human relationships develop across class lines. Fourthly, pills and condoms are now generally available, the latter openly displayed in supermarkets, which was certainly not the case during the 1960s. Fifthly, there has been a general sexual revolution in the sense that sex moved from a mildly taboo subject (Brazilians were never puritans) to an object of intense commercial exploitation via television (*novelas* and ads), cinema (the now famous Brazilian *pornochanchadas*), and magazines ranging from sexy to pornographic sold at every newspaper stand. It is interesting that in matters related to sex, censorship was practically abandoned about the same time that political censorship became intense. Some people argue that this was a ploy to give the illusion of a free press. Free pornography was an easy substitute for free speech. The unintended consequence may have been to hasten the spread of birth control by putting an intense commercial spotlight on sex and rendering legitimate the open discussion of everything related to sex, including birth control.[21]

The de facto attitude of the government is laissez-faire—private birth control initiatives are tolerated, but the official attitude is still pro-natalist. Some believe that the government would like to do a U-turn, as happened in Mexico, but that they are restrained from this by the fact that they do not want any more conflicts with the Catholic church, since they are already getting considerable criticism from the church on other matters of human rights and social justice.

In contrast to the notion that the government really wants birth control but is restrained by the political context, is the view that the government is genuinely pro-natalist and is not at all likely to change. Historically, Brazil has always followed a cheap labor policy.[22] In the early nineteenth century, slavery represented a policy of providing cheap involuntary labor from Africa. When slavery was abolished in the late nineteenth century, subsidized immigration of poor Southern Europeans provided a cheap source of labor well into the twentieth century, until such time as the natural rate of increase of the Brazilian working class was itself sufficient to guarantee cheap labor. The singular lack of enthusiasm shown by recent Brazilian governments toward a policy of spreading birth control among the working class (the upper class already practices it) may be seen as a continuation of the historical cheap labor policy, although in a passive rather than active mode.

Further support for the second view can be found in various official public pronouncements. In 1982, a study group of the Escola Superior de Guerra published a short book entitled *The Brazilian Demographic Problem*,[23] which reflects the official view, illustrated by the following quotations.

> A country of continental dimensions such as Brazil, with fabulous natural resources, abundant wealth, and without prejudice in matters of race, colour or religion needs a population sufficient to occupy and defend its territory from international greed.
>
> The demographic policy implicit in anti-natalist campaigns judged by some to be absolutely necessary for our development, would result in the stagnation or regression of the growth of our population—we who already exist in such small numbers in a country so large and with inexhaustible resources. A policy of stimulating births thereby assuring more economic development will permit us to have more Brazilian workers, technicians and scientists. In

addition to producing consumer and producer goods, with Brazil in-
dustrialized, our technicians and scientists will be able to transform
our heavy industry partially into an industry capable of producing
military goods. [p. 75]

From the military point of view, population is power,
and in Brazil, in spite of Malthusian campaigns, population growth
has historically served the country in that we have more rapid economic growth than that of countries with low natality, such as Argen-
tina, Chile, and Uruguay. [p. 72]

The authors of this booklet approvingly quote Minister João Paulo
dos Reis Veloso's statement that "a country like Brazil has no right to create birth
control programmes, because while our population grows at 2.5 per cent per year,
our economic development grows at 9 per cent" (p. 76).

Note that the last statement is precisely the misleading "rabbit
stew" aggregation considered earlier, which I was at pains to refute in my paper in
1970—and which also demonstrates that this "second look" is not uncalled for. Of
course, the economic growth of 9% proved short-lived in any case.

To summarize, the basic conclusions of this "second look, fifteen
years later" are listed below.

1. Northeast Brazil has probably the highest class difference in fertility of any society. The size of class differences in fertility was understated in my
study in 1970, and consequently the arguments based on that difference now have
stronger empirical support than was available at that time.

2. Between 1970 and 1977, fertility fell significantly in all classes.
Class differences were reduced but remained very high by international standards.
The effect of differential fertility on income distribution remains very important in
spite of the real progress made in lowering fertility.

3. A Marxian-Malthusian definition of social class, in terms of control versus non-control of both production and reproduction, fits the Northeast, and
offers a possibility for integrating the valid insights of both traditions. This is important because with the current rebirth of Marxist economics in Brazilian universities, Malthusian insights are in danger of being lost or discarded along with the brit-
tle analytical bones of value-desiccated neoclassical models. The democratization
of control over reproduction is no less (and no more) important than the democratization of land ownership in the Northeast. Everyone talks about land reform, but so
far few talk about reproduction reform. Paradoxically, reproduction reform seems to
be actually occurring faster than land reform.

International
Trade and
Sustainable
Development

Introduction

Free trade and comparative advantage were the orthodox doctrines that once had the strongest hold on my mind and were the most difficult for me to let go of. Therefore it does not surprise me that many otherwise sympathetic readers part company with me on the issue of free trade. However, I believe that the reasons which convinced me to reconsider these doctrines will also eventually convince others to do so. We have been far too uncritical in our celebration of everything global and cosmopolitan, and in our corresponding denigration of everything national and local.

I was awakened from dogmatic slumber on the trade issue by John Cobb, in 1987–88, while we were working together on our book *For the Common Good*. After twenty years of teaching the theory of comparative advantage to college sophomores, the trade issue was rather settled in my mind. But John forced me to rethink the whole question, which I did, going back to Ricardo. I was chagrined to discover the degree to which I, and the textbooks I had been using, had unthinkingly ignored Ricardo's very restrictive assumption that capital is immobile between nations. Without that assumption the principle of comparative advantage collapses. In Chapter 11 of *For the Common Good* we set our case against free trade and in defense of community, in this instance national community. I confess that I half expected that we had made some terrible mistake and that other economists would delight in destroying our arguments. But in the elapsed seven years that has not happened.

Gradually I began speaking out on the subject more boldly. While at the World Bank, Robert Goodland and I wrote an article on "An Ecological-Economic Analysis of Deregulation of International Commerce under GATT."[1] Although this paper was not well thought of within the Bank (to put it mildly), there was a notable absence of any reasoned refutation of our arguments. Since then

143

I have debated the free trade issue in *Scientific American* with Jagdish Bhagwati,[2] and at Oxford University with Francis Cairncross. In each case I learned to say a few things differently, and to avoid certain questionable formulations. But what I learned most assuredly is that the free traders had no real answers to our basic arguments. More correctly, our opponents had two replies, both of which are easily refuted: (1) that whatever problems there may be with free trade, the economic growth that it induces will outweigh them, and (2) that Ricardo's principle of comparative advantage had proved once and for all that free trade is mutually beneficial. These answers are rebutted in the first chapter of this section.

The second chapter considers the free trade issue in the context of adjustment policies urged on third-world countries by the International Monetary Fund and the World Bank, and shows how free trade is an obstacle to achievement of other goals in the adjustment package. In 1995, the IMF hosted a conference on "Macroeconomics and the Environment," after years of having maintained that the two things had nothing to do with each other. Although the IMF still resisted the connection, others at the conference pointed out that if the way countries adjust to IMF conditions is by cutting down forests, pumping up petroleum, mining minerals, and depleting topsoil as fast as possible in order to increase exports, then it is disingenuous for the IMF to pretend that there is no connection between macroeconomics and the environment, especially when free trade is a key part of macroeconomic adjustment.

Chapter 10

Free Trade and Globalization vs. Environment and Community

Lawyers are the favorite butt of professional jokes, but economists are a close second. A favorite one-liner is, "If all economists were laid out end to end, they still wouldn't reach a conclusion." However, my problem with my fellow economists is not their frequent state of disagreement, but rather their near unanimous agreement in support of basic policies that are killing us. Instead of critical debates on vital issues, what resonates from academia is the unison snoring of supine economists in deep dogmatic slumber. Economists overwhelmingly agree that (1) economic growth, as measured by GNP, is a very good thing, and (2) that global economic integration via free trade is unarguable because it contributes to competition, cheaper products, world peace, and especially to growth in GNP. Policies based on these two conceptually immaculate—and interrelated—tenets of economic orthodoxy are reducing the capacity of the earth to support life, thereby literally killing the world.

In this chapter, I will first present a summary case against the overall policy of global economic integration by free trade and free capital mobility. Then I will consider the two most usual objections to the case, namely, (1) that economic growth induced by free trade is a huge benefit that outweighs whatever costs it entails, and (2) that the principle of comparative advantage from David Ricardo gives the blessing of economic theory to free trade and globalization as currently understood. Many arguments have already been given in this book against the first objection, but the present context demands a repetition and extension of one of these before moving to a consideration of the second. Refutation of these two most common objections is surprisingly easy—and even fun.

The Case against Globalization by Free Trade

Costs of Transport, Dependence, and Reduced Range of Occupational Choice

For trade to be mutually beneficial assumes that the gains from international trade and specialization are not canceled by the immediate disadvantages: higher transport costs, increased dependence on distant supplies and markets, and a reduced range of choice of ways for citizens to make a living.

Transport costs are energy intensive, and if energy is subsidized, as it frequently is today, then so is trade. Charging full-cost energy prices would reduce the initial gains from long-distance trade, whether international or interregional, and would have the same effect as a tariff that was both efficient and protective.

The loss of independence resulting from specialization weakens a community's control over its livelihood. After specialization a country is no longer free *not* to trade, and if not careful about retaining some self-sufficiency in basics, can become vulnerable to hard bargains.

The reduced range of choice of occupations for a given population is seldom mentioned as a welfare cost, but it is important. Most people's enjoyment of life depends at least as much on how they earn their living as on how they spend their earnings. For example, a country like Uruguay, with a clear comparative advantage in cattle and sheep ranching, would afford a citizen the choice of being either a cowboy or a shepherd, if it adhered strictly to the rule of specialization and trade; however, to sustain a viable national community Uruguayans have felt that they need their own legal, financial, medical, insurance, and educational services, as well as basic agriculture and industry. Even if it entails some loss of efficiency, such diversity is necessary for community and nationhood. And from an individualistic perspective, the increased range of choice of occupation has to be counted as a welfare gain. Even for those who are cowboys and shepherds, surely their lives are enriched both by having other alternatives and by occasionally coming in contact with a compatriot who is not a *vaquero* or a *pastor*. Uruguayans consider that their community is enriched by having a symphony orchestra of their own, even though it would be cost-effective to import better symphony concerts in exchange for wool, mutton, beef, and leather. The point is that there is a community dimension to welfare that is absent completely in the one-dimensional argument that if free trade increases per capita availability of commodities, it must be good.

Standards-Lowering Competition to Externalize Costs

The increased competition resulting from free trade does indeed promote cheaper products[1]—but there are two ways of making products cheaper: by improving real efficiency, or by simply externalizing costs. Firms in a competitive environment all have an incentive to externalize costs—to the extent that they can get away with it.

Within nations there are laws and institutions that prohibit many cost externalizations. Internationally there are few such laws, and domestic laws, and their degree of enforcement, vary greatly among nations. Since lower standards mean lower costs and prices, international competition tends to be standards-lowering (i.e., cost-externalizing), and thereby destroys community life based on those higher standards. For example, a community whose standards include the avoidance of child labor will not be able to engage in free trade with a community that accepts child labor, unless it is willing to lower its standards regarding child labor or accept the bankruptcy of its businesses that have to compete with foreign child labor. Either of these alternatives is a severe disruption of its community life.

The scope of internalized costs within nations is enormous: workplace safety, minimum wage, welfare programs, social security, length of the working day, abolition of child labor, medical insurance, pollution control, liability for accidents, and so on. All of these social and environmental measures raise costs and cannot withstand the standards-lowering competition induced by free trade with countries that have lower standards. The consequence is that a greater share of total world production will move to those countries with the lowest standards—that is, those that do the poorest job of counting and internalizing costs will produce an increasing share of world output—hardly a move in the direction of global efficiency! In the quest for efficiency the most important rule is to count all costs.[2]

We therefore need a compensatory tariff to correct for differences in internalization of external costs among the nations. This is derided as "protectionism" by free traders. But protectionism traditionally has meant the protection of an inefficient domestic industry from competition with more efficient foreign firms. The compensatory tariff, by contrast, protects an efficient national policy of cost internalization against standards-lowering competition from countries that, for whatever reason, do not count all environmental and social costs. It is one thing to protect an inefficient industry—it is something else entirely to protect an efficient national policy of cost internalization! I advocate the latter, not the former.[3]

The motivation for compensatory tariffs is not to impose one country's moral standards and values on another country—rather it is to be true to one's own standards by not letting them be undercut by standards-lowering competition. To take an extreme case, even the General Agreement on Tariffs and Trade (GATT) concedes that it is too much to expect the working class in one country to freely compete with prison labor in another. But then what about child labor? Or sixteen-hour-per-day labor? Or uninsured risky labor? What about subsistence-wage labor in overpopulated countries? What about cheap goods subsidized by the uncounted divestment of natural capital?

National borders porous to the movement of goods and capital, and increasingly to labor as well, mean that nations lose control over their economic life and cease to be viable communities. Global community, a presumptive goal of free trade, is an empty slogan, and in any case should be achieved through international federation of viable national communities, not through default to a cosmopolitan vacuum left by a world without borders, a vacuum soon filled by transnational corporations. Nations weakened by economic erasure of their borders are in a poor position to carry out domestic policies, including those policies they may have agreed to undertake in support of international environmental treaties that they have signed. Such treaties are a step toward true global community, but they are rendered meaningless if nations effectively give up their ability to comply by allowing their borders to be erased in the name of free trade.

Transnational corporations have escaped the national obligations of community by becoming international, and since there is as yet no international community, they have escaped from community obligations altogether. Globalism does not serve world community—it is just individualism writ large. We can either leave transnational capital free of community constraint, or create an international government capable of controlling it, or renationalize capital and put it back under control of the national community. I favor the last alternative. I know it is hard to imagine right now, but so are the others. It may be easier to imagine after an international market crash.

With national borders permeable to the free flow of both goods and capital, and increasingly of labor as well, there will be *one* global labor market, *one* capital market, *one* market for all goods and services, and consequently *one* world price for each commodity. A single country can no longer follow a separate wage policy, or a different interest rate policy, or its own full-cost pricing policy, or even its own population control policy—unless it can convince the rest of the world to follow the same policy. Instead of hundreds of separate national "laboratories" independently trying out different policies, some of which may work, we will have just one big global experiment, which, given the reality of standards-lowering competition, is almost designed to fail.

Consider two examples of how free trade makes it hard to solve national problems. First, the problem of getting U.S. citizens off of welfare and into jobs at which they can earn a living is made unsolvable if we insist on immediately throwing them into competition with the poor masses of the world. Expecting disadvantaged fellow citizens to go right off welfare into competition with all the cheap and able labor of an overpopulated world is a denial of community with them.

Second, in a parallel way, the problem of conversion of our military production capacity to peacetime uses is made excessively difficult if the new civilian enterprise must immediately face stiff foreign competition. Our military sector is as inefficient as any centrally planned socialist economy. It needs competition—but competition must be introduced slowly. It is better for our community to employ workers and companies who, although not now competitive by world standards, are nevertheless making some positive contribution to our nation, than to demand "global efficiency" at the expense of unemployment and associated social costs—crime, drug addiction, and irresponsible procreation.

Natural Capital As Limiting Factor   As discussed in Part 2, many nations have grown to the point that the limiting factor in their further growth and development is no longer man-made capital but remaining natural capital. To cite again the clearest example, the fish catch is limited by the natural capital of remaining fish populations, not by the man-made capital of fishing boats, many of which are idle. Countries in which natural capital has become the limiting factor therefore seek to appropriate whatever natural capital remains in the international commons, and to trade for natural capital with those less developed countries still willing and able to supply it. Trade makes it possible for some countries to live beyond their geographic carrying capacity by importing that capacity—natural capital—from other countries. And this tendency in individual countries tends to push the world economy to grow beyond its optimal scale relative to the containing ecosystem. Since the initial introduction of trade eases environmental constraints relative to total economic self-sufficiency, or autarky, it creates the illusion that further trade will continue to ease those constraints. But the benefits of moving from no trade to some trade cannot be generalized to the proposition that more trade is better than less trade. And—of course—all countries cannot be net importers of natural capital.

Free trade also introduces greater geographic separation between the production benefits and the environmental costs of throughput growth, making it more difficult to compare them and consequently easier to overshoot the optimal scale defined by their equality at the margin. Furthermore, as a result of the increased integration caused by trade, countries will face tightening environmental constraints more globally and simultaneously, and less nationally and sequentially, than they would with less trade and integration. Therefore there will be less opportunity to experiment on a smaller scale and to learn from other countries' prior experience with controlling throughput.

In sum, by making supplies of resources and absorption capacities anywhere simultaneously available to demands everywhere, free trade will tend to increase throughput growth, and with it the rate of environmental degradation. It will greatly reduce the control that people in local communities have over their local environments and their livelihoods. The tendency of free trade to increase throughput growth is counted as a virtue in neoclassical growth economics. In sustainable or steady-state economics, however, any tendency for trade to push growth beyond the optimal scale is recognized as antieconomic.

Intra-Industry Trade and Intellectual Property Rights   Roughly half of world trade is intra-industry trade—that is, simultaneously exporting and importing basically the same commodity. For example, the United States imports Danish butter cookies, and the Danes import U.S. butter cookies. Somewhere on or above the North Atlantic the cookies pass each other. Surely the gains from trading such similar products cannot be large. But regardless of their size, could not these gains be had more efficiently simply by exchanging recipes?

In general, might not the free international flow of information be preferable to the flow of goods or capital? When you sell or give away information (as opposed to goods), you do not give it up—you still have it. What you give up is your monopoly, which is what gave the information its exchange value. But you still have the full use value. Once information exists, an argument can be made that its price should be zero for efficient allocation. But the cost of production of new knowledge is usually not zero, and so we reward inventors with a temporary monopoly. But might there not be a better way to reward creators of knowledge? Prizes? Grants? High salaries? Something that does not require that knowledge be kept artificially scarce?

Knowledge is so largely a social product in any case that it is quite arbitrary and unjust to give property rights for minor applications of basic knowledge but not for the discovery of basic knowledge itself. Do the genetic engineers, eager to patent new organisms, share their royalties with Watson and Crick? Or with the teachers who taught them about the double helix? Or with the heirs of Gregor Mendel?

The early Swiss economist Sismondi noted that inventions motivated by a desire to serve mankind are less likely to be socially destructive than inventions motivated by the desire for personal enrichment. Maybe he was right. Maybe the quality of the incentive is more important than the quantity. Maybe Thomas Jefferson was right in his statement, carved in stone at the University of Maryland's McKeldin Library: "The field of knowledge is the common property of mankind."

Yet free traders emphasize the importance of strengthening intellectual property rights and making knowledge less and less "the common property of mankind." Their argument is that unless new knowledge is kept expensive there will not be sufficient incentive to produce more of it. But even granting considerable force to that point, I am still inclined to favor the hypothesis that the benefit of rapid sharing of the knowledge we now have is greater than the cost of any consequent risk of slowing the creation of new knowledge. Following Schumpeter, one could argue that new knowledge has a natural but temporary monopoly by virtue of its novelty, and it is the loss of that novelty, as a result of sharing knowledge, that gives the incentive to discover ever newer knowledge. The use value of new knowledge gets imputed to the factors of production that put it into effect, as the exchange value of the knowledge is competed down to zero. Of all things, knowledge and information are what should flow most freely across national boundaries, and especially from North to South. Yet this is what today's free traders least want to be free.[4]

Refutation of Two Common Objections

Let us turn now to consider the two most common objections to the anti–free trade position. The first is that "growth will compensate." Some globalists will admit that the problems just outlined are real, but argue that whatever costs they entail are more than compensated for by the welfare increase from economic growth brought about by free trade and global integration. While it may be true that free trade increases economic growth, the other link in the chain of argument, that growth increases welfare, is devoid of empirical support in the case of the United States since 1947.

It is very likely that we have entered an era in which growth is increasing environmental and social costs faster than it is increasing production benefits. Growth that increases costs by more than it increases benefits is antieconomic growth, and should be so called.

Although economists did not devise GNP to be a direct measure of welfare, nevertheless welfare is assumed to be highly correlated with GNP. Therefore, if free trade promotes growth in GNP, it is assumed that it also promotes growth in welfare. But the link between GNP and welfare has become very questionable, and with it the argument for unregulated trade, and indeed for all other growth-promoting policies.

Evidence for doubting the correlation between GNP and welfare in the United States is taken from two sources.

First, Nordhaus and Tobin (1972) asked whether growth is obsolete as a measure of welfare and hence as a proper guiding objective of policy.[5] To answer their question they developed a direct index of welfare, called Measured Economic Welfare (MEW) and tested its correlation with GNP over the period 1929–1965. They found that for the period as a whole, GNP and MEW were indeed positively correlated—for every six units of increase in GNP there was, on average, a four-unit increase in MEW. Economists breathed a sigh of relief, forgot about MEW, and concentrated on GNP.

Some twenty years later, John Cobb, Clifford Cobb, and I (1989) revisited the issue and began our development of an Index of Sustainable Economic Welfare (ISEW) with a review of the Nordhaus and Tobin MEW. We discovered that if one takes only the latter half of their time series (the eighteen years from 1947 to 1965), the correlation between GNP and MEW *falls* dramatically. In this most recent period—surely the more relevant for projections into the future —a six-unit increase in GNP yielded on average only a one-unit increase in MEW. This suggests that GNP growth at this stage of U.S. history may be a quite inefficient way of improving economic welfare—certainly less efficient than in the past.

The ISEW was developed to replace the MEW, since the latter omitted any correction for environmental costs, did not correct for distributional changes, and included leisure, which both dominated the MEW and introduced many arbitrary valuation decisions. The ISEW, like the MEW, though less so, was correlated with GNP up to a point, beyond which the correlation turned slightly negative.[6]

Measures of welfare are difficult and subject to many arbitrary judgments, so sweeping conclusions should be resisted. However, it seems fair to say that for the United States since 1947 the empirical evidence that GNP growth has increased welfare is *very* weak. Consequently, any impact on welfare via free trade's contribution to GNP growth would also be very weak. In other words, the great benefit, for which we are urged to sacrifice national community and industrial peace, turns out on closer inspection not to exist.

The second common objection to the case against free trade is that "comparative advantage supports global integration." I am an economist, and really do admire and revere David Ricardo, the great champion of classical free trade and formulator of the principle of comparative advantage. But I argue that if Ricardo were alive now he would *not* support a policy of free trade and global integration as these are understood today.

Ricardo showed how free trade could be mutually beneficial for countries even where there were dramatic one-sided differences in how expensive it would be to produce the same goods in each country. Consider his example of England and Portugal in the eighteenth century. It was cheaper to produce both wine and cloth in Portugal, in absolute terms, than in England. But it was also true that England's cloth industry was—relative to its wine industry—significantly more efficient. England's disadvantage relative to Portugal in cloth production was less than its disadvantage relative to Portugal in wine production. England had a comparative advantage in cloth, Portugal a comparative advantage in wine. Ricardo showed that each country would be better off specializing in the product in which it had a comparative advantage and trading for the other, regardless of absolute advantage. Free trade between the countries, and competition within each country, would lead to this mutually beneficial result.

Economists have been giving Ricardo a standing ovation for this demonstration ever since 1817, as well they should.[7] But in their enthusiasm for the conclusion, modern economists seem to have forgotten one of the premises. Ricardo was very careful to base his comparative advantage argument for free trade on the explicit premise that capital was immobile between national communities. Capital, as well as labor, stayed at home, only goods were traded internationally. It was the fact that capital could not, in this model, cross national boundaries that directly led to replacement of absolute advantage by comparative advantage. Capital follows absolute advantage as far as it can within national boundaries. But since by assumption it cannot pursue absolute advantage across national boundaries, it has recourse to the next best strategy, which is to reallocate itself within the nation according to the principle of comparative advantage.[8]

For example, if Portugal produces both wine and cloth absolutely more cheaply than does England, then capital would love to leave England and follow absolute advantage to Portugal, where it would produce both wine and cloth more cheaply. But, by assumption—quite reasonable in the eighteenth century—it cannot. The next best thing is to specialize domestically in the production of English cloth and trade it for Portuguese wine.

Whatever the case in Ricardo's time, in our day it would be hard to imagine anything more contrary to fact than the assumption that capital is immobile internationally. It is today vastly more mobile than goods. Transnational corporations seeking cheap labor and resources can easily set up factories in Mexico (or Portugal), capitalizing on the absolute advantage of cheap production, with absolutely no penalty in terms of access to the markets of the countries they have just left. In today's world, linked by twentieth-century transport, communication, technologies, and financial institutions, capital will flow rapidly to the countries with absolute advantage.

The argument for globalization based on comparative advantage is therefore embarrassed by a false premise. When starting from a false premise, one would have a better chance of hitting a correct conclusion if one's logic were also faulty! But Ricardo's logic is not faulty. Therefore I conclude that he would not be arguing for free trade—at least not on the basis of comparative advantage which requires such a wildly counterfactual assumption. Unlike some of today's economists and politicians, Ricardo would *never* argue that because comparative advantage shows that free trade in goods is beneficial, one can simply extend the argument to show that free trade in capital must yield even more benefits!! To appeal to a principle that is premised on capital *immobility* in order to support an argument in favor of capital *mobility* is too illogical for words. How does one say something that is too illogical for words? Usually by burying it in the assumptions of a lot of intimidating, but half-baked mathematics.[9]

Classical Versus Neoclassical Views of Free Trade   Regardless of what Ricardo would say if he were alive, some modern neoclassical economists might still want to argue for free trade on the basis of absolute rather than comparative advantage. They could still show that total world product would increase as a result of specialization and trade according to absolute advantage, but not that *each* nation would necessarily be better off. That is the rub. Since the classical economists were nationalists, they were simply not interested in global integration for its own sake, or in trade that did not benefit their own nations. I think their position was wise. To the extent that global integration takes place, the very idea of "each nation" loses its economic meaning. But the neoclassicals do not mind that because they are individualists, not nationalists.

The reason capital stayed at home in the classical model was its adherence to national community. In Ricardo's words:

Experience, however, shows, that the fancied or real insecurity of capital, when not under the immediate control of its owner, together with the natural disinclination which every man has to quit the country of his birth and connections, and entrust himself with all his habits fixed, to a strange government and new laws, check the emigration of capital. These feelings, which I should be sorry to see weakened, induce most men of property to be satisfied with a low rate of profits in their own country, rather than seek more advantageous employment for their wealth in foreign nations.[10]

For Ricardo it is the capitalist's attachment to his national community that keeps capital at home. Adam Smith held the same view, and, interestingly, it is in the context of his discussion of the international immobility of capital that the famous "invisible hand" passage occurs. As Smith put it:

By preferring the support of domestic to that of foreign industry, he (the capitalist) intends only his own security; and by directing that industry in such a manner as its produce may be the greatest value, he intends only his own gain, and he is in this, as in many other cases led by an invisible hand to promote an end which was no part of his intention.[11]

Of course Smith's capitalist is acting in his own self-interest, but, like Ricardo's capitalist, he feels secure within the country of his birth and connections, and insecure abroad. The capitalist's very self-identity is defined with reference to his relations in community. When the self is constituted by internal relations in community it is not so surprising that pursuit of self-interest should promote the community welfare. Note that Smith takes it for granted that keeping capital at home is in the community's interest. His only problem is to explain why it is also in the capitalist's self-interest. The reason is that the self in which the capitalist is so vitally interested is largely constituted by his relations in community.[12]

Ricardo emphasized that he would be sorry to see these feelings of community weakened. But of course they have in fact been greatly weakened, in no small part by the globalist ideology ironically justified by misunderstandings of Ricardo's own comparative advantage argument.

In the classical nineteenth-century vision of free trade, held by Ricardo, the national community embraced both national labor and national capital, and these classes cooperated, albeit with conflict, to produce national goods which then competed in international markets against the goods of other nations, produced by other national capital / labor teams.

Nowadays, in the twentieth century's globally integrated view of free trade, it no longer makes sense to think of national teams of labor and capital—both become global. Formerly national capitalists in the United States now communicate with their former domestic workers by mobile telephone in the manner of the following conversation:

Sorry, old Union Joe Six-Pack, but we live in a global economy—I can buy labor abroad at one-tenth the wage your union wants, and with lower environmental and social taxes, and still sell my product in this market or any other. Your severance check is in the mail. Good luck. . . . What do you mean, "bonds of national community"? I just told you that we live in a global economy, and have abandoned all that nationalistic stuff that caused two world wars. Factor mobility is necessary for maximum efficiency, and without maximum efficiency we will lose out in global competition. . . . Yes, Joe, of course there will be a tendency to equalize wages worldwide, but profits will also equalize. . . . Well, yes, of course wages will be equalized downward and profits equalized upward. What else would you expect in a global economy that reflects world supply and demand? Don't you want the Chinese and Mexican workers to be as rich as you are? You're not a racist, are you, Joe? Furthermore, economists have proved that free trade benefits everyone. So be grateful. . . . Now that you have some extra time, Joe, sign up for Economics 101 at your local community college. You'll learn about comparative advantage. It'll help you feel better.

At this stage in the dialogue there's not much community left. We have here the abrogation of a basic social agreement between labor and capital over how to divide up the value that they jointly add to raw materials. That agreement has been reached not through economic theory, but through generations of national debate, elections, strikes, lockouts, court decisions, and violent conflicts—that agreement, on which national community and industrial peace depend, is being repudiated in the interests of global integration. That is a very poor trade, even if one calls it "free" trade.

Globalization and Immigration   The sundering of national community is carried even further now in the United States, where illegal immigration, as well as the world's most generous legal immigration and refugee policies, have the effect of bringing in poor foreign workers to domestic jobs, in addition to free trade's consequence of exporting domestic jobs to poor foreign workers by capital migration.[13] Working-class citizens by now accustomed to seeing their real wages competed down,[14] must also get used to seeing their taxes increase to provide public welfare benefits to illegal and legal immigrants, as well as loan guarantees to protect foreign currencies and the Wall Street interests that have investments denominated in these currencies.[15] Underclass citizens on welfare see their chances of getting a job diminish because the illegal immigrants are tough competition. Our government, ever sensitive to the interests of the employer class, has done little to control the border, and has even suggested that illegal immigrants are a public benefit because they pay more in taxes than they get in social welfare and public goods. This claim is quite doubtful, but in any case it is beside the point because in the absence of the illegal immigrant the job or entrepreneurial opportunity taken by the illegal immigrant would have presumably been available to a citizen previously on public welfare, who would then have become a taxpayer in addition to getting off the dole.[16]

The logic of free trade, once it is erroneously extended to free capital mobility, is by consistency also extended to free labor mobility, that is, free immigration. If we are truly in a global economy, why not? If neither capital nor the governments that serve it have any greater obligation to citizens than to foreigners, then certainly migration should be free. Free movement of goods, of capital, and of labor is the logical consequence of global economic integration. It is certainly *not* what Ricardo or Smith had in mind when speaking of free trade, but is the implicit or explicit program of today's free-trading globalists. It does not serve national community, it destroys it. And it does not create international community either.

A former Texas commissioner of agriculture, Jim Hightower, made the following suggestion: "Let's keep our factories and jobs here and move our corporate headquarters to Mexico, Korea, or wherever else we can get some reasonably priced chief executives." Or maybe we could allow free immigration of cheap chief executives along with cheap labor. Not likely. More likely is that we will witness a further writing off of the laboring class in this country, an increasing disdain toward uneducated and rural people by the corporate and university elite, and an increasing devotion by the former to the one thing about themselves that at least vaguely concerns the latter—their growing arsenal of guns.

It is considered impolite to talk about the political interest in cheap labor in this country, or about the use by the employer class of free trade and unenforced immigration laws as instruments for promoting lower wages and higher profits. Liberal intellectuals, who one might have hoped would see through the mystification, instead have advocated free trade and easy immigration as a way of being generous at someone else's expense, and of proving to themselves once again that they are not racists or even nationalists. And the economists assure them that economic growth will eventually make everyone better off, so whatever temporary cost may fall on our laboring class is a small price for "us" to pay for the gratifying illusion that we are helping starving people across the sea.

Conclusions

Free trade, specialization, and global integration mean that nations are no longer free *not* to trade. Yet freedom not to trade is surely necessary if trade is to remain mutually beneficial. National production for the national market should be the dog, and international trade its tail. But the globalist free traders want to tie the dogs' tails together so tightly that the international knot will wag the national dogs. The globalists envision this as a harmoniously choreographed canine ballet. More likely it will result in a multilateral dog fight, along with serious class conflicts within nations.

High-consuming countries, whether their high consumption results from many people or from high consumption per capita, will, in a finite and increasingly integrated world, more and more be at each other's throats. To avoid war, nations must both consume less and become more self-sufficient. But free traders say we should become less self-sufficient and more globally integrated as part of the overriding quest to consume ever more. That is the worst advice I can think of.

Chapter 11

From Adjustment to Sustainable Development: The Obstacle of Free Trade

One coming to the development literature for the first time in the early or mid-eighties would encounter the word "adjustment" with a frequency several standard deviations above its average in normal English prose. Syntactically the word cries out for two prepositions, with two objects—adjustment *of* what *to* what? These prepositions are usually suppressed for economy of expression, and sometimes for economy of thought as well. But what serious writers generally have in mind is adjustment of the real economy of a country to the theoretical model of an effecient economy as developed by mainstream neoclassical economics. Concretely this involves three main policies:

1. Adjustment of prices to make them better measures of full social marginal opportunity costs (internalization of social and environmental costs into prices), which frequently requires politically unpopular removal of subsidies and addition of taxes.

2. Adjustment of macroeconomic conditions to achieve monetary stability so that correct prices can be properly expressed in reliable monetary units of constant value over time. This means controlling inflation by eliminating fiscal deficits and restraining the money supply. Both inflation and prices that do not measure full social marginal opportunity costs induce "distortions"—that is, situations in which private gain works against public welfare. The object of "adjustment" is, then, to remove "distortions."

3. Adjustment of national markets and prices to world markets and prices so as to integrate the nation into the world trading system in order to increase productivity by specialization according to comparative advantage, and to reap the

further advantages of specialization made possible by expanding the extent of the market beyond national boundaries. Tariffs and quotas and any other restriction on international trade are considered "distortions."

There may be other criteria of adjustment, but certainly these three seem to cover most instances of so-called "adjustment lending," which invariably are for the purpose of financing a policy change aimed at rationalizing prices, dealing with macroeconomic problems of debt and deficit, and liberalizing international trade. Why a country should find it either necessary or desirable to borrow money at interest in order to adopt more reasonable national policies is not always obvious. Some tend to think of adjustment lending as bribery, although for a good cause. In any case, the faith is that the policy change, like any other investment, will add more to national welfare than the payment of interest on the loan will subtract from it.

What the Neoclassical Model Omits

The first two goals of adjustment have a great deal of merit, and, with modifications to be discussed below, should remain as key parts of sustainable development policy. The third (free trade) is highly problematic in that it partially undercuts the first two, and has other serious problems as well. Elaborating this point is the main task of what follows. The problems with adjustment, and the consequent need for a transition to sustainable development as the guiding paradigm, stem from the inadequacies of the object of the implicit preposition "to"—that is, the mainstream model to which the real economy is being adjusted. What has been left out of adjustment is what has been left out of the mainstream neoclassical model—namely, any serious concern for distribution, and any recognition whatsoever of biophysical constraints on economic growth, either from the side of finite environmental sources of raw material and energy, or from the side of finite environmental sinks for waste matter and energy. The neoclassical view does recognize externalities, but these are considered to be correctable by substitution or technology, and do not constitute a limit to the growth of the economic subsystem.

To put the matter in other terms, we have three economic problems to consider: allocation, distribution, and scale. *Allocation* refers to the apportioning of resources among alternative product uses—food, bicycles, cars, medical care. An allocation is efficient if it corresponds to effective demand, that is, the relative preferences of the citizens as weighted by their relative incomes, both taken as given. An inefficient allocation will use resources to produce a number of things that people will not buy, and will fail to produce other things that people would buy if only they could find them. It would be characterized by shortages of the latter and surpluses of the former. *Distribution* refers to the apportioning of the goods produced (and the resources they embody) among different people (as opposed to different commodities). Distributions are just or unjust; allocations are efficient or inefficient. There is an efficient allocation for each distribution of income. *Scale* refers to the physical size of the economy relative to the ecosystem. The economy is viewed, in its physical dimensions, as a subsystem of the larger ecosystem. Scale is measured as population times per capita resource use—in other words total resource use—the volume of the matter / energy throughput (metabolic flow) by which the ecosystem sustains the economic subsystem. Scale may be sustainable or unsustainable. An efficient allocation does not imply a just distribution. Neither an efficient allocation nor a just distribution, nor both, implies a sustainable scale. The three concepts are quite distinct, although relations among them exist, as noted above.

Adjustment has been seen overwhelmingly in the context of allocation—adjustment to an allocatively efficient economy. Distribution has not been totally ignored, but has certainly been a poor second in adjustment policy. Scale has been completely outside the field of vision of adjustment. Common sense sometimes compels many economists at least to recognize the importance of population limits (one factor of scale). But within the mainstream model economists become quite agnostic on population since it falls outside the domain of allocative efficiency. In any case, neither population control, nor land reform, nor any other form of wealth or income distribution are customary objectives of adjustment lending.

Transition to a sustainable development vision will put scale and distribution on center stage along with allocation. The first two features of adjustment (getting relative prices right and controlling inflation) are key to solving the allocation problem and remain fundamental in the sustainable development vision. As mentioned earlier, the third common feature of adjustment, free trade, must be rejected as a policy for sustainable development. It is time to consider the reasons why this is so, and the intense controversy surrounding this issue.

Why Free Trade Conflicts with Sustainable Development

International free trade conflicts sharply with the national policies of (1) getting prices right, (2) moving toward a more just distribution, (3) fostering community, (4) controlling the macroeconomy, and (5) keeping scale within ecological limits.
Each conflict will be discussed in turn.

1. If one nation internalizes environmental and social costs to a high degree, following the dictates of adjustment, and then enters into free trade with a country that does not force its producers to internalize those costs, then the result will be that the firms in the second country will have lower prices and will drive the competing firms in the first country out of business.

If the trading entities were nations rather than individual firms trading across national boundaries, then the cost-internalizing nation could limit its volume and composition of trade to an amount that did not ruin its domestic producers, and thereby actually take advantage of the opportunity to acquire goods at prices that were below full cost. The country that sells at less than full-cost prices only hurts itself as long as other countries restrict their trade with that country to a volume that does not ruin their own producers. That, of course, would not be free trade. There is clearly a conflict between free trade and a national policy of internalization of external costs. External costs are now so important that the latter goal should take precedence. In this case there is a clear argument for tariffs to protect not an inefficient industry, but an efficient national policy of internalizing external costs into prices.

Of course, if all trading nations agreed to common rules for defining, evaluating, and internalizing external costs, then this objection would disappear and the standard arguments for free trade could again be made in the new context. But how likely is such agreement? Even the small expert technical fraternity of national income accountants cannot agree on how to measure environmental costs in the system of national accounts, let alone on rules for internalizing these costs into prices at the firm level. Politicians are not likely to do better. Some economists will argue against uniform cost internalization on the grounds that different countries have different tastes for environmental services and amenities, and that these differences should be reflected in prices as legitimate reasons for profitable trade. Certainly agreement on uniform principles, and the proper extent of departure from uniformity in their application, will not be easy. Nevertheless, suppose that this difficulty is overcome so that all countries internalize external costs by the same rules applied in each case to the appropriate degree in the light of differing tastes and levels of income. There are two further problems arising from capital mobility and wage differentials.

2. Wage levels vary enormously between countries and are largely determined by the supply of labor, which in turn depends on population size and growth rates. Overpopulated countries are naturally low-wage countries, and if population growth is rapid they will remain low-wage countries. This is especially so because the demographic rate of increase of the lower class (labor) is frequently twice or more that of the upper class (capital). For most traded goods, labor is still the largest item of cost and consequently the major determinant of price. Cheap labor means low prices and a competitive advantage in trade. (The theoretical possibility that low wages reflect a taste for poverty and therefore a legitimate reason for cost differences is not taken seriously here.) But adjustment economists do not worry about that because economists have proved that free trade between high-wage and low-wage countries can be mutually advantageous thanks to comparative advantage.

The doctrine of comparative advantage is quite correct given the as-sumptions on which it rests, but unfortunately one of these assumptions is that cap-ital is immobile internationally. The theory is supposed to work as follows. When in international competition the relatively inefficient activities lose out and jobs are eliminated, at the same time the relatively efficient activities (those with the com-parative advantage) expand, absorbing both the labor and the capital that were dis-employed in activities with a comparative disadvantage. Capital and labor are real-located within the country, specializing according to that country's comparative advantage. However, when both capital and goods are internationally mobile, then capital will follow absolute advantage to the low-wage country rather than reallo-cate itself according to comparative advantage within its home country. It will fol-low the highest absolute profit, which is usually determined by the lowest abso-lute wage.

Of course, further inducements to absolute profits, such as low social insurance charges or a low degree of internalization of environmental costs, also at-tract capital, usually toward the very same low-wage countries. But we have as-sumed that all countries have internalized costs to the same degree, in order to fo-cus on the wage issue. Once capital is mobile, then the entire doctrine of comparative advantage and all its comforting demonstrations become irrelevant. The consequence of capital mobility would be similar to that of international labor mobility—a strong tendency to equalize wages throughout the world. Given the existing overpopulation and high demographic growth of the "third world," it is clear that the equalization will be downward, as it has indeed been during the last decade in the United States. Of course, returns to capital will also be equalized by free trade and capital mobility, but the level at which equalization will occur will be higher than at present. United States capital will benefit from cheap labor abroad followed by cheap labor at home, at least until checked by a crisis of insufficient de-mand due to a lack of worker purchasing power resulting from low wages. But that can be forestalled by efficient reallocation to serve the new pattern of effective de-mand resulting from the greater concentration of income. More luxury goods will be produced and fewer basic-wage goods. Efficiency is attained, but distributive equity is sacrificed.

The standard neoclassical adjustment view argues that wages will eventually be equalized worldwide at high levels, thanks to the enormous increase in production made possible by free trade. This increase in production presumably will trigger the automatic demographic transition to lower birthrates—a doctrine that might be considered a part of the adjustment package in so far as any attention at all is paid to population. Such a thought can only be entertained by those who ig-nore the issue of scale, as of course neoclassicals traditionally do. For all 5.4 billion people presently alive to consume resources and absorptive capacities at the same per capita rate as Americans or Europeans is ecologically impossible. Much less is it possible to extend that level of consumption to future generations. Development as it currently is understood on the United States model is only possible for a minority of the world's population over a few generations—that is, it is neither just nor sustainable. The goal of sustainable development is, by changes in allocation, distribution, and scale, to move the world toward a state in which "development," whatever it concretely comes to mean, will be for all people in all generations. This is certainly not achievable by a more finely tuned adjustment to the standard growth model which is largely responsible for having created the present impasse in the first place.

Of course, if somehow all countries decided to control their populations and adopt distributive and scale limiting measures such that wages could be equalized world wide at an acceptably high level, then this problem would disappear and the standard arguments for free trade could again be invoked in the new context. Although the likelihood of that context seems infinitesimal, we might for purposes of *a fortiori* argument consider a major problem with free trade that would still remain.

3. Even with uniformly high wages made possible by universal population control and redistribution, and with uniform internalization of external costs, free trade and free capital mobility still increase the separation of ownership and control and the forced mobility of labor which are so inimical to community. Community economic life can be disrupted not only by your fellow citizen who, though living in another part of your country, might at least share some tenuous bonds of community with you, but by someone on the other side of the world with whom you have no community of language, history, culture, law. These foreigners may be wonderful people—that is not the point. The point is that they are very far removed from the life of the community that is affected significantly by their decisions. Your life and your community can be disrupted by decisions and events over which you have no control, no vote, no voice.

Specialization and integration of a local community into the world economy does offer a quick fix to problems of local unemployment, and one must admit that carrying community self-sufficiency to extremes can certainly be impoverishing. But short supply lines and relatively local control over the livelihood of the community remain obvious prudential measures which require some restraint on free trade if they are to be effective. Libertarian economists look at *Homo economicus* as a self-contained individual who is infinitely mobile and equally at home anywhere. But real people live in communities, and in communities of communities. Their very individual identities are constituted by their relations in community. To regard community as a disposable aggregate of individuals in temporary proximity only for as long as it serves the interests of mobile capital is bad enough when capital stays within the nation. But when capital moves internationally it becomes much worse.

When the capitalist class in the United States in effect tells the laboring class, "Sorry, you have to compete with the poor of the world for jobs and

wages—the fact that we are fellow citizens of the same country creates no obligations on our part" then admittedly not much community remains, and it is not hard
to understand why a United States worker would be indifferent to the nationality of
his or her employer. Indeed, if local community is more respected by the foreign
company than by the displaced American counterpart, then the interests of community could conceivably be furthered by foreign ownership in some specific
cases. But this could not be counted as the rule, and serves only to show that the extent of pathological disregard for community in our own country has not yet been
equalled by others. In any event, the further undercutting of local and national
communities (which are real) in the name of a cosmopolitan world community
which does not exist, is a poor trade, even if we call it free trade. The true road to
international community is that of a federation of communities—communities of
communities—not the destruction of local and national communities in the service
of a single cosmopolitan world of footloose money managers who constitute not a
community, but merely an interdependent, mutually vulnerable, unstable coalition
of short-term interests.

4. Free trade and free capital mobility have interfered with macroeconomic stability by permitting huge international payment imbalances and capital transfers resulting in debts that are unrepayable in many cases and excessive in
others. Efforts to service these debts can lead to unsustainable rates of exploitation
of exportable resources, and to an eagerness to make new loans to get the foreign
exchange with which to pay old loans, with a consequent disincentive to take a hard
look at the real productivity of the project for which the new loan is being made.
Efforts to pay back loans and still meet domestic obligations lead to government
budget deficits and monetary creation with resulting inflation. Inflation, plus the
need to export to pay off loans, leads to currency devaluations, giving rise to foreign
exchange speculation, capital flight, and hot money movements, disrupting the
macroeconomic stability that adjustment was supposed to foster.

To summarize so far: Free trade sins against allocative efficiency by
making it difficult for nations to internalize external costs; it sins against distributive justice by widening the disparity between labor and capital in high-wage countries; it sins against community by demanding more mobility and by further separating ownership and control; and it sins against macroeconomic stability. Finally, it
sins against the criterion of sustainable scale, in a more subtle manner that will now
be considered.

5. As previously mentioned, part of the free trade dogma of adjustment thinking is based on the assumption that the whole world, and all future generations, can consume resources at the levels current in today's high-wage countries

without inducing ecological collapse. So, in this way, free trade sins against the criterion of sustainable scale. But, in its physical dimensions the economy really is an open subsystem of a materially closed, non-growing, and finite ecosystem with a limited throughput of solar energy. The proper scale of the economic subsystem relative to the finite total system is a very important question. Free trade has obscured the scale limit in the following way.

Sustainable development means living within environmental constraints of absorptive and regenerative capacities. These constraints are both global (greenhouse effect, ozone shield) and local (soil erosion, deforestation). Trade between nations or regions offers a way to loosen local constraints by importing environmental services (including waste absorption) from elsewhere. Within limits this can be quite reasonable and justifiable. But when carried to extremes in the name of free trade it becomes destructive. It leads to a situation in which each country is trying to live beyond its own absorptive and regenerative capacities by importing these capacities from elsewhere. Of course they pay for these capacities and all is well as long as other countries have made the complementary decision—namely, to keep their own scale well below their own national carrying capacity in order to export some of its services. In other words, the apparent escape from scale constraints enjoyed by some countries via trade depends on other countries' willingness and ability to adopt the very discipline of limiting scale that the importing country is seeking to avoid.

What nations have actually made this complementary choice? All countries now aim to grow in scale, and it is merely the fact that some have not yet reached their limits that allows other nations to import carrying capacity. Free trade does not remove carrying capacity constraints—it just guarantees that nations will hit that constraint more or less simultaneously rather than sequentially. It converts differing local constraints into an aggregated global constraint. It converts a set of problems, some of which are manageable, into one big, unmanageable problem. Evidence that this is not understood is provided by the countless occasions when someone who really should know better points to the Netherlands or Hong Kong as both an example to be emulated and as evidence that all countries could become as densely populated as these two. How it would be possible for all countries to be net exporters of goods and net importers of carrying capacity is not explained.

Of course, the drive to grow beyond carrying capacity has roots other and deeper than the free trade dogma. The point is that free trade makes it very hard to deal with these root causes at a national level, which is the only level at which effective social controls over the economy exist. The adjustment theorist will argue that free trade is just a natural extension of price adjustment across international boundaries, and that right prices must reflect *global* scarcities and preferences. But if the unit of community is the nation—the unit in which there are institutions and traditions of collective action, responsibility, and mutual help, the unit in which government tries to carry out policy for the good of its citizens—then right prices should *not* reflect the preferences and scarcities of other nations. Right prices *should* differ between national communities. Such differences traditionally have provided the whole reason for international trade in goods.

Development, Not Growth

To summarize, it has been argued that the first two goals of adjustment (right prices and price level stability) are necessary to the sustainable development era. It has been shown that the third element of adjustment, free trade, must be abandoned because it is in conflict with (a) the first two goals of adjustment that have been retained, (b) goals that were downplayed by adjustment (just distribution) but critical for sustainable development, and (c) the goal that was totally ignored by adjustment, but is the principal goal of sustainable development, namely a scale of the economic subsystem that is within the carrying capacity of the ecosystem. It remains to try to spell out a bit more the positive vision of sustainable development.

As already indicated, the basic vision underlying sustainable development is that of the economy as a physical subsystem of the ecosystem. A subsystem cannot grow beyond the scale of the total system of which it is a part. If the total system provides services that the subsystem cannot provide for itself, then the subsystem must avoid impinging on the parent system to an extent and in ways that would impair its ability to provide those services. The scale of the economy must remain below the capacity of the ecosystem sustainably to supply services such as photosynthesis, pollination, purification of air and water, maintenance of climate, filtering of excessive ultraviolet radiation, recycling of wastes, etc. Adjustment in the service of growth has pushed us beyond a sustainable scale.

To maintain the present scale of population and per capita consumption we are consuming natural capital and counting it as income. The effort to overcome poverty by further growth in scale of throughput is self-defeating once we have reached the point where growth in scale increases environmental costs faster than it increases production benefits. Beyond this point, which we have, in all likelihood, already passed, further growth makes us poorer, not richer. The alternative is to stop growth in scale, and seek to overcome poverty by redistribution and qualitative improvement in efficiency of resource use, rather than further quantitative increase in the resource throughput. A policy of limiting throughput will automatically redirect energies toward increasing the efficiency with which it is used. If technology can easily and greatly increase efficiency, then the transition could be relatively painless. If not, it will be more difficult. In either case it remains necessary. The basic policy is the same whether one is a technological optimist or pessimist.

In an effort to avoid facing these realities, those wedded to the adjustment paradigm have come up with one more adjustment which they contradictorily call sustainable *growth*.

Much confusion is generated by using the term "sustainable growth" as a synonym for sustainable *development*. Respect for the dictionary would lead us to reserve the word "growth" for quantitative increase in physical size by assimilation or accretion of materials. "Development" refers to qualitative change, realization of potentialities, transition to a fuller or better state. The two processes are distinct—sometimes linked, sometimes not. For example, a child grows and develops simultaneously; a snowball or a cancer grows without developing; the planet Earth develops without growing. Economies frequently grow and develop at the same time but can do either separately. But since the economy is a subsystem of a finite and non-growing ecosystem, then as growth leads it to incorporate an ever larger fraction of the total system into itself, its behavior must more and more approximate the behavior of the total system, which is development without growth. It is precisely the recognition that growth in scale ultimately becomes impossible—and already costs more than it is worth—that gives rise to the urgency of the concept of sustainable development. Sustainable development is development without growth in the scale of the economy beyond some point that is within biospheric carrying capacity.

Many believe that the present scale is beyond long-term carrying capacity and that sustainable growth in its initial phase will require a period of negative growth. Even if one is a technological optimist and believes that development in the productivity of the resource throughput can increase faster than the volume of the throughput needs to diminish, this is still very radical. The term "sustainable growth" aims to deny this radical transformation, and to suggest that growth is still the number one goal, that growth just needs to be a bit more environmentally friendly. Sustainable *growth* is just one more adjustment to the standard view. Sustainable *development* is an alternative to the standard growth ideology and is incompatible with it.

Sustainable development, development without growth, does not imply the end of economics—if anything, economics becomes even more important. But it is a subtle and complex economics of maintenance, qualitative improvement, sharing, frugality, and adaptation to natural limits. It is an economics of better, not bigger.

Two Pioneers
in the
Economics of
Sustainable
Development

Introduction

This section is a change of pace, a shift to the literary mode of intellectual biography, an exposition of the ideas of two thinkers whose enormous and early contributions to the economics of sustainability have been insufficiently recognized. Reading about ideas in the context of the real people who developed and championed them is often more interesting and informative than studying just the ideas themselves, abstracted from their human origins. For a fascinating discussion of other earlier pioneers, see Juan Martinez-Alier's book *Ecological Economics* (1987).[1]

Frederick Soddy is especially important for two reasons. First, he recognized back in the 1920s the critical importance of the laws of thermodynamics for economics, a theme which Nicholas Georgescu-Roegen developed in much more depth and detail fifty years later. Second, Soddy argued that money leads us to confuse debt (the symbol) with wealth (the reality symbolized), and to forget that while the former can grow forever, the latter cannot. If one should think that this particular form of "money illusion" is unlikely, one has only to read the newspaper to be convinced otherwise. Recently there was a Ponzi scheme called the New Era Foundation, operating out of Philadelphia, that stung some of the richest and most financially astute people in the country. How could these sophisticated people fall for that nonsense? was my first reaction. On reflection, however, I had to ask myself, Were they not just being consistent with the canonical faith in growth? They were quite accustomed to having their money double every seven years. After all, that reflects a rate of return of only 10% annually. If someone promises to double your money in six months instead of seven years, what *a priori* reason is there to kick him out of your office? If money can already grow fast, then why can't it grow still faster? Since money has not elsewhere been treated in this volume, except briefly in Chapter 1, a discussion of Soddy and his ideas is convenient for this reason as well.[2]

Nicholas Georgescu-Roegen has been cited frequently in this volume (recall the "entropy hourglass" in the introduction to Part 1). He died last year (1994). I include my obituary essay about him here because it explains in a simple way the overall nature of his contributions, and their relevance to sustainability. The coherence of this contribution is not evident from the scattered, though frequent, references to him throughout this book. Georgescu-Roegen's life also illustrates the extreme difficulty that even a consummate economist faces in making the discipline of economics take seriously any new insight that fundamentally challenges its customary presuppositions.

Chapter 12

The Economic Thought
of Frederick Soddy

Almost always the men who achieve these fundamental inventions of a new paradigm have been either very young or very new to the field whose paradigm they change.
—Thomas S. Kuhn,
The Structure of Scientific Revolutions

Frederick Soddy (1877–1956) is best known as a pioneering chemist who collaborated with Rutherford in studying radioactive disintegration, predicted the existence of and coined the name for isotopes, and was a major contributor to the modern theory of atomic structure. For these achievements he was elected a Fellow of the Royal Society in 1910 and was awarded the Nobel Prize in 1921. He was a member of the Swedish, Italian, and Russian academies of science. During his career he held university positions at McGill, Glasgow, Aberdeen, and, from 1919 onward, Oxford (Fleck 1957).

Although an enthusiastic believer in scientific progress and in the possibility of a society in which the fruits of scientific knowledge would be shared by all, Soddy was acutely aware that history supported the view that science has proved as much a curse as a blessing to humanity. Nor could he accept the comfortable view that scientists have no responsibility for the uses to which their work is put. Even though others (bankers and economists) bore, in his view, a far greater burden of guilt for the misuse of knowledge, scientists could not plead innocent. The world's real problem was faulty economics, not faulty chemistry, and for the second half of his nearly eighty years economics replaced chemistry as the center of his intellectual life.

Soddy realized earlier than most the theoretical possibility of atomic energy. Since his own work had contributed to the discovery that this vast energy potential existed, it was natural for him to ask what sort of a world it would be if atomic energy ever became available. His answer (written in 1926) was clear:

> If the discovery were made tomorrow, there is not a nation that would not throw itself heart and soul into the task of applying it to war, just as they are now doing in the case of the newly developed chemical weapons of poison-gas warfare. . . . If [atomic energy] were to come under existing economic conditions, it would mean the *reductio ad absurdum* of scientific civilization, a swift annihilation instead of a none too lingering collapse. [Soddy 1926, p. 28]

For Soddy, the problem was to change economic conditions in order eventually to make the world safe for atomic energy and other fruits of science: there must be something radically wrong with economic thought and institutions in order for the gift of scientific knowledge to have become such a threat. Soddy was thus led to a radical critique of economics.

It is interesting that Soddy's concern about the destructive potential of atomic energy was considered extreme at the time. Another Nobel laureate, Robert A. Millikan, commented,

> Since Mr. Soddy raised the hobgoblin of dangerous quantities of available subatomic energy [science] has brought to light good evidence that this particular hobgoblin—like most of the bugaboos that crowd in on the mind of ignorance—was a myth. . . . The new evidence born of further scientific study is to the effect that it is highly improbable that there is any appreciable amount of available subatomic energy for man to tap. [Millikan 1930, p. 121]

Millikan, of course, turned out to be wrong, but the underlying faith that he went on to express is still held by many, namely that one may "sleep in peace with the consciousness that the Creator has put some foolproof elements into his handiwork, and that man is powerless to do it any titanic physical damage" (ibid.). As R. L. Sinsheimer recently noted, "Scientific endeavor rests upon the faith that our scientific probing and our technological ventures will not displace some key element of our protective environment and thereby collapse our ecological niche" (Sinsheimer 1978, p. 24). It now seems evident that the only protective element the Creator put into his handiwork is man's capacity for moral insight and restraint, which is far from foolproof. With the benefit of hindsight we can see that Soddy was the true prophet and that the scientific establishment, represented by Millikan, was whistling in the dark.[1] Far from believing in providential "foolproof elements" built into creation, Soddy was convinced that the economic system contained built-in elements for assuring the destruction of Creation, once science gave man the power. The key problem, therefore, was to discover and correct the errors in our economic thinking and institutions, a task which Soddy tackled with both moral fervor and the systematic logic of an experienced scientist.

Perhaps the most intriguing thing about Soddy the economist is that he started his inquiry with a mind both highly intelligent and completely free from the preconceived paradigm of the orthodox economists, for whom he had an undisguised contempt. The contempt was mutual. With the significant exception of Frank Knight, to be discussed later, Soddy's work was ignored by economists. Unlike the American positional astronomer Simon Newcomb, who also came to economics from the physical sciences, Soddy came as a critic, not a student, and remained an outsider. Newcomb liked economics, did not believe that his pre–World War I America was in mortal danger from an increasingly powerful but misdirected application of science, and wrote a fairly orthodox *Principles of Political Economy* (1885), which demonstrated that he had done his economics homework, and had earned the right to try to make economics just a bit more scientific. Soddy, on the other hand, considered economics a pseudoscience in need of a totally new beginning. John Ruskin, not Ricardo, Mill, or Marshall, was his inspiration.

The not surprising consequence of this approach was that Soddy was and continues to be written off as a crank. In fact, Soddy's economics seems to have been something of an embarrassment to everyone but Soddy. In 1926, the *Times Literary Supplement* (26 August, p. 565), in reviewing his major economic work *Wealth, Virtual Wealth, and Debt*, remarked that it was sad to see a respected chemist ruin his reputation by writing on a subject about which he was quite ignorant. Nor had the verdict changed thirty years and several books later, when in 1956 an obituary in *Science* lamented, "Some ... knew him only as ... a 'crank' on the subject of monetary policy. ... His fanatical devotion to schemes of this sort, derided by the orthodox economists, ... was surprising to many who knew him first as a pioneer in chemical science" (Russell, p. 1069). This neglect of Soddy's economics is unfortunate because, although Soddy is admittedly unconvincing in his frequent attribution of war and all other evils to fractional reserve banking, he nevertheless has much to teach us, and in fact anticipated the recent contribution of Nicholas Georgescu-Roegen (1971) in providing economics with a partial foundation in thermodynamics, the physics of usefulness.

The fact that Soddy might have learned more from economists than he did does not mean that economists have nothing to learn from Soddy. The approach here taken is to think of him somewhat as an intelligence from Mars who looked at economic issues in a different way, and to try sympathetically to understand him and render him intelligible to modern economists. In what follows I attempt to summarize and explain Soddy's critique of economics.

The Neglected Physical Basis of Economics

Soddy's basic philosophical approach to economics might be called materialism without reductionism. We must recognize the fundamental dualism of the material and the spiritual and resist "monistic obsessions" (Soddy 1922, p. 6). Economics occupies the middle ground between matter and spirit, between the electron and the soul:

> In each direction possibilities of further knowledge extend *ad infinitum*, but in each direction diametrically away from and not towards the problems of life. It is in this middle field that economics lies, unaffected whether by the ultimate philosophy of the electron or the soul, and concerned rather with the *interaction*, with the middle world of life of these two end worlds of physics and mind in their commonest everyday aspects, matter and energy on the one hand, obeying the laws of mathematical probability or chance as exhibited in the inanimate universe, and, on the other, with the guidance, direction and willing of these blind forces and processes to predetermined ends. [ibid.]

Soddy rejects the monism of "ultra-materialism":

> I cannot conceive of inanimate mechanism, obeying the laws of probability, by any continued series of successive steps developing the powers of choice and reproduction any more than I can envisage any increase in the complexity of an engine resulting in the production of the 'engine-driver' and the power of its reproducing itself. I shall be told that this is a pontifical expression of personal opinion. Unfortunately, however, for this argument, inanimate mechanism happens to be my special study rather than that of the biologist. It is the invariable characteristic of all shallow and pretentious philosophy to seek the explanation of insoluble problems in some other field than that of which the philosopher has first hand acquaintance. [ibid., p. 7]

Yet a proper materialism must be one of the foundation stones of economics. In fact, "without phosphorus no thought" (Soddy 1949, p. 129) is an axiom that all philosophers and ethicists should be required to memorize. What mechanical science teaches economics is that

> life derives the whole of its physical energy or power, not from anything self-contained in living matter, and still less from an external

deity, but solely from the inanimate world. It is dependent for all the necessities of its physical continuance primarily upon the principles of the steam-engine. The principles and ethics of human law and convention must not run counter to those of thermodynamics. [Soddy 1922, p. 9]

The last sentence is very significant because it provides the basis for many of Soddy's criticisms of the economy as a presumed perpetual motion machine. For humans, like other heat engines, the physical problems of life are energy problems. Pre-nineteenth-century man lived on energy revenue (sunlight captured by plants, the "original capitalists"). Present-day man augments this revenue by consuming energy capital (coal, the "stored sunlight of Paleozoic summers"). While man can use fuel-fed machinery to lighten labor, he can feed his internal fires only with new sunshine, or rather the energy of new sunshine as transformed through the good offices of the plant.

Life thus depends on a continuous flow of energy, and hence the enabling requisites of life must partake of the nature of a flow rather than only a stock. There are limits to the degree that this flow can be stored for future use. A significant part of the requisites of life must come to us as a current flow or "revenue" that cannot in any physical sense be converted to a stock and indefinitely stored for later use. Like the manna which God sent to the Hebrews in the wilderness, the revenue is renewed daily, must be gathered in amounts sufficient for the day (neither too much nor too little), and breeds worms and becomes foul if accumulated too much in excess of current needs (Exodus 16:17–20). Stocks of assets, to the extent that we can maintain them against the ravages of entropy, are aids and accessories in improving our ability to tap the energy revenue, but the revenue itself cannot be significantly increased, and it cannot be saved except to a limited degree. Indeed, the very maintenance of our accumulated stock of physical wealth against the destructive force of entropy requires the renewing power of the low-entropy "revenue" flow. True, nature has stored energy in coal, but it took geologic epochs of time, and we are only able to unstore it. Furthermore, the "flamboyant period" of using up the capital stock of coal was perceived by Soddy as a "very passing phase," after which the constraints imposed by living on energy revenue would be more clearly seen and unmistakably felt.

For Soddy the basic economic question was, How does man live? and the answer was, By sunshine. The rules that man must obey in living on sunshine, whether current or palaeozoic, are the first and second laws of thermodynamics. This, in a nutshell, is "the bearing of physical science upon state stewardship." Wealth is for Soddy "the humanly useful forms of matter and energy" (Soddy 1943, p. 6). Wealth has both a physical dimension, matter/energy subject to the laws of inanimate mechanism, and a teleological dimension of usefulness, subject to the purposes imposed by mind and will. Soddy's concept of wealth reflects his fundamental dualism and his belief that the middle world of life and wealth is concerned with the interaction of the two end worlds of physics and mind in their commonest everyday aspects. That Soddy concentrated on the physical dimension in order to repair the consequences of its past neglect should not be allowed to lead one to suppose that he proposed a monistic physical theory of wealth, a misinterpretation which, we will see, was fostered by Frank Knight.

The Major Confusion: Wealth Versus Debt

The fundamental error of economics is the confusion of wealth, a magnitude with an irreducible physical dimension, with debt, a purely mathematical or imaginary quantity. The positive physical quantity, two pigs, represents wealth and can be seen and touched. But minus two pigs, debt, is an imaginary magnitude with no physical dimension:

> Debts are subject to the laws of mathematics rather than physics. Unlike wealth, which is subject to the laws of thermodynamics, debts do not rot with old age and are not consumed in the process of living. On the contrary, they grow at so much per cent per annum, by the well-known mathematical laws of simple and compound interest. . . . For sufficient reason, the process of compound interest is physically impossible, though the process of compound decrement is physically common enough. Because the former leads with the passage of time ever more and more rapidly to infinity, which, like minus one, is not a physical but a mathematical quantity, whereas the latter leads always more slowly towards zero, which is, as we have seen, the lower limit of physical quantities. [Soddy 1926, p. 70]

The ruling passion of the age is to convert wealth into debt in order to derive a permanent future income from it—to convert wealth that perishes into debt that endures, debt that does not rot, costs nothing to maintain, and brings in perennial interest (Soddy 1933, p. 25). No individual could amass the physical requirements sufficient for maintenance during his old age, for like manna it would rot. Therefore he must convert his non-storable surplus into a lien on future revenue, by letting others consume and invest his surplus now in exchange for the right to share in the increased future revenue. The revenue is "a river of perishable and consumable wealth, steadily flowing to waste whether consumed by human beings or by rats and worms" (Soddy 1924, p. 24). But since future annual revenue is limited, there is a corresponding limit on the extent to which present surpluses can be exchanged for perennial streams of future revenue. Soddy emphasizes that the present surplus accumulation can never be changed into future revenue in any physical sense, but only *ex*changed for it under social conventions. Although it may comfort the lender to think that his wealth still exists somewhere in the form of "capital," it has been or is being used up by the borrower in either consumption or investment, and no more than food or fuel can it be used again later. Rather it has become debt, an indent on future revenues to be generated by future sunshine. "Capital," says Soddy, "merely means unearned income divided by the rate of interest and multiplied by 100" (Soddy 1922, p. 27).

Although debt can follow the law of compound interest, the real energy revenue from future sunshine, the real future income against which the debt is a lien, cannot grow at compound interest for long. When converted into debt, however, real wealth "discards its corruptible body to take on an incorruptible" (Soddy 1933, p. 28). In so doing, it appears "to afford a means of dodging Nature" (p. 24), of evading the second law of thermodynamics, the law of random, ravage, rust, and rot. The idea that people can live off the interest of their mutual indebtedness (Soddy 1926, p. 89) is just another perpetual motion scheme—a vulgar delusion on a grand scale.

Soddy seems to be saying that what is obviously impossible for the community—for everyone to live on interest—should also be forbidden to individuals, as a principle of fairness. If it is not forbidden, or at least limited in some way, then at some point the growing liens of debt holders on the limited revenue will become greater than the future producers of that revenue will be willing or able to support, and conflict will result. The conflict takes the form of debt repudiation. Debt grows at compound interest and as a purely mathematical quantity encounters no limits to slow it down. Wealth grows for a while at compound interest, but, having a physical dimension, its growth sooner or later encounters limits. Debt can endure forever; wealth cannot, because its physical dimension is subject to the destructive force of entropy. Since wealth cannot continually grow as fast as debt, the one-to-one relation between the two will at some point be broken—there must be some repudiation or cancellation of debt. The positive feedback of compound interest must be offset by counteracting forces of debt repudiation, such as inflation, bankruptcy, or confiscatory taxation, all of which breed violence. Conventional wisdom considers the latter processes pathological, but accepts compound interest as normal. Logic demands, however, that we either constrain compound interest in some way, or accept as normal and necessary one or more of the counteracting mechanisms of debt repudiation.[2] As Soddy put it, "You cannot permanently pit an absurd human convention, such as the spontaneous increment of debt [compound interest], against the natural law of the spontaneous decrement of wealth [entropy]" (Soddy 1922, p. 30).

The perpetual motion delusion of living on debt has arisen in the following way, Soddy says.

> Because formerly ownership of land—which, with the sunshine that falls on it, provides a revenue of wealth—secured, in the form of rent, a share in the annual harvest without labor or service, upon which a cultured and leisured class could permanently establish itself, the age seems to have conceived the preposterous notion that money, which can buy land, must therefore itself have the same revenue-producing power. [Soddy 1926, p. 106]

If debt and money are the units of measure by which we account for and keep track of the production and distribution of physical wealth, then surely the units of measure and the reality being measured cannot be governed by different laws. Soddy's "acid test is that no monetary accountancy be allowed that could not be done equally well by physical counters" (Soddy 1943, p. 24). If wealth cannot grow at compound interest for long, then debt should not either. If wealth cannot be created *ex nihilo* then how can we allow money (debt) to be created *ex nihilo* (and just as easily destroyed)? Worse, how can we tolerate the fact that money is both created *ex nihilo* and lent at compound interest, while at the same time serving as a unit of measure for wealth which is incapable of either of those "conjuror's tricks"? This brings us to money, the topic which most occupied Soddy's attention.

The Monetary Flaw

The main defect in the economic system was, for Soddy, the practice of fractional reserve banking, whereby the private banking system was enabled to create money, thus appropriating what he called "the Virtual Wealth of the community," which it then lent at interest. The concept of "virtual wealth" plays a key role in Soddy's analysis. Essentially, it is the aggregate value of real wealth which individuals in the community voluntarily abstain from holding in order to hold money instead. In order to escape the inconvenience of barter everyone must hold money, which could be exchanged for real wealth, but is not. In Soddy's words, "This aggregate of exchangeable goods and services which the community continuously and permanently goes without (though *individual* money owners can instantly demand and obtain it from other individuals) the author terms the Virtual Wealth of the community" (Soddy 1934, p. 36).

If everyone tried to exchange their money holdings for real assets it could not be done, because all real assets are already owned by someone, and in the final analysis someone has to end up holding the money. So virtual wealth does not really exist as actual wealth over and above the value of real assets, which is why it is called "virtual." Yet people behave as if virtual wealth were real, because at an individual level money is easily exchangeable for physical assets. The phenomenon of virtual wealth must occur in a monetary economy, unless the money is itself a commodity that circulates at its commodity value.

The value of each unit of money, or the inverse of the "price-index," is simply the virtual wealth divided by the total aggregate of money held.

Soddy gives the following summary of the nature and importance of virtual wealth:

> Money is now a form of national debt, owned by the individual and owed by the community, exchangeable on demand for wealth by transference to another individual. Its value or purchasing power is not directly determined by any positive or existing quantity of wealth, but by the negative quantity or deficit of wealth, the owner-ship and enjoyment of which is voluntarily abstained from without the payment of interest, by the owners of the money, to suit their individual business and domestic affairs and convenience. The aggregate of this deficit is called the Virtual Wealth of the community, and it measures the value of all the money owned by the community, which is forced by the necessity of exchanging its produce to act as though it possessed this amount of wealth more than it actually does possess. The Virtual Wealth of a community is not a physical but an imaginary negative wealth quantity. It does not obey the laws of conservation, but is of psychological origin. [Soddy 1926, p. 295]

Virtual wealth varies with the size of population and national income and the business and payment habits of the community. It is only when virtual wealth is constant that we can equate the value of a unit of money to the ratio of virtual wealth to aggregate money held. Soddy believed that virtual wealth, though not constant, was far less variable than the money supply.

Who benefits from virtual wealth? In a sense the whole community does, since it is the price of avoiding barter, or more precisely the price of avoiding the waste of a full commodity currency which uses costly resources (gold) to perform a function that could be performed by paper or by abstract accounting units. In another sense, virtual wealth is like seigniorage, the difference between the monetary value and the commodity value (cost of production) of the money token. With the advent of credit money, the commodity value of the token becomes nil and seigniorage or virtual wealth is the full monetary value of the money issued—or rather the equivalent in foregone utility. The analogy with seigniorage suggests a further answer to the question of who benefits from virtual wealth. It is the issuer of fiat money, whoever first puts it in circulation, that gets the seigniorage. The ancient prerogative of the crown has been usurped, not by the modern state, the crown's legitimate heir, but by the private banking system, which "has corrupted the purpose of money from that of an exchange medium to that of an interest-bearing debt" (Soddy 1926, p. 296). Moreover, the very existence of the bulk of our money depends upon this debt never being liquidated. The very existence of money now becomes a source of private income, and the total money supply becomes a "concertina," expanding to fuel a boom, and contracting with debt repayment and default, thereby reinforcing a slump.

Soddy's concept of virtual wealth bears an interesting relation to the modern debate about whether fiat money is a part of the net wealth of the community. Pesek and Saving (1967) argue that it is, whereas others, such as James Tobin (1965), argue that it is not. Soddy says that fiat money is virtual wealth. Individuals voluntarily hold money balances rather than an equivalent value in real assets in order to escape the enormous inconvenience of barter. Virtual wealth is the utility cost of holding money. The fact that the benefits are worth more than the costs does not make the costs disappear, and does not convert money into wealth. The social institution of money may be regarded as a form of collective patrimony in the same sense as we so regard an efficient legal code or an advanced technology. But the money commodity itself need not be, and in the case of fiat money is not, a productive asset. Indeed, the very advantage of fiat money is to free resources from being tied up in money so that more real assets may be produced with the resources. We count the extra real assets made possible by fiat money as a part of the aggregate wealth of the community, but not the paper chits themselves. Soddy's notion of virtual wealth is actually very close to what James Tobin terms the "fiduciary issue":

> The community's wealth now has two components: the real goods accumulated through past real investment and fiduciary or paper 'goods' manufactured by the government from thin air. Of course, the nonhuman wealth of such a nation 'really' consists only of its tangible capital. But, as viewed by the inhabitants of the nation individually, wealth exceeds the tangible capital stock by the size of what we might term the fiduciary issue. This is an illusion, but only one of the many fallacies of composition which are basic to any economy or society. The illusion can be maintained unimpaired as long as the society does not actually try to convert all of its paper wealth into goods. [Tobin 1965, p. 676]

For Soddy, banks do not really make loans, because a loan implies that the lender gives up what the borrower receives. When a bank lends money it gives up nothing, creating the deposits *ex nihilo* up to the limit set by reserve requirements.[3] The real "lender" is the community at large, whose money balances lose in purchasing power with the issue of new money. We know the new money will be spent and increase demand, because the borrower who gets it would not pay interest just to increase his idle balances. Prices are bid up since *ex nihilo* creation of money (demand) can increase much more rapidly than can the *ex materia* creation of new physical wealth (supply). But the more direct line of causation is simply that relatively constant virtual wealth divided by more pounds sterling means each pound is worth less. Money should not bear interest as a condition of its existence, but only when genuinely lent by an owner who gives it up to a borrower. Banks are like counterfeiters who lend false money, accept their own false money in repayment and destroy it, but receive the interest in real money transferred to them by the rest of the community and which is not destroyed. Banks create and destroy money with no understanding of the "laws that correlate its quantity with the national income" (Soddy 1926, p. 296). Also, by continually changing the value of money as they create and destroy it, the banking system converts the pound sterling into a rubber yardstick, in effect making a mockery of all physical measurement standards, since "yards per pound" or "gallons per pound" become variable magnitudes, even though yards and gallons be fixed.

At first sight it may seem odd that one who analyzes the economy with the concepts of physical science should focus so much on money, instead of real resources, matter, energy, and the rest. But of course it is precisely the fact that money seems to have escaped the laws of conservation and entropy that led Soddy to conclude that the flaw in the system must lie with the "conjuror's tricks" of modern bankers, who

> have been allowed to regard themselves as the owners of the virtual wealth which the community does *not* possess, and to lend it and charge interest upon the loan as though it really existed and they possessed it. The wealth so acquired by the impecunious borrower is not given up by the lenders, who receive interest on the loan but give up nothing, but is given up by the whole community, who suffer in consequence the loss through a general reduction in the purchasing power of money. [Soddy 1926, p. 296]

A further contradiction arises from the interest-bearing national debt being used as collateral security by bondholders who borrow from banks. Banks create a deposit (new money) for the borrowing bondholder and charge him interest. The public is taxed to enable the government to pay interest on the bond to the bondholder who, in effect, passes the interest on to the bank. Soddy draws the conclusion that "taxes are thus paid to the bank for doing what the taxes were imposed to prevent being done, namely, the increase of the currency. Otherwise, there would have been no reason for the State to borrow at interest if it had not wished to prevent the increase of the currency" (Soddy 1926, pp. 195, 298). Soddy considers this the final *reductio ad absurdum* of the monetary system.

Reform Measures

Three basic reforms are suggested by Soddy to restore honesty and accuracy to the economic system: a 100% reserve requirement for banks, a policy of maintaining a constant price-index, and freely fluctuating exchange rates internationally.

With a 100% reserve requirement banks could no longer create money, and that basic function, along with the seigniorage prerogative, or the ownership of virtual wealth, would be restored to the state, which would again become the sole "utterer" of money. Banks would have to exist by charging for their legitimate services, that is, those that do not require the creation of money.

What principle is to govern the state in issuing money? Money is to be created or destroyed by the state as needed in order to keep the purchasing power of money constant. A price index will be devised by a national statistical authority. If the index has a tendency to fall over time, the government will finance its own activities by printing money. Alternatively it might lower taxes, or use the newly created money to redeem interest-bearing national debt. In other words, deflation would be corrected by some form of money-creating government deficit. If the index shows a rising tendency the government will raise taxes (or issue interest-bearing national debt) and not spend the revenue. Inflation would be corrected by a money-destroying government surplus. Soddy makes an analogy between the price index and the governor on a steam engine. Both provide a mechanism of stabilizing feedback. The then existing system suffered from destabilizing feedback, since the money supply would expand during a boom and contract during a slump, thereby reinforcing the original tendency.

Equilibrium in balance of payments with the rest of the world would be achieved by freely fluctuating exchange rates which would tend to establish a kind of purchasing power parity among currencies. International flows of gold and the consequent inflationary and deflationary pressures on national economies would thereby be eliminated, thus easing the task of keeping the internal purchasing power of the currency constant. Furthermore, the need for tariffs and other interferences with free trade designed to correct international payments imbalances, major causes of international conflict in Soddy's view, would have been eliminated.

Soddy's proposals have nothing in common with those of Silvio Gesell or Major Douglas, or other famous "monetary cranks." Soddy respected these men for raising important questions, but concluded that in their proposals for reform they were just as guilty of appealing to "conjuror's tricks" as were the orthodox money men. Far from advocating "funny money schemes," Soddy considered the existing canons of sound finance to be elaborate mystifications obscuring the most blatant "funny money" practices carried on in the interest of the bankers and their class, to the detriment of society. These socially dishonest though perfectly legal practices, along with the attempt to convert wealth into debt internationally and live off the interest received from other countries, plus the waning of the "flamboyant period" of energy capital consumption, of which "imperialism marks its final bid for survival" (Soddy 1922, p. 12), would lead inexorably to international conflict and to the misuse of the gifts of science in warfare.

Reform of both economic understanding and the economic system in the light of physical and moral first principles is the sine qua non of a civilization capable of using knowledge for good rather than evil. "Let us have an end of the pretence that economics should not be concerned with morals" (Soddy 1934, p. 214). As a minimum morality, economics must surely insist on a system of honest weights and measures underlying exchange; yet the current monetary system with its fluctuations in purchasing power subverts honest measure and gives a false accounting of the physical realities underlying the production and distribution of wealth.

The Relevance of Soddy's Economic Thought Today

Soddy's insistence that the first and second laws of thermodynamics must be the starting point of economics (Soddy 1934, pp. 4, 5) is a fundamental insight the relevance of which has grown as we have come to discover that neither the sources of low-entropy inputs nor the sinks for high-entropy waste outputs are infinite. Probably the most important economic treatise of the last fifty years is Nicholas Georgescu-Roegen's *The Entropy Law and the Economic Process* (1971), which demonstrates that the economic process is entropic in its physical coordinates; that wealth is an open system, a structure maintained in the midst of a throughput that begins with the depletion of low-entropy matter/energy and ends with the return of an equal quantity of polluting high-entropy matter/energy back to the environment; that in contrast to the reversibility of mechanical phenomena, entropic phenomena are characterized by irreversibility, a fatal weakness of the mechanistic epistemology of standard economics; and that there is a critical asymmetry between our two sources of low entropy. The last point refers to the fact that solar low entropy (Soddy's revenue) is nearly infinite in total amount but strictly limited in its rate of flow to earth, whereas terrestrial low entropy (concentrated minerals in the earth's crust) is strictly limited in total amount, but can be used up at a rate of our own choosing. Economic development since the Industrial Revolution has been in the direction of ever less reliance on the abundant solar flow and towards this dependence on the relatively scarce terrestrial stock. That is what Soddy called the "flamboyant period," destined to be short-lived.

Evidently Georgescu-Roegen was unaware of the writings of Soddy on this subject, because he never cites Soddy. No one is more scrupulously honest and painstaking in citing the work of others than Georgescu-Roegen, and this omission is pointed out only to indicate the extent of Soddy's obscurity as an economist. Similar comments apply to Kenneth Boulding, who has also related economics to thermodynamics without mentioning Soddy, and to the present author as well.[4] This omission is understandable because, after all, Soddy was a chemist not an economist, and his economic writings all bore titles indicating only the monetary nature of his economic work, or such uninformative titles as *Cartesian Economics*. Only the subtitle of the latter, *The Bearing of Physical Science upon State Stewardship*, gives any hint of the nature of his most important and original contribution to economics. But the fact remains that Soddy anticipated the basic insights of Georgescu-Roegen and Boulding regarding the relation of economics and thermodynamics, and deserves recognition as a pioneer in a line of thinking which I believe will one day be dominant.

Soddy was also a pioneer in recognizing the moral responsibility of science, and in realizing ahead of others that new knowledge, while it might not be permanently "forbidden," can certainly be "inopportune" under existing social and moral conditions, even to the extent of being lethal to the civilization that made it possible (Sinsheimer 1978, p. 24).

Was Soddy successful in his effort to discover the flaws in the economic system that corrupted the fruits of science and led to war? Would 100% reserves, a constant price index, and flexible exchange rates make the world safe for atomic energy? Is it true that whether science emancipates or destroys humanity depends on a "minor technical point in a banking system," as Soddy claimed (Soddy 1924, p. iv)? One may reasonably doubt it. In fact, it seems that at this point Soddy himself was "seeking the solution to insoluble problems in some field other than that of which the philosopher has first-hand acquaintance"—to recall his own jibe at the mechanistic biologists. But the fact that Soddy exaggerated the efficacy of his suggested reforms does not mean that his analysis is unimportant. Neither the specific proposals nor the reasoning underlying them can fairly be dismissed as those of an outsider or a monetary crank who just does not understand economics.[5] Flexible exchange rates have come into being already, and Soddy was arguing their virtues at a time when most economists were wedded to the gold standard. The new humility born of the theoretical anomaly of simultaneous inflation and unemployment and the demonstrated inability of orthodox "monetary cranks" to deal with persistent inflation could conceivably lead to a reconsideration of the constant price-index and 100% reserve requirements. Of course, some of these policies have had other champions besides Soddy, some with very respectable academic credentials, such as Henry Simons and Irving Fisher (see Simons 1948 and Fisher 1935).

It is curious that Irving Fisher never mentions Soddy in his writings on 100% money. Soddy, however, in a pamphlet written in 1943, refers to Fisher: "Some years later, after the great depression in the U.S.A., an American economist, Professor Irving Fisher at Yale University, put forward a scheme which in its original form was practically identical [to Soddy's 'pound for pound banking' plan] and which he termed 100% money" (Soddy 1943, p. 11). Soddy's plan was published in

1926, Fisher's in 1935. Soddy seems to regard the near identity of plans as an interesting and encouraging coincidence and in no way suggests that Fisher had copied or even been influenced by him.

Although a great enthusiast for science and technology, Soddy could not share the popular obsession with unlimited growth. Even if continual economic growth were possible, it would at some point become senseless. On this point Soddy quotes John Ruskin, whom he greatly admired as an economist: "Capital which produces nothing but capital is only root producing root; bulb issuing in bulb, never in tulip; seed issuing in seed never in bread. The Political Economy of Europe has hitherto devoted itself to the multiplication . . . of bulbs. It never saw or conceived such a thing as a tulip" (Soddy 1933, p. v).

Soddy held that "economic sufficiency is the essential foundation of all national greatness and progress" (ibid., p. 12). But sufficiency means "enough" and growth beyond "enough" is just "seed issuing in seed never in bread." Soddy does not define "sufficiency," but it is clear that any definition must respect the limits of energy revenue from the sun as captured by plants, and the entropic limits on the possibility of storing up wealth for future use, as well as the teleological constraint implied by a defined (i.e., limited) purpose from which low-entropy matter / energy derives its value dimension, and thus becomes wealth. Not all matter / energy is capable of becoming wealth; only low-entropy matter / energy has the physical potential for usefulness, for receiving the imprint of information and purpose. Since the entropy law says in effect that potential gets used up, then scarcity must increase over the long run. But what bothered Soddy was not the scarcity implications of entropy, since he believed that science could more than offset increasing scarcity for a very long time yet. The truly scarce factor for Soddy was not low entropy, but our ability keep from blowing up scientific civilization with the increasing power that science made available. We persist in applying those powers toward the impossible goal of making the real world of matter / energy conform to the purely mathematical law of compound interest. This leads to debt cancellation, conflict, and war. Orthodox growth economics notwithstanding, the best evidence is that the earth is not growing at all, much less at a rate equal to the rate of interest. The attempt to pit an absurd human convention against a natural law is not only foolish, but highly dangerous.

The absurdity of infinite growth has been the most carefully ignored anomaly in the paradigm of modern economics. As Soddy put it,

> If Christ, whose views on the folly of laying up treasures on earth are well known, had put by a pound at this rate, it should now be worth an Octillion, and Tariff Reform would be of little help to provide that, even if you colonized the entire stellar universe. . . . It is this absurdity which inverts society, turns good into evil and makes ortho-

dox economics the laughing stock of science. If the consequences were not the familiar atmosphere of our daily lives they would be deemed beyond the legitimate bounds of the most extravagant comic opera. [Soddy 1924, p. 17]

A contemporary unsympathetic reviewer, economist A. G. Silverman, was at least forthright enough to face the issue and to attempt a reply:

> In criticism of the above theory, it may be asked how can the receivers of interest, if they live on this income, take advantage of the law of compound interest; and if they reinvest this 'unearned' income why cannot the law of compound interest approximately hold for physical capital as well as debt? [Silverman 1927, p. 277]

The first question is sensible but irrelevant because Soddy never suggested that one could take advantage of compound interest without reinvesting at least part of the interest income. The second part of the question, however, reveals that the questioner had no conception of the difference between physical and purely mathematical quantities, and must have made Soddy despair of ever communicating with economists. Perhaps by "approximately" Professor Silverman meant "for a limited time period." But then we must ask what happens at the end of that limited time period, and how long it is.

Probably the most favorable review that Soddy got from an economist came from none other than Frank Knight, who began by confessing,

> Somewhat to the reviewer's surprise this book [*Wealth, Virtual Wealth, and Debt*] has proven well worth the time and effort of a careful reading. Surprising because, in general, when the specialist in natural sciences takes time off to come over and straighten out the theory of economics he shows himself even dumber than the academic economist, and because, in particular, Soddy's pamphlet on *Cartesian Economics* which we read some years ago did not promise to set a new precedent in this regard. [Knight 1927, p. 732]

Knight went so far as to call the book "brilliantly written and brilliantly suggestive and stimulating." I would like to be able to appeal to the authority of Frank Knight to support my own favorable evaluation of Soddy's economics, but unfortunately our particular appreciations of Soddy conflict. Knight considers Soddy's practical theses concerning money to be "highly significant and theoretically correct" (Knight 1927, p. 732), a judgment with which I do not basically disagree but consider a bit too kind, since Soddy certainly exaggerated the significance of his practical theses, however correct they may be. Concerning the physical basis of economics and the relation to thermodynamics, however, Knight is very negative: "His effort to establish a conception of physical wealth, subject to a principle of conservation and interpretable in relation to physical energy, must be briefly dismissed" (ibid.).

Knight's grounds for dismissal are opaque:

> Magnitudes of wealth and productive capacity . . . change absolutely whenever a human being changes his (or her!) mind; and the mass-energy relations of mind-changes are as unimportant in this connection as they are obscure—if their very existence is anything but a metaphysical inference based on the monistic bias of the scientific intellect. [Knight 1927, p. 732]

Whatever that may mean, it is surely odd that anyone who read *Cartesian Economics* (recall the first two quotations under the subhead "The Neglected Physical Basis," above) could even obliquely accuse Soddy of "monistic bias." Furthermore, Soddy had no theory of conservation of the *value* dimension of wealth (which may change with mental states), but only insisted that the physical dimension of wealth is subject to the laws of thermodynamics regardless of mind changes or financial conventions, and that this fact is not trivial. If the fact that magnitudes of wealth and productive capacity change absolutely whenever a human being changes his mind were the whole truth, then how easy it would be to make everyone wealthy—all we would need do to double wealth would be to change our minds! Then wealth could grow as fast as debt, since it would be free from its physical body. It would be quite unfair to accuse Knight of such simple-minded angelism, but it strikes me as equally unfair of Knight to treat Soddy as a simple-minded physical reductionist. It is true that Soddy emphasized the physical aspect of wealth in order to correct for its neglect by economists, a procedure which, if Knight's attitude is representative, Soddy was certainly justified in adopting.

In view of the fact that Soddy's critique of money stemmed directly from his prior physical analysis, it is strange that Knight could so categorically reject the latter while enthusiastically embracing the former, although it is conceivable that one could arrive at the right monetary conclusions for the wrong physical reasons. Knight offers the following support for Soddy's views on money:

> In the abstract, it is absurd and monstrous for society to pay the commercial banking system 'interest' for multiplying severalfold the quantity of medium of exchange when (a) a public agency could do it at negligible cost, (b) there is no sense in having it done at all, since the effect is simply to raise the price level, and (c) important evils result, notably the frightful instability of the whole economic system. [ibid.]

Knight deserves much credit for having been the only reputable economist to have taken Soddy seriously, even though in my opinion he missed Soddy's main contribution. But then so did everyone else until now, when, in the light of both Georgescu-Roegen's masterly reuniting of economics with its physical base and the current recognition of the critical importance of energy, the prior contribution of Soddy has become visible enough for anyone to see. Soddy was in many ways fifty years ahead of his time.

Chapter 13

On Nicholas Georgescu-Roegen's Contributions to Economics: An Obituary Essay

Nicholas Georgescu-Roegen died 30 October 1994 at his home in Nashville, Tennessee. He was born in Constanza, Romania, in 1906, where he grew up during the difficult years of World War I. His outstanding performance in Romania's best schools won him a scholarship to the Sorbonne in Paris, where he received a doctoral degree in mathematical statistics, awarded with highest honors. His scholarship grant was extended for two years of postdoctoral study with Karl Pearson in London. In 1934 he came to the United States as a Visiting Rockefeller Fellow at Harvard, where he became an economist under the influence of Joseph Schumpeter. Two years later he returned to serve his native country in both academic and government positions, including that of secretary general of the Romanian Armistice Commission in 1944–1945. That post obliged him to defend, albeit without success, the interests of Romania against the arbitrary violations of the Armistice Convention by the civilian and military representatives of the USSR. He had been president of the Romanian Association for Friendship with the USA and a member of the National Council of the Peasant Party. All this was more than sufficient for the Communist regime to go after his head. Early in 1948, with great risks, he fled together with his wife, Otilia, stowed away on a foreign freighter. He was thus able to return to Harvard in 1948. In 1949 he accepted a position at Vanderbilt, where he stayed for twenty-seven years, and where it was my great privilege, along with many others, to be his student.

Georgescu-Roegen's contributions to economics are numerous and varied, but can usefully be grouped into two categories made popular by the philosopher Thomas Kuhn: normal science and revolutionary science. His normal science contributions include fundamental work in utility and consumer choice, measurability, expectations, production theory, input-output analysis, and economic development. He was truly a pioneer in mathematical economics, and therefore it may be misleading to class that part of his contribution as "normal science." It was rather revolutionary while he was doing it, and appears now as normal science only because the revolution was successful and became the new norm. What I am here calling his contribution to revolutionary science, namely his work in *The Entropy Law and the Economic Process*, has not yet been victorious, and is revolutionary in the sense that it still faces opposition from the reigning paradigm, the very paradigm which Georgescu himself helped to solidify.

Others of his students might in my place choose to write mainly of his earlier contributions to what is now standard economics. That would certainly be appropriate. But I have chosen to write about his revolutionary contributions because I think they are far more important, and certainly more relevant to ecological economics. I confess that it is a matter of some consternation and distress to me that twenty-two years after the publication of *The Entropy Law and the Economic Process*,[1] and twenty-eight years after the publication of the introductory essay to *Analytical Economics*,[2] one can still find no trace of their influence in the standard principles textbooks. Recognition of the importance of these new ideas has not been lacking in other fields. Writers in science, engineering, and philosophy journals have wondered aloud why economists have not paid more attention to Georgescu's later work. The lack of influence might be taken as evidence that his arguments have simply not withstood the criticism of other economists. But that is manifestly not the case. His challenge has not been met with reasoned refutation, but rather with silence, or at most with the lame remark that his recent work is "not really economics." It has been said that the best measure of a scientist's influence is the number of years he can hold back progress in his own discipline. By that measure we have too many influential economists writing textbooks and editing journals!

But the situation is more complicated because Georgescu's recent contributions have in a sense been recognized by economists, yet without really being taken seriously.[3] After all, Stefano Zamagni wrote an entire book on Georgescu's contributions to consumer theory, and in 1976 a *festschrift* was published in his honor, with contributions from leading economists including four Nobel laureates, and edited by his colleagues and former students, Anthony Tang, Fred Westfield, and James Worley.[4] Also, Georgescu was a Distinguished Fellow of the American Economic Association, and in 1965 Paul Samuelson in his preface to *Analytical Economics* referred to him as a "scholar's scholar, an economist's economist." And Samuelson was not referring only to Georgescu's normal science work, reprinted in *Analytical Economics*, but also to the long introductory essay that was the first expression of the revolutionary position later given definitive form in *The Entropy Law and the Economic Process*. Samuelson went on to say, "I defy any informed economist to remain complacent after meditating over this essay." And yet remain complacent is just what most economists did! In fact, twenty-eight years later, even in

Samuelson's influential textbook, we have yet to find a trace of the ideas contained in that essay.

Of course, a beginning text does not discuss advanced topics, and one certainly does not expect to find there any mention of Georgescu's highly technical contributions to standard economics. But his revolutionary insights regarding economics and entropy are really elementary by virtue of being so fundamental. Nor do they require anything beyond a non-technical exposition of the entropy law. These basic insights could certainly be included in an elementary text. But the rub is that their inclusion has so many implications that are so upsetting to the standard viewpoint that extensive revisions throughout the text could not be avoided.

Suppose one were to try to rewrite a basic principles text incorporating the paradigm shift of *The Entropy Law and the Economic Process*—what would one have to do? How different would it be? This is the main question I want to consider. It is worth trying to answer because it forces one to explain Georgescu-Roegen's insights in the simplest way one can, and to trace their broad consequences into various branches of economics.

The first thing to change would be the circular flow diagram that conveys the preanalytic vision of the economic process as an isolated circular flow from firms to households and back again, with no inlets or outlets. This diagram has its uses in analyzing exchange, but it fails badly as a framework for studying production and consumption. Maintenance and replenishment, in this picture, would seem to be accomplished internally, requiring no dependence on an environment. It is exactly as if a biology textbook proposed to study an animal only in terms of its circulatory system, without ever mentioning its digestive tract! An animal with an isolated circulatory system and no digestive tract would be a perpetual motion machine. Unlike this imaginary circular-flow animal, real animals have digestive tracts that connect them to their environment at both ends. They continuously take in low-entropy matter/energy and give back high-entropy matter/energy. An organism cannot recycle its own waste products. Of course biology textbooks do not omit the digestive tract. They usually discuss it before the circulatory system, probably because of its prior evolutionary emergence.

But in economics there is only the circulatory system. This is as true of Marxist economics as it is of neoclassical economics. What concept in economics ties the economy to its environment? Circulation of blood is to circulation of money as the digestive tract is to . . . (*what?*). It is not too big a simplification to say that Georgescu filled in the blank with the analogous concept: the one-way flow beginning with resources and ending with waste. To this concept he gave the name "entropic flow." Others, such as Kenneth Boulding, have called it "throughput." It is a simple and obvious concept that anyone can grasp, and that everyone recognizes as descriptive of the real world. But previously it was not thought to involve scarcity, and therefore was excluded from the economist's preanalytic vision of his subject.

The conclusion is that our revised textbook must begin with a different preanalytic vision: namely, a diagram showing the entropic throughput in bold solid lines as a one-way flow from environmental sources, through firms and households, and back to environmental sinks. The circular flow would be depicted as a faint dotted loop from firms to households and back again. The entropic throughput of matter / energy is more basic than the circular flow of exchange values. No economy can conceivably exist without the entropic flow, while it is easy to conceive of an economy with no circular flow—for example, an economy of self-sufficient peasants engaging in no exchange.

Surely it would be a simple matter to correct our basic preanalytic vision of the economic process in this way. But, as already indicated, the concept of the entropic throughput is a Trojan horse. Once it is admitted within the hardback covers, its hidden army of implications attacks nearly every section of the book.

Let us first look at the general epistemological implications, and then consider some more specific consequences.

Standard economics is mechanistic, it is "the mechanics of utility and self-interest," in Jevons's words. Mechanics studies reversible and quality-less phenomena. The circular flow of exchange is quality-less and reversible, and thus fits the mechanistic view. But the entropic flow is irreversible and qualitative. Entropy is the measure of the qualitative difference between useful resources and useless waste. This qualitative change is irreversible. Therefore, mechanistic models cannot deal with the most basic fact of economic life. Furthermore, the presence of the entropic flow, necessary for the maintenance of the economic process, necessarily induces qualitative change into the very environment on which it depends, since what is given back to the environment is qualitatively different from what is taken in. As the environment changes, the economy must re-adapt—a co-evolutionary process.

Qualitative change cannot be adequately studied by the analytical or arithmomorphic concepts proper to mechanistic models because these concepts are rigidly and precisely defined and forever self-identical. To study change requires dialectical concepts whose nature is that they have evolving penumbras in which B can be both A and non-A: e.g., an age at which one is both young and old, a credit card which is both money and non-money, an amphibian which belongs to both land and sea. If we are to capture the real qualitative change that is essential to the economic process, we must reason with dialectical concepts, making use of mechanical models (analytical similes) only as a test of dialectical argument. Our revised text must correct the current overemphasis on arithmomorphic analytical thinking to the near exclusion of dialectical reasoning.

The circular flow vision is congenial to the mechanistic epistemology because it sees only locomotion, reversible and quality-less. Nor is this vision contradicted by the first law of thermodynamics (conservation of matter / energy), which tells us that the building blocks of matter and energy are indestructible. In this view, production consists of arranging indestructible building blocks so as to provide utility, while consumption consists in disarranging those same blocks as a result of use, eventually destroying the artifact's capacity to yield utility. But then production rearranges them again, and the cycle continues. Looking at the first law alone presents no obstacles to, and in fact invites, the inclusion within the circular flow of physical dimensions as well as purchasing power. And so we even find some texts telling us that the flow of *output* is circular, self-renewing, and self-feeding! But the inclusion of physical dimension in the circular flow is flatly ruled out by the second law of thermodynamics, the entropy law, which says that the quality of matter / energy that gives rise to usefulness is used up and is not recyclable. The ultimate value produced is the experience of life enjoyment. Neither the ultimate means of low-entropy matter / energy nor the ultimate end of life enjoyment can be expressed as a circular flow.

In the revised text the special topic chapters on natural resources and environment (usually tacked on at the end of the book) would probably not exist because these would no longer be "special topics," but would be integrated into the very center of economics.

In addition to this general epistemological reorientation away from mechanism and arithmomorphism, there are a number of more specific consequences that follow from putting the entropic flow at the core of economic theory. These implications mainly center around the feasibility of continuous economic growth (in real GNP) as the norm of a healthy economy and the main goal of economic policy. The circular flow can theoretically grow forever because abstract exchange value (debt, purchasing power) has no physical dimension. But growth in the entropic flow encounters the physical barriers of depletion, pollution, and ecological disruption.

In peasant agricultural economies this conflict is smaller since they depend on solar energy, the abundant source of low entropy, and also focus on the accumulation of concrete use values, such as pigs, which impose their own limits to accumulation. The modern industrial economy, however, depends more on the relatively scarce terrestrial source of low entropy (fossil fuels and minerals) and focuses on the accumulation of abstract exchange value (debt, "negative pigs") for which more is always perceived as better. But debt should not for long grow faster than real assets. The industrial economy thus will at some point strain against the limits of the entropic flow. Therefore, in the new paradigm increasing depletion and pollution become expected, necessary consequences of economic growth, not surprising externalities as viewed from the circular flow paradigm. Of course, technological adaptation is possible. But technologies that squeeze more welfare (more life enjoyment) out of a given entropic flow become more interesting than technologies which simply increase the volume of throughput. Our revised chapter on technology would stress the point that the former technologies benefit the future as well as the present, while the latter benefit the present at the expense of the future.

This last observation suggests a reorientation in our chapter on distribution toward more concern for intergenerational distribution. The standard view seems to go along with Barnett and Morse's intergenerational invisible hand: "By devoting itself to improving the lot of the living, therefore, each generation, whether recognizing a future-oriented obligation to do so or not, transmits a more productive world to those who follow" (1963, p. 249).[5] The reason for this view is that man-made capital and labor are conventionally considered to be the sources of value added, while that to which value is added is made of the indestructible building blocks of nature, to which nature itself has added no value. While not at all denying conventional value added, Georgescu considered that nature also adds value, and that the value added by nature is what distinguishes resources from wastes. This primacy of nature's value added (low entropy) leads to Georgescu-Roegen's view that "every time we produce a Cadillac we irrevocably destroy an amount of low entropy that could otherwise be used for producing a plow or a spade. In other words, every time we produce a Cadillac, we do it at the cost of decreasing the number of human lives in the future." In the circular flow paradigm we have an intergenerational invisible hand and harmony. In the entropic flow paradigm we have an intergenerational "invisible foot," and conflict of interest. It can hardly be a matter of indifference which view is correct, even though we already know which is politically more popular.

In addition to highlighting intergenerational conflicts, our chapter on distribution would point out that the "miracle of compound interest" can no longer be appealed to as the way to "grow" everyone in the present generation out of poverty. Growth cannot forever substitute for redistribution and population control in fighting poverty.

Our chapter on economic development would undergo a similar reorientation. It would not hold out the vision of development as a worldwide generalization of the U.S. standard of living. Rather it would start with the recognition that, due to the limits of the entropic flow, it is unrealistic to think that the standard of per capita resource use of that 5% of the world's population in the United States could ever be generalized to 100% of the world's 5.5 billion people. We must either admit that such development is only for a minority or else redefine development in a way that is generalizable to all. The new concept of development would not be virtually synonymous with growth in real GNP, as it is today, but would emphasize population control, limits to inequality in distribution, and production for sufficiency in basic needs. The idea that poor countries can simply grow their way out of poverty and debt by spinning their circular flows of exchange ever faster would itself be retired from circulation, along with other Ponzi schemes.

The chapter on national income accounting, with its conventions on how to measure the circular flow, would be expanded to include some measured index of the entropic flow—a "gross national throughput." Also, this chapter could consider the curious asymmetry in present national accounts whereby we write off the value of man-made assets against current production as they depreciate, but make no such deduction for the depreciation of natural assets. A country could exhaust its mines, cut down its forests, erode its topsoil, and exploit its wildlife and fisheries to extinction, and measured income would rise steadily as these assets disappeared. Putting the entropic flow at the center of analysis should force us to pay attention to the natural capital stocks that yield this vital flow. We would emphasize the Hicksian definition of income as the maximum amount an individual or a community could consume over some time period and still be as well off at the end of the period as at the beginning. Being as well off means having maintained capital intact—only now that must include natural capital as well as man-made.

The chapters on production in our new text would be based on Georgescu-Roegen's fund-flow model. Capital and labor are conceived of as funds or agents that transform the flow of natural resources into a flow of products. The dominant relation between funds and flows is complementary. Substitutability between fund and flow is strictly marginal, limited to reducing process waste. To conceive of capital as a near-perfect substitute for resources, as is frequently done under the influence of Cobb-Douglas type production functions, is to believe that one can make the same house with twice as many saws, but half the lumber. Not to mention the problem that more saws require more resources for their production. The prevalent neoclassical idea that we can escape the resource constraints of the entropic flow by substituting capital for resources would be retained as an amusing but edifying example of the power of mechanistic models to mislead—a classic case of A. N. Whitehead's "fallacy of misplaced concreteness," which Georgescu considered the cardinal sin of economics (see note 1, Chapter 3).

Our chapter on population would have a much revised discussion of the concept of optimum population. The issue would not be how many people, but how many people for how long? Or rather, how many people, for how long, living at what level of per capita resource use? The relevant question would be how to maximize the cumulative person-years ever to be lived over time at a standard of per capita resource use that is sufficient for a good life. The difficult dialectical concept of sufficiency would be as important as the concept of efficiency in the revised text.

Of course some topics would remain relatively unchanged: supply and demand, elasticity, marginal cost and marginal revenue, how banks create money, monopoly, pure competition, etc. Although price theory may not change radically, we would have to emphasize more the temporally parochial nature of prices. Future generations cannot bid in present markets. Also, relative prices measure relative scarcity of particular resources, but they do not adequately reflect the absolute dimension of scarcity, the scarcity of the entropic flow as a whole (i.e., the scarcity of its environmental sources and sinks, which until recently have been thought of as free goods).

I believe I have said enough to show that the introduction of the entropic flow into the standard text would require so many revisions as to make the text no longer standard, even though many chapters would still look familiar. Perhaps this is why such changes are glacially slow in coming. One does not expect fundamental change to occur overnight. But twenty-five years is a reasonable time over which to hope for progress. What is the matter with our discipline?

Perhaps part of the answer was given in 1853 by another great economist, one whose contribution was entirely ignored during his lifetime, Herrmann Heinrich Gossen. It is doubly appropriate to quote Gossen because Georgescu and his colleague, Rudolph Blitz, gave us the definitive English translation and introduction to Gossen's work. At the end of his preface Gossen says,

> I close with the wish that my work should receive rigorous but impartial examination. I am in a strong position to insist on this request because I was forced to fight so many mistaken ideas generally considered correct, ideas that have thus become so much more dear to the heart of many, yes, very many people, because their position in life is partly or wholly dependent upon accepting these ideas as true. Giving up these ideas would put them in the situation in which I now find myself, namely, at a mature age to have to look for a new position.

I am glad that at a mature age Nicholas did not have to look for a new position. Along with others of his friends I was saddened that his latter years were so marked by bitterness and withdrawal, brought on in part by the failure of the profession to give his work the recognition that it truly merited, and in part by his own irascible and generally demanding personality. So great was his bitterness that he even cut relations with those who most valued his contribution. But none of that diminishes the great importance of his lifework, for which ecological economists must be especially grateful. He demanded a lot, but he gave more.

PART VII

Ethics, Religion, and Sustainable Development

Introduction

Sustainable development will require a change of heart, a renewal of the mind, and a healthy dose of repentance. These are all religious terms, and that is no coincidence, because a change in the fundamental principles we live by is a change so deep that it is essentially religious whether we call it that or not. And among our proudly secular intelligentsia there is strong resistance to calling it that—indeed the best way to marginalize an issue in academia is to classify it as religious.[1] We no longer call for repentance, or even for progress. The strongest prophetic utterance one hears today is a call for change. We no longer have the courage to use the value-dependent term "progress," since values are considered mere "epiphenomena" by the intelligentsia. The more neutral term "change" is preferred, because it implies no direction or intentionality. It is just something objective that happens, and we, of course, are assumed to have some vestigial sense of duty to adjust to it, or at least not oppose it. An example of "change" in this sense is the thrust toward globalization, discussed in Part 5.

On the one hand, resistance to religion is not hard to understand when we realize that most people's image of religion is some TV evangelist emoting and pleading for money to build a Disney-like biblical theme park. (I was startled to learn that more people visit Disneyland every year than visit Mecca or Jerusalem, so maybe these evangelists are trying to learn from the competition!) On the other hand, if those who reject traditional religion—for example, scientific materialists—can find within their purposeless, deterministic universe some good reason for caring about the capacity of the earth to support life, then I am very happy to make alliance with them in the urgent task of conserving it, and will temporarily put aside my belief that they are in fact sawing off the branch on which they are sitting.

The first chapter in this section focuses on the principle of limited inequality, and argues that this principle has a strong biblical basis. It may seem quaint to appeal to biblical authority in support of an ethical principle, rather than to John Rawls, Robert Nozick, Amartya Sen, or the social contract, as is the current academic vogue. But as a matter of historical fact most of the moral principles that have force in the United States came straight from the Bible, and were spread throughout this land by churches and universities. And the universities were themselves overwhelmingly founded by churches, usually protestant ones, even though little trace of that origin remains in most universities today.[2] Those who would prefer to ground ethical principles in culture and history will find in our culture and history mainly various understandings of the Bible as bases for ethical principles. So I see no need to apologize to them for basing a moral principle directly on the Bible, rather than indirectly through our eroding cultural heritage. If secular ethicists can arrive at the principle of limits to inequality by their own deep moral intuition and reason, then by all means let them do it, and let us hope they will be influential. But any claims they might make to originality or priority in discovery of this principle would be hard to take seriously.

Some years ago, I advocated a minimum and a maximum income as part of the institutional basis appropriate to a steady-state economy.[3] The minimum income, of course, has a great deal of political support (despite the periodic attempts of politicians to undermine it). The notion of a maximum income has none, and seems to strike people as mean, petty, and invidious. I believe this is because growth in total wealth is assumed to be unlimited. As the very rich get richer, the poor at least are not hurt, in this view, and are probably even helped by the expenditures of the wealthy. I argue to the contrary—that there *is* a limit to the total material production that the ecosystem can support, and that it would be clearly unjust for 99% of the limited total product to go to only one person. I conclude, therefore, that there must implicitly be some maximum personal income. What I hear in reply is the familiar refrain "That's not the right way to look at it." Anyone raising this issue in the media is immediately accused by the pontificating pundits of wanting to foment class warfare.

But inequality is increasing in the United States and will become an issue again in spite of political efforts to deny its importance. The idea of a maximum as well as a minimum income has recently surfaced again in a very interesting little book by Sam Pizzigati, *The Maximum Wage* (actually it is a maximum personal income that he proposes).[4] Although written in a very popular and breezy style, the book is well argued and documented. It advocates a factor-of-ten range between maximum and minimum income, and discusses many beneficial effects for the vast majority of citizens. A range of inequality permitting a factor-of-ten difference between the richest and poorest would serve the need for legitimate differences in rewards and incentives while respecting the fact that we are persons-in-community, not isolated, atomistic individuals. There is nothing sacred about a factor of ten, but it does have some empirical basis in a number of large organizations such as the civil service, the military, and universities. If a factor of ten is too egalitarian for our individualistic society, one could substitute a factor of twenty.

A step in this direction has come from Congressman Martin Sabo of Minnesota, whose proposed "Income Equity Act" would limit the eligibility for tax deduction on executive compensation to salaries no more than twenty-five times that of the lowest-paid full-time worker in the same organization. Thus if the CEO is to make $500,000 as a deductible corporate business expense, then the lowest-paid worker in that firm must make at least $20,000. Even that modest measure is not likely to be enacted by the present (1995) Congress.

But at some point distribution *must* become an issue. In 1960 after-tax average pay for chief executives was about twelve times that of the average factory worker. By 1974 the factor had risen to thirty-five. In 1995 it is well over one hundred (*Business Week*'s number is 135). And those figures compare the top to the average, not to the bottom. Also, they compare only wages and salaries—if they included returns to capital ownership the income difference would be much larger.

No one is arguing for an invidious, forced equality. A factor of ten in inequality would be justified by real differences in effort and diligence, and would provide sufficient incentive to call forth these qualities. To be conservative make it a factor of twenty. But bonds of community break at or before a factor of one hundred. Class warfare is already beginning. The devotion of many rural and working-class people to their guns, and the resulting clout of the National Rifle Association, stems from the usually unarticulated but very real feeling that "although this government has written me off as an ignorant, working-class redneck, there is a limit to how far they can push me if I have my guns. If they take my guns, there is no limit." I recognize that there is considerable political and religious fanaticism in these militia movements, but they are also an expression of class conflict bred from growing inequality.

The second chapter in this section was written for a World Council of Churches (WCC) conference held in parallel with the United Nations Conference on Environment and Development (UNCED) in Rio de Janeiro in June of 1992. The WCC conference was held outside Rio, in the working-class suburb of Nova Iguaçu, as an expression of solidarity with the poor. This was a worthwhile gesture, and afforded a great contrast to the posh hotels in Rio where official delegates were housed. However, it also revealed the extent of class division worldwide, because international participants at the WCC conference were virtual prisoners in the monastery at which the conference was held; the real likelihood of a foreigner getting mugged on the streets of Nova Iguaçu was sufficiently high that we had to be bussed everywhere, including to a structured but worthwhile meeting with local people in a Catholic base community. These were honest, decent folks, trying hard to survive in a country where inequality is as great as it is anywhere in the world. That their rebellion so far has been limited to a small percentage of their number taking to mugging outsiders is testimony to their fundamental goodness. They were not very interested in the UNCED conference, and unfortunately the UN-CED conference recognized their existence only in the context of defending the growth-as-usual paradigm against the environmentalists, who were alleged not to care about helping the poor. The idea of limits to inequality got even less discussion at UNCED than did the idea of limits to growth. While UNCED accomplished some good things, growth was still the dominant theme. The fact of increasing inequality was recognized, but met only with calls for more growth. Few official participants, I think, saw the absurdity of the slogan over the conference booth of the Italian energy company ENI, which boasted, in letters two feet high, "We Are Growing With The Planet."

Chapter 14

A Biblical Economic Principle and the Sustainable Economy

Everyone claims biblical support for his own pet economic ideas. Like the devil, the economist can quote scripture to prove what he wants to prove. Some have argued that God is a socialist, a corporate syndicalist, a supply-sider, a single-taxer, a Reaganite, and so on. Now here I come trying to convince you that what God really likes best is a sustainable or steady-state economy. Isn't this all rather tiresome and shouldn't we be doing something else?

On the contrary, I think we need far more of this discussion precisely because it is so muddled and contradictory. Christianity and other religions have coexisted with a wide range of economic systems, but do all economic systems merit their blessings (or condemnation) in equal measure? Do we not have some guidelines regarding what kind of economic order merits God's approval, or more frequently, disapproval? I believe that we have a duty to try to influence the economic institutions and policies of our community, our nation, and our world.

But we need some principled way of getting from religious belief to economic principle, and any such principle must be general and fundamental enough to be translated from the agrarian economies of biblical Palestine and the Roman Empire to the modern industrial economies of today. In this chapter, I attempt a translation of one specific—and radical—economic principle from the specific context of the Old and New Testaments. In the last chapter, I conclude the book by looking a bit more broadly at religious context: I suggest the ways in which the principal features of the economics of sustainable development come naturally out of and are crucially sustained by a religious view of the world.

My task here is twofold: first, to discover basic principles behind the economic situations of the Bible's covenant people; second, to give those same principles a new institutional body through which to influence or leaven our modern economy.

For example, it makes no sense for farmers today not to harvest the corners of their fields in order to leave something for wayfarers, sojourners, widows, and orphans. The practice is outdated, but the principle is timeless: make some provision for the poor. The old way is obsolete, so we look for a more fitting way. Even categories of the needy change—in our times widows and orphans are frequently rather well-off heirs. Perhaps the colorless census term "unmarried heads of household" comes closer to naming our disadvantaged brothers and sisters—usually sisters. I think everyone will agree on the twofold nature of the translation problem: What was the real meaning in the original setting? What in the modern setting means the same thing?

I propose to deal with just one biblical economic principle, the one which seems to me most basic, most easily discerned, and most in need of a better institutionalization in today's world. It also partially overlaps with the institutions needed for a sustainable economy. In what follows I will first state the principle and present evidence that it in fact was the guiding economic norm of the groups whose values are incorporated in the Hebrew Scriptures and that its validity is reaffirmed in the New Testament. Secondly, I will suggest a new institution for better reincorporating that principle into the modern economy. Thirdly, I will suggest some further implications of the principle and its relevance to a steady-state economy.

The principle, if it could be stated in the form of an eleventh commandment, would read: *Thou shalt not allow unlimited inequality in the distribution of private property.*

The Principle and Its Biblical Basis

The "eleventh commandment" presupposes the legitimacy of private property and of some inequality in its distribution. It simply insists that the degree of inequality be limited. Before considering the range of such limits, let us first say a word about private property itself, since its legitimacy is often contested. Christianity and Judaism both regard human persons as free and responsible agents, accountable for their own actions. Without private property the arena of individual freedom and responsibility would be exceedingly small. Also, the eighth commandment, "Thou shalt not steal," is often cited as an oblique support for private property.

Land was the primary factor of production, the basic source of wealth, in the economy of biblical Palestine. It was considered to belong to God, who created it. But the land was held, worked, and administered by families who had the right of usufruct as God's tenants in perpetuity. Some families prospered more than others. There were rich and poor. Riches were considered a blessing, poverty a misfortune.

Absolute equality was neither a fact nor a goal, but the community could not tolerate unlimited inequality. There were definite limits to the degree of inequality. First, the distribution of land among families was equal, or at least just in some more inclusive sense. Second, if property is necessary for the exercise of freedom and responsibility, then it is clear that everyone should have some, or at least the right to glean the fields and harvest the corners, an attenuated form of property. The obverse of this position is the classical justification for private property as a bulwark protecting the individual against exploitation by others. A property owner has an independent livelihood and need not accept whatever conditions of employment are offered. If the legitimacy of property is based on either of these reasons, it is clear that its ownership should be widespread, indeed universal.

But the workings of an economy over time naturally generate inequality. Both success and failure tend to be cumulative. Ability is not evenly distributed, nor is soil fertility, nor good luck. Marriages are not economically random and usually result in further concentration of wealth. Dishonesty and exploitation are not required to explain inequality, although they certainly contribute to it.

The Levitical answer to how much inequality is permissible was basically this: no more than could accumulate over fifty years, starting with a just initial distribution, and following basic laws of fair dealing, zero interest rate, sabbatical fallow, minimal rights of the poor, religious tithes, and the like. The jubilee —the sabbath of sabbaths, the fiftieth year—was a time for returning to the original distribution. The mere existence and expectation of the jubilee year tended to slow down the accumulation of the very inequalities that it would eventually correct. As the jubilee year approached, the incentive to accumulate was reduced, since current gains would soon have to be surrendered. Immediately after the jubilee, when the gains could be enjoyed for forty-nine years, the incentive to accumulate was greatest, just when the actual equality of distribution was also greatest. These considerations were reflected in the price of land, which was lowered as the jubilee approached, on the very modern principle that capital is the present value of a discounted future income stream: "for what he is selling you is a certain number of harvests" (Lev. 25:13–17). In conformity with the prohibition on interest, the future income stream is discounted at a zero rate, which is to say not discounted at all.

In addition to the overall long-run limits on social inequality implicit in the jubilee year, were there individual minimum and maximum limits in the short run? It seems that there were. Certainly at a minimum there were gleaning, and alms, and the rights of slaves and of widows, all of which can be interpreted as providing a floor below which no one was allowed to fall. Was there a corresponding ceiling on personal wealth? I submit that there was, because even the king, the person most likely to have unlimited rights of accumulation, was expressly denied such a right. Neither horses, wives, nor gold and silver must be increased excessively by the king (Deut. 17:16ff.). The fact that from Solomon on this law was broken (as was the jubilee itself) simply gives rise to further support for the law in the repeated rebukes of the prophets. The basic philosophy of sufficiency, "enoughness," and limited inequality at the individual level is expressed in Proverbs:

> Give me neither poverty nor riches, but give me only my daily bread, otherwise I may have too much and disown you and say, "Who is the Lord?" Or I may become poor and steal, and so dishonor the name of my God. [Prov. 30:8ff.]

The prohibition on interest, at least among members of the community, was a strong force for limiting inequality. Interest-bearing debt, with its explosive exponential compounding, is a powerful instrument of accumulation for the lender, and sometimes of impoverishment for the borrower.

Biblical scholars have a great deal more to say on these matters. My knowledge is limited and so is my purpose, namely to offer some evidence that the general principle underlying the culturally specific laws of Israel's covenant community was that of limited inequality. In further support I will cite one Old Testament scholar, C. J. H. Wright:

> There is, then, a strong link between Israel's theocratic monotheism (the central arch of her faith) and her tendency towards her own brand of socio-political and economic "egalitarianism." This did not obliterate differentials but attempted to confine them within the proper limits of functional necessity for the harmony and peace of society.[1]

And one further supporting conclusion, from Cambridge economist A. B. Cramp, can be cited:

> The fundamental principle enshrined in the many-sided, detailed provisions, then, seems to be one that would set limits to the accumulation of capital by individuals (not necessarily the same thing as limiting total accumulation by society as a whole), and would make serious provision for the difficult matter of redistribution of capital when, inevitably, some citizens fare better than others in the economic process.[2]

I have concentrated on the Old Testament because that is where economic organization is most explicitly discussed. The New Covenant not only is a general reaffirmation of the Old, but provides a much sharper and more personal warning on the danger of riches and an even stronger injunction to have a special concern for the poor. It seems to me therefore that the Old Testament principle of limited inequality is forcefully reaffirmed in the New Testament, albeit in a less legalistic and more personal way. Legal structures are necessary, but not sufficient, for community and *shalom*. A change of heart, a renewal of the mind at the individual level, is also required lest the law become dead. This renewal of the mind is urged at the individual or local level by Paul in 2 Corinthians 8:13–15:

> This does not mean that to give relief to others you ought to make things difficult for yourselves: it is a question of balancing what happens to be your surplus now against their present need, and one day they may have something to spare that will supply your own need. That is how we strike a balance: as scripture says: "The man who gathered much had none too much, the man who gathered little did not go short."

Here is a New Testament affirmation of the principle of limited inequality based on an explicit reference to its Old Testament roots (Exod. 16:18): "The man who had gathered more had not too much, the man who had gathered less had not too little." The gathering refers to manna, which also had the property of spoiling if accumulated beyond need, thus reinforcing the idea of limits to accumulated inequality.

That no one has a right to luxury while others lack necessities is a basic requirement of community, whether the basis of community is God's gift of the land or of the entire ecosystem that supports the fertility of the land. How might we incorporate the principle of limited inequality in today's economy in some reasonable and effective way? What are the further implications of doing so?

The Principle in the Modern World

Before searching for new institutional forms of the limits-to-inequality principle, we should ask whether the jubilee year itself could be revived in our time. I think not, even though international debtors and creditors may be forced to arrange something like a "jubilee" forgiveness of international debt in the near future! But the jubilee presupposes an initial just distribution of land among particular families that was established by God's authority within historical memory. That is not the case now. Furthermore, most wealth today is not in the form of land, but rather in the form of capital, including human capital (skills, education). Because of the enormous importance of capital and the associated complex debt structure, the imposition of a zero interest rate would be unrealistic, to put it mildly.

Also, the jubilee system seems to assume a sustainable economy, which we emphatically do not have now, no matter how strongly some of us advo-

cate it as a goal. The initial distribution can be reestablished only if the size or number of families does not grow, and if the resource (the land) is not depleted over
time. These two conditions were more closely approximated in ancient Israel than
in our day. Naturally high death rates kept population from growing very fast, and
a pastoral-agrarian economy did not deplete the resource base rapidly, especially
when supplemented by laws requiring sabbatical fallow for the land.[3] Today the
prior existence of a steady-state economy cannot be taken for granted, but must be
taken as a goal of policy—as something to be reestablished in modern form. Estab-
lishing the principle of limited inequality is a necessary, but not sufficient, condition for achieving a modern steady state. But more of that in the next section. For
now we must look for a way to institutionalize limits to inequality without a God-
given initial distribution. What range of inequality is necessary to reward real differences in irksomeness of work, and in initiative and responsibility? What is the
actual range of inequality? How might the actual be brought into conformity with
the functionally necessary and just degree of inequality?

We must begin by admitting that we have no God-given definition
of what the limits to inequality should be. Do we therefore face a hopeless task? I
don't think so. A democracy has no clear-cut objective rule for determining the
minimum voting age; we feel that it should be early adulthood, but whether that
should be defined as eighteen or twenty-two could be argued endlessly. The point
is that the exact limit is largely arbitrary. The important thing is that there be some
defined and accepted minimum age—whether eighteen or twenty-two is not really
significant. Likewise, the exact limits to inequality are much less important than
the principle that limits be placed somewhere corresponding to a reasonable, functional, and just degree of inequality. But what is that reasonable, functional range?
The minimum income would be some culturally defined amount sufficient for
food, clothing, shelter, and basic health and education. The maximum might be ten
times the minimum. Plato thought the factor should be four. Why do I suggest ten?

There is some evidence that a factor of ten is sufficient to reward real
differences and to provide sufficient incentive so that all necessary jobs are filled
voluntarily. In the U.S. military, for example, the highest-paid general makes ten
times the wages of the lowest private. Probably the general has extra fringe benefits
that may result in a factor of eleven or twelve. The same range is found in the Civil
Service—a GS-18 makes about ten times the salary of a GS-1. In the university a
distinguished professor is paid about ten times the salary of a graduate student in-
structor. In corporations the range is much greater, but this is largely because the
top officers have the privilege of setting their own salaries, unlike generals, senior
civil servants, and distinguished professors.

I take a factor of ten, then, as a benchmark. The important thing is
the change from unlimited to limited inequality. The exact limits are arbitrary and
can be adjusted on the basis of experience. Maybe the factor should be five, maybe
twenty. After all, seven is a rather arbitrary number also. Would it matter so much if

the "sabbatical" were the sixth or the eighth year, or if the jubilee were every forty-five years?

What is the actual range of inequality? What does the actual distribution of income look like? Economists use Lorenz curves, Gini coefficients, Pareto distributions, lognormal distributions, etc., to describe the income distribution. But the most graphic and imaginative description I have seen comes from Dutch economist Jan Pen, who organizes a parade of dwarfs and giants. All income recipients will be shrunk or stretched so that their height is proportional to their income. They will then pass by in a parade, shortest first, tallest last. The parade will last exactly one hour and will be observed by you and me, persons of presumed average height.

What would be see? At first, there are a few people of negative height, their heads may be as much as ten yards underground. These are people who made losses that year—not necessarily poor, but they soon will be if they keep that up. Then come lots of gnomes, about the size of a matchstick. Many are part-time workers, students, or housewives, who earn very little but share in a family income, so they are not as badly off as one might think. The gnomes file by for about five minutes. Then people become noticeably larger, about three feet tall—old-age pensioners, divorced women without alimony, many handicapped, some artists. They take another five minutes. The parade has been going on for fifteen minutes before we see people four feet tall, unskilled workers. Quite a few are women, many are dark-skinned. And now we continue seeing dwarfs for a long time. Then come some office workers, educated folks—not dwarfs but definitely short from our perspective. Only after the parade has been going for forty-eight minutes, twelve minutes before the end, do we see people our own height, the average-income people. We see teachers, civil servants, insurance agents, farmers, some skilled workers. Six minutes later we see the first of the top ten percent, people about six feet, six inches tall, mostly university graduates. In the last few minutes the giants very suddenly emerge. A lawyer, a doctor, and some accountants about eighteen feet tall, other doctors, judges and executives around sixty feet tall. Then comes Prince Phillip, one hundred and eighty feet tall, and the director of Shell Oil, more than double that. Then, at the very end of the parade, come a few people whose height has to be measured in miles, like rock singer Tom Jones. At the very end comes John Paul Getty, some ten miles tall at least.

As you can guess, Professor Pen's parade took place in Britain around 1970. Such a parade in the United States in 1990 would show greater inequality. A similar parade in our proposed limited-inequality world might begin with three- or four-footers and end with thirty- or forty-footers. The great majority would fall between these limits, in any case, so the number of people affected would be relatively few: a very few at the top, more at the bottom, but fewer than the number in the first ten minutes of the parade, since many of them were dependents with adequate family income but very low part-time personal earnings.

We should adopt a range-based rather than a variance-based concept of inequality. Even though the variance-based concept is more usual in statistics, it is an average measure which does not correspond to particular individuals. The range concept is more in the biblical spirit of focusing on the concrete situation of particular individuals—too poor, too rich. It is these extremes that we wish to avoid. The average of deviations from the mean is not so relevant. Hence the emphasis on maximum and minimum limits.

But should the maximum and minimum limits be applied to income or wealth, or, as scripture seems to suggest, a minimum income coupled with a maximum wealth? Let us consider the possibilities. The minimum limit clearly cannot be placed on wealth, since one always has the option of consuming one's wealth and could hardly expect to have it restored year after year. So the minimum limit must be placed on income. The maximum limit could be placed on income, or wealth, or on both. A maximum on wealth, with no maximum on income, would lead to very lavish consumption of all income for one who has reached the wealth maximum. This would simply channel increasing inequality into larger consumption disparities once wealth disparities are limited and, by encouraging consumption, would work against the larger conservation ideals of a sustainable society. Putting a maximum on income avoids that problem, but may be thought to give rise to the opposite problem of fostering excessive wealth inequality.

But this symmetry does not hold on closer analysis. Limiting income directly will also indirectly limit wealth in two ways. First, wealth will be accumulated out of income less rapidly if income is limited. Second, previously accumulated wealth will be devalued for those whose income from other wealth or work has reached the maximum income limit. They will have an incentive to consume or divest themselves of wealth the return on which they are not allowed to keep. Thus it would seem that direct limits, both maximum and minimum, are most effectively applied to income rather than wealth, although an additional maximum on wealth may be worth further consideration. The simplest and most obvious institution for limiting inequality is, therefore, also the best one—namely, maximum and minimum limits on income.

The Principle and the Steady-State Economy

So far, the principle of limited inequality has been discussed in terms of a single time period. But does not the principle also apply over time? Present people collectively should not be too rich if that implies that future people will be too poor. Or, conversely, present people should not be made too poor for the purpose of making future people richer than they need to be. In an era dominated by the idea of economic growth, with its necessary squeezing of present consumption for the sake of investment, the second error has occasionally been recognized. We wonder if the costs of accumulation borne by the early generations in the Soviet Union's industrialization drive are worth the benefits to today's Soviet citizens, or if the cost to the generation living in Britain during the Industrial Revolution was really recompensed by the subsequent higher consumption of their grandchildren. But it is the former question that concerns us here. Are we producing and consuming on a scale which the biosphere cannot sustain and which will impoverish the future? The principle of justice as limited inequality, when extended into the future, implies sustainability—justice extended to future people. Closely related to sustainability is the question of the scale of economic activity (involving depletion and pollution) relative to the natural rates of assimilation and replenishment in the ecosystem.

To the extent that economic growth (development) is based on qualitative improvement, squeezing more welfare out of the same resource flow, then there is no apparent limit to that growth. But neither is there any reason not to share that kind of growth equally. If knowledge is the ultimate resource, then by all means let knowledge grow forever. Shared knowledge is multiplied rather than divided!

But before getting carried away with the idea that the human mind is an ultimate resource that can guarantee endless economic growth, let us remember that, while certainly not reducible to physical terms, the mind is not independent of the body and the body is physical. "No phosphorous, no thought," Frederick Soddy reminds us. As Loren Eiseley put it, "The human mind, so frail, so perishable, so full of inexhaustible dreams and hungers, burns by the power of a leaf." Minds capable of such insight ought to be capable of showing more restraint towards leaves and phosphorous than is usually exhibited by our growth-bound economy. The economist Kenneth Boulding reminds us that capital is knowledge imposed on the physical world in the form of improbable arrangements. But knowledge cannot be imprinted on any kind of matter by any kind of energy—it must be low-entropy matter / energy. Otherwise we could harness the sea breeze with windmills made of sand and use the energy to extract gold from the ocean.

Suppose that an economy stayed within the ten-to-one limits to inequality, but was growing in absolute scale: more people and higher per capita consumption. Although at every point in time the limits to inequality would be respected, over time these limits would not be maintained. Either growth would eventually make the future vastly richer, or ecological collapse would make it vastly poorer—or, likely, the first followed by the second. Since the issues of overpopulation and ecological destruction were not important in biblical times we have little specific guidance about these issues in the Judeo-Christian religious tradition. As mentioned earlier, sustainability was more or less taken for granted. Ancient Israel's economy was pastoral or agricultural, small scale, and solar-based—almost automatically sustainable. I say "almost" because the laws mandating fallow for the land, not taking the bird that is hatching eggs, not destroying trees in war, for instance, indicate a concern for sustainability that suggests it was not totally automatic, nor taken for granted. High death rates naturally kept the population from growing very rapidly, so that overall the economy was in a near steady state, as it would have to be in order to return to the initial historical circumstances of the jubilee. Under these conditions it could not be argued that no maximum was needed as long as everyone was getting richer and that it mattered little if the rich got richer faster than the poor got richer. In a steady state, if the rich get richer the poor must get poorer, not only relatively but absolutely. If the total is limited there must be a maximum limit on individual income. If there is also a minimum, then, by and large, the higher the minimum the lower must be the maximum.

Many would argue that a steady-state economy among the covenant people was a fortuitous circumstance of history having nothing to do with divine revelation. Science and technology have since removed the natural limits that necessitated the steady state and in particular the need for a maximum income. Keep the minimum income, they say, but once poverty is abolished we need not worry about inequality. Furthermore, increasing inequality may be necessary to stimulate growth, which can be used to raise the minimum.

There are two points to make in reply. First, it really does matter how far apart the rich and the poor are from the point of view of community. Unlimited inequality is inconsistent with community, no matter how well-off the poorest are. Even relative poverty breeds resentment, and riches insulate and harden the heart. Conviviality, solidarity, and brotherhood weaken with economic distance. Political power tends to follow relative income and cannot be allowed to concentrate too far in either a theocracy or a democracy without leading to a plutocracy.

Second, the idea that science and technology, because they have greatly increased our power, have removed all limits comes close to being the opposite of the truth. Indeed, it is precisely because science and technology have given us such power that the scale of our economy has been able to grow to the point where we now must consciously face the fundamental limits of creaturehood: finitude, entropy, and ecological dependence. Science can help us adjust to these limits in the best manner, but to think that we will overcome them is to claim authority to remake God's Creation on our blueprint, rather than to maintain and care for it according to God's.

That we are actively engaged in building this new tower of Babel is beyond doubt. How could it be otherwise when most of our generation rejects the very idea of the world as a creation, even one of a Creator who has made considerable use of random mutation and natural selection as a process design principle? My point is not antiscience, since if we are to maintain and care for God's Creation we must surely learn how it works. The first and second laws of thermodynamics, joined by finitude and ecological interdependence, make nonsense of the notion that the economy can continue to grow forever, or even for very long, in its physical dimensions. It is unscientific not to take seriously the most basic laws of science, most of which are statements of impossibility: it is impossible to travel faster than

the speed of light, or to create or destroy matter / energy, or to have perpetual motion, or spontaneous generation of life, and the like.

Long before we have reached ultimate biophysical limits to growth
in the scale of our economy, we will have passed the economic limit beyond which
the marginal costs of growth exceed the marginal benefits. No one can be sure that
we have not already passed that point, since we do not even bother to count costs
and benefits of growth. We just count economic activity in GNP and presume that
its beneficial aspects outweigh its regrettable aspects.

The limits-to-growth debate that started in the late sixties and disappeared with the election of Ronald Reagan needs to be rekindled. It stopped
precisely when people realized that limits to growth imply limits to inequality (if
poverty is to be reduced) and, specifically, a maximum limit. But, the thinking
went, that is clearly impossible, so there must have been a mistake in our reasoning
or our premises. Let us therefore reject the premise of finitude and entropy and return to the unlimited-growth vision that does not call for political impossibilities.
That it calls for physical impossibilities instead can be overlooked, since most vot-
ers have never heard of the laws of thermodynamics, and with the advent of the
space age we all know that finitude has been abolished by the "high frontier."
There is no limit to how many towers of Babel we can build and economic growth
remains the summum bonum. But this is a pipe dream. Historically the steady state
is the normal condition; growth is an aberration. I certainly want to stop short of arguing that the ideal of a sustainable economy is a part of divine revelation. I would
argue only that the principle of limited inequality has biblical authority and that
when we try to institute that principle in the modern world (especially if we extend
it to include future generations) we will find the concept of a steady-state economy
increasingly more relevant than that of the existing growth economy. It is meaning-
ful as a way to keep the rich from leaning too heavily on the poor and the present
generations from leaning too heavily on future generations. It is also relevant to
keeping human beings from leaning too heavily on other creatures whose habitats
must disappear as we convert more and more of the finite ecosystem into a source
for raw materials, a sink for waste, or living space for humans and warehouses for
our artifacts. Stewardship requires that we move off the unsustainable growth path
to which we cling precisely in order to avoid limiting inequality. And we will not be
able to shift from growth to the steady state without instituting limits to inequality.

Chapter 15

Sustainable Development:
From Religious Insight to Ethical
Principle to Public Policy

To go from religious or spiritual insight to the concrete economic policies most in conformity with that insight is a big jump. We need an intermediate step: the formulation of ethical principles—general principles of right action in the world. Then we can ask what concrete economic policies in our specific historical context best serve these ethical principles, and thus indirectly serve the insight from which these principles were derived.

Errors can of course be made at each of the three steps. Our religious insight might be wrong, perhaps too insensitive, or perhaps too fanatical. The translation of a basic religious insight into an ethical principle may be historically biased or too one-sided, even if the basic insight is true. The derivation of specific economic policies from a general principle of right action in the world could be mistaken. Even when our ethical principle is sound, our faulty understanding of how the world works sometimes leads to policies that have effects opposite from those we desired.

The Religious Foundations of Sustainable Development

Although I will draw mainly on Christian traditions in speaking of religious foundations, it is my belief that most other religious traditions give similar insights regarding Creation and stewardship. (This is to be expected for Judaism and Islam, which share early biblical roots with Christianity.) Buddhism, for example, teaches moderation and the virtue of living lightly on the world. I focus on Christianity because I am a Christian, not out of any exclusivist wish to deny the truth of other traditions. I find it enormously encouraging that there is so much agreement among traditional religions on the issue of stewardship. It is less encouraging that we all share a common need for repentance for our various failures to take stewardship seriously in practice.

We are taught that God created the world and all therein. In the Genesis story, Creation was declared good by God even before Adam and Eve were created, and Creation was pronounced *very* good after human beings were added. Man is special, but not the only creature valued by the Creator. The world and our lives within it are the gifts of God, for which we should be grateful. Our gratitude and thanksgiving are expressed in worship, but should also be expressed in restraint. If we love God we will love God's world. If we are grateful for God's gift of life we will not waste the capacity of God's world to support life. If we love God's world we will try to understand how it works, so that we will not ignorantly harm it, like a curious child playing with a grasshopper. We will learn self-control before presuming to control Creation—taking seriously the Buddhist meditation "Cut down the forest of your greed, before cutting real trees."

Not only humans matter, although we matter most. A person is worth many sparrows, but for that statement to mean anything a sparrow's worth cannot be zero. All living things have both instrumental value for other living things and intrinsic value by virtue of their own sentience and capacity to enjoy their own lives. We customarily value subhuman species in terms of their instrumental value to us, neglecting both their intrinsic value and their instrumental value to other subhuman species. We grant ourselves intrinsic value, as well as instrumental value to each other (often the source of conflict). But we do not count our instrumental value to other species, which is too often negative but could be positive if we cared about it. Even a first cataloging of types of value in the world leads to an environmentalist insight.

There are heresies in Christianity that tend to despise the world (Manicheanism, Gnosticism), and despising the world is indeed a heresy for a religion that teaches not only that God created the world, but also that God was and is incarnate in that world. Is the church in the grip of such a heresy today? Is that what explains its slowness to speak out on issues of environmental protection? I do not think so. Rather, I believe, it is the failure of the church to understand that Creation really is under severe threat.

It is difficult to see this, not only for Christians but for many people of goodwill, because the threat comes from growth (both demographic and economic), and growth is something long considered benign. Growth was supposed to spread the benefits of abundant life to all. It promised to cure poverty and misery without demanding too much in the way of sharing. Technological solutions to poverty would succeed in the future where moral solutions had failed in the past. This was the hope of the Enlightenment and the modern scientific establishment, including especially its Marxist heresy of recent demise. Christianity was in agreement with secular culture for a change, and that was comforting—a bit too comforting, in retrospect.

217

Exponential growth has taken us, in a surprisingly short time, as I have argued, from a relatively empty world to a relatively full world—full of people and their furniture. Economic growth made the world full of us and our things, but relatively empty of what had been there before—that which now has been assimilated into us and our things, namely, the natural life-support systems that we have recently started calling "natural capital" out of belated recognition of both their utility and their scarcity. Further expansion of the human niche now frequently increases environmental costs faster than it increases production benefits, thus ushering in a new era of antieconomic growth, growth that impoverishes rather than enriches because it costs more at the margin than it is worth. This antieconomic growth makes it harder, not easier, to cure poverty and protect the biosphere. GNP continues to grow while the welfare of the people declines. Out of confusion, or perhaps out of idolatry, we continue to mistake the symbol for the reality symbolized. Even after the symbol has become a gross misrepresentation of reality we continue to serve it.

The religious insight here affirmed, namely that this is God's world and we are responsible for how we treat it, is so elementary that it is hard to say more about it. One clarification needs emphasis—in speaking of Creation I am not implying acceptance of the antievolutionist, biblically literalist doctrine that has come to be called "scientific creationism." God's creation of a creative evolutionary process is, to me at least, even more awesome than would be the creation of a world of static forms of life. Nor in making this clarification do I wish to endorse the imaginative "just-so stories" and circular speculations concocted by the dogmatic Darwinists who have made themselves irrelevant to issues of ethics and policy by their mechanistic denial of the reality and efficacy of purpose itself, as discussed in this book's introductory essay. A. N. Whitehead's remark is worth repeating: "scientists animated by the purpose of proving that they are purposeless constitute an interesting subject for study."

Just how God created the world is an important question closely related to understanding how the world works, a question we must take seriously if we are to avoid damaging that creation through ignorance. But this question comes later. The prior issue is our acceptance of God's gift of the living world and our obligation to care for it. This obligation exists regardless of the particular divine technology or blueprint with which God made the world, and regardless of the present state of our understanding of how randomness and purpose interact in the divine technology. Of course the obligation to care for the created world would not exist if randomness explains everything and purpose is declared a mere hallucination—if intentionality is not causative then we need not be concerned with ethics.

There is a further insight, however, that is very important. Although it is not necessarily a religious insight, it nevertheless may come easier to people who see themselves more as creatures than as creators. This is the preanalytic vision—elaborated in the book's introduction and in Part 1—that sees the economy as an open subsystem of a larger but finite, non-growing, and closed ecosystem on which it is fully dependent for sources of low-entropy raw materials and for sinks to absorb high-entropy waste materials. Completely nonreligious people may hold this vision simply because it conforms to the facts of experience. The alternative preanalytic vision, the one that supports most economic analysis today, is that the economy is the total system and is unconstrained in its growth by anything. This vision concedes that nature may be finite, but sees it as just a sector of the economy, for which other sectors can substitute without limiting overall growth in any important way. The latter vision somehow fits with the idea that human beings are fundamentally creators rather than creatures. I hesitate to call these visions religious insights. But preanalytic visions share with religious ones the feature that ensures that we can never escape them by analysis: they define the terms of analysis and therefore cannot provide us with a perspective that could refute their own viewpoints. Their hold on us is in part one of faith and commitment. The vision of economy as subsystem is not the same as the fundamental religious insight that the world is God's Creation, and that we and all our little creations are part of and limited by that larger creation, but it is certainly more in harmony with that insight than the vision of man's economy as the total system with nature a subsector whose services can be substituted by other sectors. The analytical consequences of these two preanalytic visions are, as I have argued, enormously different: the economy-as-subsystem vision leads to the quest for an optimal scale of the human niche, beyond which growth should cease; the economy-as-total-system vision leads to growth forever as the norm.

The Ethical Principle of Sustainable Development

If we accept the religious insight that the world is God's Creation, and are able to discern that we too are creatures of God with creaturely limits on our own creativity, then what conclusions should we draw about how to act rightly in the world? Should we convert as much as possible of the matter / energy of the world into ourselves and our artifacts? Should that be the "central organizing principle" of society, to use Vice President Gore's term? Indeed, growth has been and still is our central organizing principle. That is precisely our problem. We need a new central organizing principle—a fundamental ethic that will guide our actions in a way more in harmony with both basic religious insight and the scientifically verifiable limits of the natural world. This ethic is suggested by the terms "sustainability," "sufficiency," "equity," "efficiency." Growth has become unsustainable. It has never been equitable in that some live far above sufficiency, while others live far below. And no system that uses resources at a rate that destroys natural life-support systems without meeting the basic needs of all can possibly be considered efficient.

To capture the cluster of values expressed by "sustainability/sufficiency/equity/efficiency" in one sentence, I suggest the following: *We should strive for sufficient per capita wealth—efficiently maintained and allocated, and equitably distributed—for the maximum number of people that can be sustained over time under these conditions.*

Some clarifications are needed. Note that the goal is *sufficient*, not maximum, per capita wealth. Sufficient for what? Sufficient for a good life. I will not try to define "good life," but I will note that not only man-made wealth but also preserved natural capital is necessary for a good life. What is maximized is cumulative number of lives over time lived in sufficiency. This is very different from maximizing the population simultaneously alive. Too many people alive at one time overloads and destroys the earth's carrying capacity, resulting in fewer lives, or lives lived below sufficiency, in subsequent time periods, and consequently a smaller cumulative total of lives lived in a condition of sufficiency. Too much consumption per capita at any one time leads to the same result. The value of efficiency, both technical and allocative, is affirmed because it allows more people to exist over time in conditions of sufficiency. Wealth "efficiently maintained" means that wealth as it depreciates is replaced by new production that gives greater (maximum) use or satisfaction per unit of resource used. Equitable distribution means that sufficiency is attained by all, and that the range of inequality above sufficiency is limited. It does not mean equal wealth for all. Some degree of inequality of wealth is necessary for justice, efficiency, and community. But, as discussed in the previous chapter, the present range of inequality is vastly greater than what is consistent with community or necessary for economic incentive. The idea of sustainability, of course, is captured by the insistence on maximizing cumulative lives *over time.*

Since utilitarianism is the basic ethic underlying economics, it is useful to compare the above statement with Jeremy Bentham's utilitarian guide of "the greatest good for the greatest number." Bentham's rule has the virtue of brevity, but unfortunately it contains an impossible double maximization. You cannot have two "greatests" because it is possible to have either more people at a lower per capita good or greater per capita good for fewer people. Logically it would have to be either "greatest good for a sufficient number" or "sufficient good for the greatest number." The principle here advocated is the latter, with "number" defined as cumulative number over time.

The reason for that choice is that we have no notion of what is a sufficient number over time—that would imply deciding when the world should end. Standard economics, however, by its practice of discounting the future, is implicitly willing to say that beyond some point the future is worth nil and might as well end. Rejection of this view is part of the thrust of the concept of sustainability. Although both Christianity and thermodynamics teach that the world is not perpetual, we nevertheless affirm that life and longevity are good gifts of God and should not be wasted. Also, we do have some notion of how much is sufficient for a good life, even though there will be disagreement. Much thought and clarification is needed here, but, clearly, at one extreme life can be stunted by poverty, and just as clearly, at the other extreme life is not improved and is even harmed by surfeit and excess. It is not too much to expect that we could come up with a reasonable range of inequality limits, notwithstanding the chorus of econo-sophists who will ask, Who are *you* to impose your personal tastes on everyone else? etc., etc., ad nauseam. If the cluster of values affirmed above were logically reducible to "personal tastes," and if continual growth were biophysically possible, then this common objection would have force. The fact that both presuppositions of this objection are clearly wrong is indicative of the low level of argument that is customary in what currently passes for serious economic discourse.

The product of population and per capita resource use at any point in time represents the *scale* of the human presence in the biosphere—the rate of total resource throughput. It is this total scale that is limited by the regenerative and absorptive capacities of the ecosystem, and that is sustainable or unsustainable. For a given sustainable scale of throughput we could choose to have many people consuming small amounts of resources per capital, or fewer people consuming correspondingly more resources per capita. This is the choice of "sufficient good," subject to which cumulative lives would be maximized.[1]

If something like the ethic offered above is accepted, then we will have to find economic policies for putting it into practice. Without such an ethic we will be led astray by sophists who argue that we have no obligations to the future because future people do not exist, and rights cannot inhere in nonexistent people, and without rights there can be no obligations. Therefore we have no obligations to future people. And even if we did, it is sometimes added, the best way to serve the future is to maximize present riches. The invisible hand, it is argued, not only converts personal greed into social benevolence, it also transforms generational selfishness into intergenerational generosity. The bequest to the future of manmade capital is thought to more than compensate for the depreciation and liquidation of natural capital.

But the value of a sawmill is zero without forests; the value of fishing boats is zero without fish; the value of refineries is zero without remaining deposits of petroleum; the value of dams is zero without rivers and catchment areas with sufficient forest cover to prevent erosion and siltation of the lake behind the dam. Empty verbiage about the intergenerational invisible hand and the near-perfect sustainability of man-made for natural capital is just the usual confused attempt to give a technical nonanswer to a moral question.

I believe that God the Creator exists now, as well as in the past and future, and is the source of our obligation to Creation, including other creatures, and especially including members of our own species who are suffering. Our ability and inclination to enrich the present at the expense of the future, and of other spe-

221

cies, is as real and as sinful as our tendency to further enrich the wealthy at the expense of the poor. To hand back to God the gift of Creation in a degraded state capable of supporting less life, less abundantly, and for a shorter future, is surely a sin. If it is a sin to kill and to steal, then surely it is a sin to destroy carrying capacity—the capacity of the earth to support life now and in the future. Sometimes we find ourselves in an impasse in which sins are unavoidable. We may sometimes have to sacrifice future life in order to preserve present life—but to sacrifice future life to protect present luxury and extravagance is a very different matter.

Many will share the sense of obligation for Creation affirmed in the preceding paragraph but will recoil from grounding it in theism of any kind. One has a right to expect, however, that they will make an effort to ground their sense of obligation in something more basic than their own subjective personal preferences—even if (especially if) the latter are thought to be mechanically derived from a process of random genetic mutation and natural selection. In particular, one has a right to expect sufficient discernment and clarity on their part to avoid mistaking a vestigial sense of obligation, inherited from an age of theistic belief, for a new sense of obligation presumably derived from the modern cosmology of scientific materialism.

Economic Policies for Sustainable Development

Economic policy for sustainable development must no longer seek solutions to economic problems in terms of the modern central organizing principle of growth, but in terms of the traditional principles of sustainability, sufficiency, equity, and efficiency.

The first step in this change is to recognize, as I have argued in Chapter 2, that there are three economic problems—allocation, distribution, and scale. These three economic problems represent separate goals—and solving one does not solve the others. Today we are trying to kill three birds with two stones. The first goal is the problem of allocation, the division of the resources among their alternative commodity uses—that is, how many resources to allocate for cars, for bicycles, for shoes, for beans. An optimal allocation is one that is efficient in giving people what they want and are able to pay for. The instrument for attaining efficiency is relative prices, which measure marginal opportunity costs. The second goal is distribution, the division of the resources in their final product embodiments among alternative people—that is, how many bicycles or beans are distributed to you, to me, and to other people. An optimal distribution is one that is within the bounds of equity and sufficiency. The policy instrument is transfer payments and limits to inequality. Economic theory has long recognized these two problems, even though the efficiency problem has received far more attention than the equity problem. The scale problem has not traditionally been recognized by economic theory or policy—it is the newly recognized third goal for which we have no policy instrument.

But today the problem of optimal scale can no longer be avoided. It was avoided in the past because as long as scale was small it was possible for economic growth to be a central organizing principle of society. Growth was put in first place because it would presumably wash away the problem of poverty in a cascade of abundance vouchsafed by the amazing grace of compound interest. There would be no need for redistribution; indeed, premature redistribution would only slow the growth machine. Growth would also wash away inefficiency without the political discipline of getting relative prices to reflect full social and environmental costs. But scale too has its limits. It has a maximum, and well before the maximum it has an optimum—a point beyond which further growth costs more than it is worth. Evidence increases daily that we have passed that optimum scale.

The existence of such an optimal scale follows closely from the pre-analytic vision of the economy as an open subsystem of a larger but finite and non-growing ecosystem. As the economy expands physically, it assimilates into itself an ever greater proportion of the total life space and the total matter/energy of the ecosystem. Less is therefore available to all other species to provide the services we depend upon, such as photosynthesis, to mention only the most important. At some point well before the boundaries of the growing subsystem coincide with the total system, we will have sacrificed life-support services that are far more valuable than the extra commodity services that we got in return.

Since the earth itself is developing without growing, it follows that a subsystem of the earth must eventually conform itself to the same behavioral mode of development without growth, alias "sustainable development." This could happen at any scale which is below carrying capacity. The optimal scale, following our basic ethic, would be the one that maximizes lives ever lived over time at a sufficient level of per capita resource use for a good life. At present all we know for sure is that the optimal scale must be sustainable, that the economic subsystem must not overload the ecosystem to the point of reducing future life. For now it is a sufficient challenge to strive for a sustainable scale. Later we can worry about which sustainable scale is optimal.

The notion of optimal scale in the preceding paragraph is totally anthropocentric in that the human niche is constrained only by the necessity to preserve other forms of life for their instrumental value to us—that is, their ecological life-support service. No intrinsic value of other species was recognized. If we do recognize the intrinsic value of other living things—as Scripture does and as I think we should—that will give an additional reason for setting aside life space, or habitat, for them, and would result in a smaller optimal scale for humans than if the instrumental value of other creatures is counted.[2]

In terms of specific economic theory, the paradigm policy for solving the allocation, distribution, and scale problems seems to me to be the tradable permits plan, as discussed in Chapter 2. The great virtue of the tradable permits scheme is that it forces us to distinguish three independent policy goals and to recognize that they require three independent policy instruments. Moreover, it also requires that the first two goals (scale and distribution) be decided socially before the third (allocation) can be worked out individualistically by the competitive market.

Summary and Conclusion

We are creatures endowed with creativity but also subject to limits, and we have obligations to our Creator to care for Creation, to maintain intact its capacity to support life and wealth. Specifically this means to act so as to maximize cumulative lives ever to be lived over time in a state of sufficiency. This in turn means not destroying carrying capacity—which implies that sustainability, not growth, should become the ruling ethic for a Creation-centered economy. In this vision, along with sustainability, the associated values of sufficiency, equity, and efficiency become the central organizing principles of the economy. Growth in population or per capita resource use would be encouraged or discouraged according to their favorable or unfavorable effects on sustainability, sufficiency, equity, and efficiency. The type of concrete policy for best doing this, I have argued in Chapter 2 and elsewhere, is the tradable permits scheme which forces a clear separation of scale, distribution, and allocation.

The technical and economic problems involved in achieving sustainability are not that difficult. The hard problem is overcoming our addiction to growth as the favored way to assert our creative power, and the idolatrous belief— whether we think in religious terms or not—that our derived creative power is autonomous and unlimited. Such idolatry cannot admit that the elimination of poverty requires recognition of *limits*, not faster growth—*limits* to growth in per capita resource use, *limits* to population growth, *limits* to the growth of inequality. Refusal to recognize these creaturely limits results in growth beyond the carrying capacity of the earth, with its consequent destruction, followed by a reduction in cumulative number of lives ever to be lived in conditions of material sufficiency, as well as in the premature deaths of many people now living below sufficiency.

We must face the failures of the growth idolatry. We must stop crying out to the growing economy, "Deliver me, for thou art my god!" Instead, we must have the courage to ask with Isaiah, "Is there not a lie in my right hand?"

Notes

Introduction   The Shape of Current Thought or Sustainable Development

1. See Wilfred Beckerman, *Small Is Stupid: Blowing the Whistle on the Greens* (London: Duckworth, 1995). See also my review in *Population and Development Review*, September 1995.

2. See Nicholas Georgescu-Roegen, *The Entropy Law and the Economic Process* (Cambridge: Harvard University Press, 1971), chapters 2 and 3.

3. Herman Daly, *Steady-State Economics* (second edition, Washington, D.C.: Island Press, 1991; first edition, W. H. Freeman Co., 1977).

4. *Environmentally Sustainable Economic Development: Building on Brundtland*, ed. Robert Goodland, Herman Daly, Salah El Serafy, and Bernd von Droste (UNESCO, 1991), reissued as *Population, Technology, and Lifestyles: The Transition to Sustainability* (Washington, D.C.: Island Press, 1992).

5. I sent MIT Press, at their solicitation, a collection of essays on sustainable development, an earlier incarnation of this book. They sent it out for review, and on the basis of three positive reviews, wrote a contract to publish, subject to my doing further editing work. This I did, and sent in the revised manuscript. Some months later I was informed that a distinguished economist on their editorial advisory committee was not happy with the book and wanted more reviews. Did the distinguished economist have specific criticisms? No, I was told, he had not read the manuscript, but just wanted more reviews as a matter of procedure. Not to worry, MIT Press was still committed to publishing the book. So they sent the manuscript out for two more reviews. One was positive, the other was extremely negative. That made a total of five reviewers, all of MIT Press's own choosing, of which four said publish, and one said do not publish. The negative review "trumped" the four positive reviews, and the press broke its contract. The basic thrust of the negative review, leaving aside *ad hominem* irrelevancies, was "That is not the right way to look at it." All of this was the more surprising because I had recently published a collection with MIT Press that was well received (*Valuing the Earth: Economics, Ecology, Ethics*, ed. H. Daly and K. Townsend [Cambridge, Mass.: MIT Press, 1993]).

The professional staff of the MIT Press was embarrassed by the unexpected and high-handed actions of the distinguished economist on their editorial advisory board. Neither that economist nor the anonymous negative reviewer, whose identities were not hard to deduce, have ever reviewed or criticized in print any of my previous books, which from their perspective are as bad as this one. I do not object to their disagreeing with me—I am sure that they are sincere in their heartfelt opposition. I just think their criticisms should be public in the form of signed, published reviews from which I and others might conceivably benefit. What upset these important economists sufficiently to cause them to engage in such shabby behavior? I tell this story to show that academia is every bit as doctrinaire as the World Bank.

6. K. Arrow et al., "Economic Growth, Carrying Capacity, and the Environment," *Science*, 28 April 1995.

7. See Clifford W. Cobb and John B. Cobb, Jr., *The Green National Product: A Proposed Index of Sustainable Economic Welfare* (Lanham, Md.: University Press of America, 1994). See also Herman E. Daly and John B. Cobb, Jr., *For the Common Good* (Boston: Beacon Press, 1989).

8. See Herman E. Daly, "Alternative Strategies for Integrating Economics and Ecology," in *Integration of Economy and Ecology: An Outlook for the Eighties*, ed. AnnMari Jansson (Stockholm: University of Stockholm Press, 1984), 19–29.

9. Al Gore, *Earth in the Balance: Ecology and the Human Spirit* (New York: Houghton Mifflin, 1992).

10. President's Council on Sustainable Development, Washington, D.C., *Status Update*, April 1995, 11.

11. John F. Haught, *The Promise of Nature: Ecology and Cosmic Purpose* (Mahwah, N.J.: Paulist Press, 1993), 9, 7. See also, Charles Birch, *On Purpose* (Kensington, Australia: New South Wales Press, 1980).

12. Stephen J. Gould, "Unenchanted Evening," *Natural History*, September 1991, 14. For an insightful discussion see David Orr, *Earth in Mind* (Washington D.C.: Island Press, 1994), chapter 20.

13. Haught, *The Promise of Nature*, 15.

14. Alfred North Whitehead, *The Function of Reason* (Princeton, N.J.: Princeton University Press, 1929), 16.

Part 1   Introduction

1. Nicholas Georgescu-Roegen, *The Entropy Law and the Economic Process* (Cambridge, Mass.: Harvard University Press, 1971). For a defense of the view that entropy is highly relevant to economics, against arguments to the contrary by some economists, see my articles "Thermodynamic and Economic Concepts as Related to Resource-Use Policies: A Comment," *Land Economics* 62, no. 3 (August 1986): 319–21; "Is the Entropy Law Relevant to Natural Resource Scarcity?—Reply," *Journal of Environmental Economics and Management* 23 (July 1992): 91–95. See also G. A. Lozada, "Georgescu-Roegen's Defense of Classical Thermodynamics Revisited," *Ecological Economics* 14, no. 1 (July 1995): 31–44. Another theoretical issue not treated in these articles, yet relevant to

sustainability, is temporal discounting. The topic is touched on occasionally throughout this book, especially in Part 7, but not dealt with thematically. A good exposition and guide to the large literature on this topic is Colin Price, *Time, Discounting, and Value* (Oxford: Blackwell, 1993).

Chapter 1   Moving to a Steady-State Economy

1. Frederick Soddy's ideas on finance and banking are further discussed in Part 6.

Chapter 2   Elements of Environmental Macroeconomics

1. See the following: R. Dornbusch and S. Fischer, *Macroeconomics*, 4th ed. (New York: McGraw-Hill, 1987); R. E. Hall and J. B. Taylor, *Macroeconomics*, 2nd ed. (New York: W. W. Norton, 1988); R. J. Barro, *Macroeconomics*, 2nd ed. (New York: Wiley and Sons, 1987).

2. What has macroeconomics contributed to environmental economics so far? As we have seen, the textbooks make no claim to any contribution whatsoever, but that is too modest. National income accounting is a part of macroeconomics, and there has been an effort to correct our income accounts for consumption of natural capital. Current national accounting conventions also treat environmental cleanup costs as final consumption rather than intermediate costs of production of the commodity whose production gave rise to those costs (Hueting 1980; Leipert 1986; Repetto 1987; Ahmad et al. 1989). Traditional national income accountants have not exactly been in the forefront of the effort to correct these two errors, and may even be said to be dragging their feet. However, the conservatively motivated and impeccably orthodox attempt to gain a closer approximation of true Hicksian income (maximum available for consumption without consuming capital stock) will surely make this effort an important foundation of environmental macroeconomics.

Inter-industry or input-output analysis is also a useful tool of environmental analysis, although it is hard to classify it as either micro or macro. But because of its close relation to national accounts, let us call it macro and credit it as an existing part of environmental macroeconomics. Certainly it has been important in elucidating total (direct and indirect) requirements of materials and especially energy that must be extracted from the environment in order to increase any component of the economy's final bill of goods by some given amount. The concept of carrying capacity is also emerging as a tool of environmental macroeconomics (see Chapter 8, on the Ecuadoran Amazon and Paraguayan Chaco).

3. Any analogy has its limit, and the Plimsoll line is used here mainly to clarify the difference between optimal allocation and optimal scale. But the analogy might be pressed just a bit more regarding the obvious difficulty of determining just where to draw the analogous line for the economy. Drawing the line on a ship's bow seems comparatively easy, and indeed it is. But carping academic relativists can point out that there would be different Plimsoll lines for fresh and salt water, that the line is not just a physical measurement but involves some social judgment of acceptable risk, that the technical design of the ship will influence the position of the line, etc. Yet in spite of all these difficulties we do manage to draw a reasonable line somewhere, to the immense benefit of generations of seafarers. Likewise for the economy, it is more important that a limit be placed somewhere than that the limit be at exactly the right place.

4. For economists this can be illustrated in terms of the familiar microeconomic tool of the Edgeworth box. Moving to the contract curve is an improvement in efficiency of *allocation*. Moving along the contract curve is a change in *distribution* which may be deemed just or unjust on ethical

grounds. The *scale* is represented by the dimensions of the box, which are taken as given. Consequently, the issue of optimal scale of the box itself escapes the limits of the analytical tool. A microeconomic tool cannot be expected to answer a macroeconomic question. But, so far, macroeconomics has not answered the question either—indeed has not even asked it. The tacit answer to the implicit question seems to be that a bigger Edgeworth box is always better than a smaller one!

5. See, for example, David Pearce et al. 1989, p. 135.

6. See Herman E. Daly and John B. Cobb, Jr., *For the Common Good* (Boston, Mass.: Beacon Press, 1989; 2d ed., 1994).

7. See Richard Norgaard and Richard Howarth, "Sustainability and Discounting the Future," in *Ecological Economics: The Science and Management of Sustainability*, ed. R. Costanza (New York: Columbia University Press, 1991).

8. The definition of human appropriation underlying the figures quoted includes direct use by human beings (food, fuel, fiber, timber), plus the reduction from the potential due to ecosystem degradation caused by humans. The latter reflects deforestation, desertification, paving over, and human conversion to less productive systems (such as agriculture).

Chapter 3   Consumption

1. N. Georgescu-Roegen (1979) deserves to be quoted at length on this point because so few people have understood it. He writes the "Solow-Stiglitz variant" of the Cobb-Douglas function as:

$$Q = Ka^1 \, Ra^2 \, La^3 \qquad\qquad (1)$$

Where Q is output, K is the stock of capital, R is the flow of natural resources used in production, L is the labor supply, and $a^1 + a^2 + a^3 = 1$ and of course, $a^i > 0$.

From this formula it follows that with a constant labor power, Lo, one could obtain any Qo, if the flow of natural resources satisfies the condition

$$Ra^2 = \frac{Qo}{Ka^1 Loa^3} \qquad\qquad (2)$$

This shows that R may be as small as we wish, provided K is sufficiently large. Ergo, we can obtain a constant annual product indefinitely even from a very small stock of resources R > 0, if we decompose R into an infinite series $R = \Sigma Ri$, with $Ri \rightarrow 0$, use Ri in year i, and increase the stock of capital each year as required by (2). But this ergo is not valid in actuality. In actuality, the increase of capital implies an additional depletion of resources. And if $K \rightarrow \infty$, then R will rapidly be exhausted by the production of capital. Solow and Stiglitz could not have come out with their conjuring trick had they borne in mind, first, that any material process consists in the transformation of some materials into others (the flow elements) by some agents (the fund elements), and second, that natural resources are the very sap of the economic process. They are not just like any other production factor. A change in capital or labor can only diminish the amount of waste in the production of a commodity: no agent can create the material on which it works. Nor can capital create the stuff out of which it is made. In some cases it may also be that the same service can be provided by a design that requires less matter or energy. But even in this direction there exists a limit, unless we believe that the ultimate fate of the economic process is an earthly Garden of Eden.

The question that confronts us today is whether we are going to discover new sources of energy that can be safely used. No elasticities of some Cobb-Douglas function can help us to answer it.

2. The contribution of these two pioneers is the subject of Part 6.

3. Differential rent would equalize the price of both oil sources if demand were sufficient for them to be used simultaneously. But they are used sequentially, and the differential rent is never charged against the earlier subsidy. The demand from future generations is not felt until after they are born. The energy rate of return on investment in petroleum has been declining, so that the real subsidy to the economy has been declining, even while the contribution of higher priced petroleum to the GNP has been rising, See J. Gever et al., *Beyond Oil* (Cambridge, Mass.: Ballinger, 1986); and C. Cleveland et al., "Energy and the U.S. Economy: A Biophysical Perspective," *Science* 225 (1984): 890–97.

4. Marginal benefits fall because, as rational beings, we use resources to satisfy our most pressing wants first. Marginal costs rise because, in like manner, we use the best and most accessible resources first.

5. This is a simpler version of the identity discussed in Chapter 4.

6. This is the definition of a sustainable scale. Sustainability does not imply optimality—we may prefer another sustainable scale, one with more or less natural capital, but still sustainable. I think it would be reasonable to consider sustainability as a necessary but not sufficient condition of optimality. But in current economic theory sustainability is not implied by optimality—maximizing present value at positive discount rates implies writing off the future beyond some point and liquidating it for the benefit of the present and near future.

7. Reasoning in terms of broad aggregates has its limitations. Converting natural into man-made capital embraces both the extravagant conversion of tropical hardwoods into toothpicks and the frugal conversion of pine trees into shelters for the homeless. The point is not that all conversions of natural into man-made capital simultaneously cease being worthwhile, but rather that ever fewer remain worthwhile as growth continues.

Part 2   Introduction

1. For a discussion employing traditional economic theory in the service of sustainable development at the World Bank, see J. Kellenberg and H. Daly, "Counting User Cost in Evaluating Projects that Deplete Natural Capital: World Bank Best Practice and Beyond," World Bank working paper (ENV Working Paper no. 66, April 1994).

2. There are two institutions that use the term "ecological economics" in their name; they have overlapping interests and associates, but also many differences that cause some confusion about the meaning of the term "ecological economics." The International Society for Ecological Economics (ISEE) was founded earlier and truly is the pioneer. It has held three international biennial

conferences, and published the proceedings of the first two, with the third due out soon. It has a membership base of around 1,500 world-wide, and is a participatory, broad-based organization, with all the problems that entails. Its growth was due both to the importance of the ideas addressed and issues that it raised, and to the exceptional energy and leadership of its president, Robert Costanza. Its stance toward mainstream economics has been more critical than that of the other institution, the Beijer Institute for Ecological Economics. The latter is a part of the Swedish Royal Academy of Science, and is run by Karl-Goran Maler and Partha Dasgupta, with a board of directors that, although diverse and well-qualified, is nevertheless dominated by an establishment point of view. It is an elite, top-down institution with no participatory base. Its leadership's orientation is difficult to distinguish from environmental economics of the most neoclassical kind. However, it does foster a relatively open research agenda, focusing to date on biodiversity, common property, and complex systems. It also serves other useful functions, such as engineering the consensus statement by economists and ecologists discussed in the introduction to this book.

Chapter 4   Operationalizing Sustainable Development by Investing in Natural Capital

1. *Maintaining capital intact* when technology is constant is the same as maintaining *physical capital intact*. When technology increases the productivity of capital, then it is not so clear what "keeping capital intact" means. The maximum amount that the community can sustainably consume has increased. To count that increase as income, we must continue to maintain the same physical capital intact. This would be the prudent course. We could, however, opt to maintain the old smaller income and take the benefits of the technological improvement in the form of a one-time increase in consumption (of capital), while maintaining only the capital needed to produce the former income stream. Capital includes both natural and man-made. We should avoid the error, common in the past and even now, of consuming the benefits of increased productivity of man-made capital by running down natural capital. As will be argued here, the two forms of capital are complementary. Furthermore, the main reason for the historical increase in the productivity of man-made capital has been that it has had increasing amounts of natural resources to work with, resulting in a decline in the productivity of natural resources (and natural capital). The historical increase in man-made capital productivity has been partly at the expense of reduced natural capital productivity resulting from its extravagant use—as if it were free. Therefore, the historical increase in man-made capital productivity cannot be taken as evidence for an increase in natural capital productivity, or as a reason for optimistic expectations in that regard.

2. Regarding the house example I am frequently told that insulation (capital) is a substitute for resources (energy for space heating). If the house is considered the final product, then capital (agent of production, efficient cause) cannot end up as a part (material cause) of the house, whether as wood, brick, or insulating material. The insulating material is a resource like wood or brick, not capital. If the final product is not taken as the house but the service of the house in providing warmth, then the entire house, not only insulating material, is capital. In this case, more or better capital (a well-insulated house) does reduce wasted energy. Increasing the efficiency with which a resource is used is certainly a good substitute for more of the resource. But these kinds of waste-reducing efficiency measures (recycling prompt scrap, sweeping up sawdust and using it for fuel or particle board, or reducing heat loss from a house) are all rather marginal, limited substitutions.

3. The usual definition of complementarity requires that for a given constant output, a rise in the price of one factor would reduce the quantity of both factors. In the two-factor case, both factors means all factors, and it is impossible to keep output constant while reducing the input of all factors. But complementarity might be defined back into existence in the two-factor case by avoiding

the constant output condition. For example, two factors could be considered complements if an increase in one factor will not increase output, but an increase in the other factor will—and *perfect* complements if an increase in neither factor alone will increase output, but an increase in both will. It is not sufficient to treat complementarity as if it were nothing more than "limited substitutability." The latter means that we could get along well enough with only one factor and less well with only the other, but that we do not need both. Complementarity means we need both, and that the one in shortest supply is limiting.

4. At the margin a right glove can substitute for a left glove by turning it inside out. Socks can substitute for shoes by wearing an extra pair to compensate for thinning soles. But in spite of this marginal substitution, shoes and socks, or right and left gloves are overwhelmingly complements. The same is basically true for man-made and natural capital. Picture their isoquants as L-shaped, having a 90° angle. Erase the angle and draw a tiny 90° arc connecting the two legs of the L. This seems close to reality.

5. The figures are mainly suggestive, but do have an empirical basis in the estimate that humans currently preempt 40% of the net primary product of photosynthesis for land-based ecosystems. In other words, 40% of the solar energy potentially capturable by plants and available to other living things passes through the human economy, or is in some way subject to human purposes. This seems a reasonable index of how full the world is of humans and their possessions.

6. Peter G. Brown, *Restoring the Public Trust* (Boston: Beacon Press, 1994).

7. From the familiar biological yield curve below it is clear that a sustainable harvest of *H* will be yielded either at a stock of *P1* or *P2*.

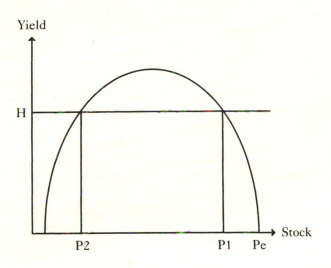

In general, *P1* is the natural capital mode of exploitation of a wild population. *P2* is the cultivated capital mode of exploitation of a bred population. At *P1* we have a large population taking up a lot of ecological space, but providing, in addition to a yield of *H*, other natural services, as well as maintaining a larger amount of biodiversity. Costs are basically harvest cost of the wild population. At P_2, we have a much smaller stock giving the same yield of H, requiring much less ecological space, but requiring greater maintenance, breeding, feeding, and confinement costs if viewed as cultivated natural capital. The appeal of cultivated natural capital is to get H from a low P_2, making ecological room for other exploited (or wild) populations. But management costs are high. The appeal of P_1 and the mode of natural capital proper is that management service is free, and the biodiversity of larger stocks is greater.

Chapter 5   Fostering Environmentally Sustainable Development

1. See J. Kellenberg and H. Daly, "Counting User Costs in Evaluating Projects that Deplete Natural Capital: World Bank Best Practice and Beyond," World Bank working paper (ENV Working Paper no. 66, April 1994.) User cost is calculated as the estimated additional cost per unit of the substitute resource (backstop) discounted back to the present from the estimated future date exhaustion of the resource in question.

2. The term "throughput" is an inelegant but highly useful derivative of the terms input and output. The matter/energy that goes into a system and eventually comes out is what goes through— the "throughput" as engineers have dubbed it. A biologist's synonym might be "the metabolic flow" by which an organism maintains itself. This physical flow connects the economy to the environment at both ends, and is of course subject to the physical laws of conservation and entropy.

3. See Ernst von Weizsacker, *Ecological Tax Reform* (London: Zed Books, 1992).

4. Both goods and factors of production can be either complements or substitutes. For consumer goods, shoes and socks are complements (used together); shoes and boots are substitutes (one used instead of the other). In building a house, bricks and wood are substitutes; bricks and masons are complements. If factors are good substitutes the absence of one does not limit the usefulness of the other. For complements, the absence of one greatly reduces the usefulness of the other. The complementary factor in short supply is then the *limiting factor*.

5. Keep in mind that no one questions that some resources can be substituted for others, e.g., bricks for wood. But to substitute capital stock (saws and hammers) for wood is only very marginally possible if at all. Capital is the agent of transformation of the natural resource flow from raw material into finished product. Resources are the *material cause* of the finished product; capital is the *efficient cause*. One material cause may substitute for another (bricks for wood); one efficient cause may substitute for another (e.g., power saws for hand saws, or capital for labor); but efficient cause and material cause are related as complements rather than substitutes. If man-made capital is complementary with the natural resource flow, then it is also complementary with the natural capital stock that yields that flow.

6. Forgone consumption is the essence of investment. Consumption is reduced by reducing either per capita consumption or population. Therefore investment in natural capital regeneration includes investment in population control, and in technical and social structures that demand less resource use per capita.

7. See Herman E. Daly, "The Perils of Free Trade," *Scientific American*, November 1993.

8. J. M. Keynes (1933), "National Self-Sufficiency," in *The Collected Writings of John Maynard Keynes*, vol. 21, ed. Donald Moggeridge (London: Macmillan and Cambridge University Press).

Part 3   Introduction

1. Herman E. Daly and John B. Cobb, Jr., *For the Common Good* (Boston, Mass.: Beacon Press, 1989; second edition, 1994).

2. Clifford W. Cobb and John B. Cobb, Jr., have continued this work. See their book *The Green National Product* (Lanham, Md.: The University Press of America and The Human Economy Center, 1994). Cobb and Cobb sent the original (1989) ISEW to numerous experts likely to be critical of it (e.g., Carol Carson, Robert Eisner, and E. J. Mishan). These eminent critics were offered a small honorarium and publication of their criticisms, with the understanding that Cobb and Cobb would then redo the ISEW in the light of those criticisms, or else explain why not. That is basically the plan of the book, and I recommend it both for its substance and as an example of generosity and fairness in dealing with one's critics. Many good criticisms were made, the index was revised, but the basic pattern described above remained. For an application of the ISEW to England, with similar findings, see Tim Jackson and Nick Marks, *Measuring Sustainable Economic Welfare—A Pilot Index: 1950–1990* (Stockholm: Stockholm Environmental Institute, 1994), published in cooperation with the New Economics Foundation, London, England. For a survey of the relations of ISEW to GNP in the U.S., the U.K., Germany, Austria, and the Netherlands, with preliminary evidence for a threshold beyond which increasing GNP no longer leads to increasing ISEW, see Manfred Max-Neef, "Economic Growth and the Quality of Life: A Threshold Hypothesis," *Ecological Economics* 15/2 (November 1995): 115–18.

Chapter 7   On Sustainable Development and National Accounts

1. For a recent critique of GNP see Roefie Hueting (1980). Hueting does not adopt Fisher's concepts, but offers many insightful comments on the shortcomings of GNP.

2. In the language of benefit-cost analysis, S becomes benefit and T becomes cost. Hence, S/T is the same thing as the benefit-cost ratio. The objective function is then to maximize the benefit-cost ratio, a familiar enough mechanical welfare function, but not, of course, expressed in the same units we are using here.

3. It is ironic that when Keynes introduced the concept of user cost applied to man-made capital, he appealed to the analogous case of "raw materials (where) the necessity for allowing for user cost is obvious" (Keynes 1936, p. 73). Nowadays, in trying to introduce user cost on raw materials into national accounts, we appeal to the analogous case of man-made capital where allowing for user cost is obvious! I am indebted to Mr. Salah El Serafy for this observation.

4. For more on the relevance of Irving Fisher, see Daly 1991.

Part 4   Introduction

1. Herman E. Daly, "The Population Question in Northeast Brazil: Its Economic and Ideological Dimensions," *Economic Development and Cultural Change* (University of Chicago), July 1970; and "A Marxian-Malthusian View of Poverty and Development," *Population Studies* (London School of Economics), March 1971.

Chapter 9   Marx and Malthus in Northeast Brazil

I am grateful to the Fulbright Commission for a lectureship that allowed me to spend three months in Northeast Brazil in 1983. Also, for discussions and suggestions I am indebted to my colleagues at the Universidade Federal do Ceará, the Fundação Joaquim Nabuco, and the Instituto Brasileiro de Geografia e Estatística. Responsibility for all points of view and any errors, of course, rests with me.

1. "The Population Question in Northeast Brazil: Its Economic and Ideological Dimensions," *Economic Development and Cultural Change*, July 1970; "A Marxian-Malthusian View of Poverty and Development," *Population Studies*, May 1971.

2. *Perfil Estatístico de Crinacas e Mães no Brasil: Caracteristicas Socio-demográficas, 1970–1977* (Rio de Janeiro, IBGE), 99. This study will henceforth be cited as *"Perfil."*

3. *Perfil*, 89.

4. See comment by Yony Sampaio, with my reply, in *Economic Development and Cultural Change*, January 1976.

5. PNAD is an acronym for Pesquisas Nacionais por Amostra de Domicilio (National research based on household sample).

6. See no. 3, above.

7. Total fertility is the number of live births per woman if she survived to menopause and were subject to the age-specific fertility rates currently prevailing in the population in question.

8. For 1970 the child mortality below two years of age was 192.3 per thousand, and in 1977 154.7 per thousand (*Perfil*, 55).

9. Thomas W. Merrick and Elsa Berquo, *The Determinants of Brazil's Recent Rapid Decline in Fertility* (Washington, D.C.: National Academy Press, 1983), 24.

10. Charles H. Wood and José Alberto Carvalho, "Population Growth and the Distribution of Household Income: The Case of Brazil," *The Sociological Quarterly* 23 (Winter 1982): 53.

11. J. Mayone Stycos, "Social Class and Differential Fertility in Peru," *Proceedings of the International Population Conference, New York, 1961*, vol. 2 (London, 1963), 123–38.

12. Jorge H. Zambrano Lupi, "Fertility and Educational Status in Mexico City" (in Spanish), *Demografía y Economía* 13 (4), no. 40 (1979): 442.

13. Kanti Pakrasi and Ajit Halder, "Fertility in Contemporary Calcutta: A Biosocial Profile," *Genus* 37 (3–4), (July–Dec. 1981): 201–19.

14. William Petersen, *Population* (New York: Macmillan Co., 1975), 527.

15. Wood and Carvalho, "Population Growth," n. 11, see their Table 1, 54.

16. *Perfil*, 157.

17. João Lyra Madeira, "Migrações Internas no Planejamento Economico," in *Migrações Internas no Brasil*, ed. Manoel A. Costa (Rio de Janeiro: Instituto de Planejamento Economico e Social, 1971), 42.

18. See n. 1, above.

19. See Karl Marx, *Capital*, chapter 33, "The modern theory of colonization," pp. 379–83 in Great Books edition (University of Chicago, 1952).

20. Merrick and Berquo, *Determinants*, 82, 83.

21. For an interesting study of changing sexual attitudes in different social classes, see Rose Marie Muraro, *Sexualidade de Mulher Brasileira* (Editora Vozes, Petropolis, R. J., Brazil, 1983).

22. Nathaniel H. Leff, *Underdevelopment and Development in Brazil*, 2 vols. (London: George Allen and Unwin, 1982). See especially chapter 4, volume 1.

23. *O Problema Demográfico Brasileiro* (Associação dos Diplomandos da Escola Superior da Guerra, Grupo 05, Belo Horizonte, MG, 1982). (My translations.)

Part 5   Introduction

1. Herman Daly and Robert Goodland, "An Ecological-Economic Analysis of Deregulation of International Commerce under GATT," *Ecological Economics* 9, no. 1 (February 1994).

2. *Scientific American* 269, no. 5 (November 1993): 50–57.

Chapter 10   Free Trade and Globalization vs. Environment and Community

1. *Definition of free trade*: the deregulation of exchanges and transfers by individuals and corporations across national boundaries. The contrary of free trade is not autarky; it is regulated trade—i.e., the regulation by the national community of the exchanges that its members make with those outside the community. The purpose of such regulation is to protect the common interests of the national community.

2. Some economists argue that all costs are internalized and that what may look like uncounted costs simply reflect values for which willingness to pay is low. Country X has no pollution controls simply because they are not willing to pay the price for cleaner air or water. Their willingness to pay

may be low because of their low desire for the value in question or because of their low income. Differences in willingness to pay, for whatever reason, are held to be legitimate reasons for competitive advantage, whereas differences in degree of cost internalization are not. Two points need to be made in response. First, there really are large differences in degree of cost internalization, independent of differences in willingness to pay. Second, even if the issue is restricted to willingness to pay, it is quite possible for one country's willingness to pay to be so far out of line with that of another country as to constitute a good reason for restricting trade. If Country X has a very low willingness to pay to avoid sixteen-hour-per-day child labor, that fact creates in Country Y no obligation to subject its own citizens to similar conditions, or even to accept the effect that such a low willingness to pay would, through free trade, exert on its own employment structure and community life. That world resources would be more efficiently allocated by free trade, when evaluated on the basis of prices reflecting willingness to pay in Country X, is not the relevant criterion for Country Y.

3. See Tim Lang and Colin Hines, *The New Protectionism: Protecting the Future against Free Trade* (London: Earthscan, 1993).

4. In this context I cannot resist reciting my favorite quote from John Maynard Keynes: "I sympathize therefore, with those who would minimize, rather than those who would maximize, economic entanglement between nations. Ideas, knowledge, art, hospitality, travel—these are the things which should of their nature be international. But let goods be homespun whenever it is reasonably and conveniently possible; and, above all, let finance be primarily national" (J. M. Keynes [1933], "National Self-Sufficiency," in *The Collected Writings of John Maynard Keynes*, vol. 21, ed. Donald Moggeridge [London: Macmillan and Cambridge University Press]).

5. "Is Growth Obsolete?" in *Economic Growth*, National Bureau of Economic Research, general series, no. 96E (New York: Columbia University Press, 1972).

6. Neither the MEW nor the ISEW considered the effect of individual country GNP growth on the *global* environment, and consequently on welfare at geographic levels other than the nation. Nor was there any deduction for harmful products, such as tobacco or alcohol. Nor was any adjustment made for the diminishing marginal utility of aggregate income. Such considerations would further weaken the correlation between GNP and welfare. Also, the fact that personal consumption is the major component of both the GNP and the ISEW (as well as the MEW) introduces a strong autocorrelation bias, thus making the observed lack of correlation more dramatic.

7. Comparative advantage has been called the "deepest and most beautiful result in all of economics." See Ronald Findlay, "Comparative Advantage," in John Eatwell et al., editors (The New Palgrave: A Dictionary of Economics), *The World of Economics* (New York: W. W. Norton, 1991), 99.

8. Absolute advantage is the rule for maximizing returns to capital when capital is mobile. Comparative advantage is the rule for maximizing returns to capital subject to the constraint that capital stays at home. This remains true in spite of an improvement in the definition of cost from Ricardo's labor cost to the modern concept of opportunity cost. The difficulty about assumed capital immobility remains. Opportunity cost is the correct concept—but the opportunity set, out of which the opportunity cost (next best alternative) is defined, is the whole world when capital is mobile, and the nation when capital is immobile. When the opportunity set for capital is the whole world, then absolute advantage governs; when it is the nation, then comparative advantage governs.

9. In their July 1993 draft "Trade and Environment: Does Environmental Diversity Detract from the Case for Free Trade?" Jagdish Bhagwati and T. N. Srinivasan reaffirm the view that free trade remains the optimal policy in spite of environmental issues. But their conclusion is based on what they call "a fairly general model . . . but one where resources, such as capital, do not move across countries" (p. 11). Of course, if capital is immobile between nations comparative advantage arguments still hold. The point is that in today's world capital is highly mobile. Nor do the authors advocate restricting capital mobility to make the world conform to the assumptions of their argument— much the contrary! Their willingness to draw concrete policy conclusions from such an injudiciously abstracted model is a classic example of what A. N. Whitehead called "the fallacy of misplaced concreteness." At least they honestly stated their assumption, albeit without flagging its critical importance to their argument.

10. David Ricardo, *Principles of Political Economy and Taxation*, Sraffa edition (Cambridge, England: 1951), 136–37.

11. Adam Smith (1776), *The Wealth of Nations* (New York: Random House, 1971), 423.

12. Sir James Goldsmith, in *The Trap* (New York: Carroll and Graff, 1993), has made cogent arguments in opposition to free trade in the modern sense of free movement of goods, capital, and people. Sir James seems to argue for keeping labor and goods at home, while letting capital flow internationally. This would, I think, be a great improvement over the present system, but I believe I would still prefer Ricardo's original solution of keeping capital at home and letting goods flow internationally. This is because control of production usually inheres in capital, and it is in the interest of community to keep that control as local as feasible.

13. W. J. Baumol, *Environmental Protection, International Spillovers, and Trade* (Stockholm: Almqvist and Wicksell, 1971). Economists tend to dismiss such wage effects as merely "pecuniary externalities" which deserve less attention than "technological externalities." The latter refer to costs or benefits shifted to third parties in a manner external to the price system; the former refers to third party effects that operate through the price system. Since lowering the price of labor by free migration is a cost to the preexisting labor force, and a benefit to employers and foreign laborers, which is mediated by the wage rate, it is classed as a pecuniary externality and not given much consideration in economic theory—i.e., it is "merely a matter of distribution."

14. The category "nonsupervisory employees" accounts for 80% of the labor force in the United States. Between 1973 and 1990 their real wages fell by 17%. Labor productivity did not fall over this period—in fact it continued to rise, although at a diminished rate. But the price of manufactured goods fell as a result of the United States moving to a more open economy. After 1972, the trade / GNP ratio moved above its usual historical level of about 13%, reaching 25% in the 1980s. In spite of these facts, we are continually told that free trade benefits everyone by reducing the prices that consumers pay. True enough, except that it has caused the wages of 80% of the workforce to fall faster than prices, so that their *real* wages have fallen by 17%. No doubt the remaining 20% of the population has done very well indeed. A mere question of distribution, economists tell us. But there is no prospect of a significant redistribution, and even if there were, it is hard to believe that the gains to the upper 20% would be sufficient to compensate the losses of the lower 80%. See Ravi Batra, *The Myth of Free Trade* (New York: Scribners, 1993).

15. In the United States the free traders won the fight over NAFTA. U.S. citizens were assured that the nation would gain more jobs than it lost because we exported more to Mexico than we im-

ported from them. Yet it is exactly that Mexican payments deficit in current account that caused a drain of reserves and a flight of both the foreign and domestic capital that was financing the Mexican deficit, resulting in a 40% devaluation of the peso relative to the dollar. Now U.S. citizens are being told that they have to serve as guarantors for some 20 billion dollars worth of Mexican debt. Never mind that the 20 billion comes from a fund that is supposed to be used to stabilize the dollar, not the peso. Never mind that the guarantee is to protect the bad investments of many on Wall Street who so enthusiastically promoted NAFTA and were earning very high returns. And never mind that the devaluation has resulted in a trade surplus for Mexico and a reversal of the net job gain argument used to sell NAFTA in the first place. The threat of more illegal immigration from Mexico, previously used to help pass NAFTA, is once again pressed into service (by the global integrationists!) to argue for the loan guarantee.

16. Humanitarian advocates for the poor illegals often argue that they only take menial jobs that Americans would not take, and therefore cause no harm. I wish it were that simple. But the reason no American will take such jobs is that competition from illegals has lowered wages and working conditions below the acceptable minimum standards. Many Americans used to work their way through college at menial jobs because those jobs paid enough. Now that is not the case and students have to go into debt instead. Alternatively it is argued that the U.S. unemployed are just not qualified for the new jobs generated by our economy, and therefore qualified immigrants are needed. But if those qualified immigrants were not available we would invest more in raising the quality of skills among our own unemployed.

Part 6   Introduction

1. Juan Martinez-Alier, with Klaus Schlüpmann, *Ecological Economics: Energy, Environment, and Society* (Oxford, England: Basil Blackwell, 1987).

2. For more on money, and Soddy, see the afterword in Herman E. Daly and John B. Cobb, Jr., *For the Common Good*, 2nd ed. (Boston: Beacon Press, 1994).

Chapter 12   The Economic Thought of Frederick Soddy

Reprinted from *History of Political Economy* 12, 4 (1980), Duke University Press.

1. In fairness to Millikan it should be noted that in concluding his vigorous defense of science he did temper his optimism with the following caution: "I am not in general disturbed by expanding knowledge or increasing power, but I begin to be disturbed when this comes coincidentally with a decrease in the sense of moral values. If these two occur together, whether they bear any relationship or not, there is real cause for alarm" (Millikan 1930, p. 129).

2. This point has been forcefully made by the biologist Garrett Hardin. See Garrett Hardin and Carl Bajema, *Biology: Its Principles and Implications*, 3d ed. (San Francisco: 1978), 257.

3. When a bank lends to A it forgoes the opportunity of making the same loan to B, so in that sense there is an opportunity cost in allocating the virtual wealth among borrowers, but there is no opportunity cost to the bank in acquiring the virtual wealth in the first place.

4. In fact, Boulding told me he was very much aware of Soddy the scientist, having slept through his chemistry lectures at Oxford, but knew nothing of his economic writings. As for sleeping through chemistry lectures, even the writer of one obituary tribute remarked that it would be idle to pretend that Soddy was a successful classroom teacher.

5. For such a dismissal see A. G. Silverman (1927).

Chapter 13   On Nicholas Georgescu-Roegen's Contributions to Economics

1. Nicholas Georgescu-Roegen, *The Entropy Law and the Economic Process* (Cambridge, Mass.: Harvard University Press, 1971).

2. Nicholas Georgescu-Roegen, *Analytical Economics* (Cambridge, Mass.: Harvard University Press, 1966).

3. As noted by Mark Blaug in *Great Economists Since Keynes* (Totawa, N.J.: Barnes and Noble, 1985), 71: "It is only fair to add that Georgescu-Roegen's later books have not been well received, or rather, have been respectfully received and quickly put away. For various complex reasons, not to mention the difficult style in which they are written and the intimidating references they contain to theoretical developments in physics and biology, these works have received virtually no critical discussion from economists."

4. *Evolution, Time, and Welfare in Economics*, ed. A. M. Tang et al. (Lexington, Ky.: D. C. Heath Co., 1976).

5. Harold Barnett and Chandler Morse, *Scarcity and Growth* (Baltimore, Md.: Johns Hopkins University Press for Resources for the Future, 1963).

6. Herrmann Heinrich Gossen, *The Laws of Human Relations and the Rules of Human Action Derived Therefrom*, translated by Rudolph C. Blitz, with an introductory essay by Nicholas Georgescu-Roegen (Cambridge, Mass.: MIT Press, 1983).

Part 7   Introduction

1. See the cogent discussion by Phillip E. Johnson, *Reason in the Balance: The Case against Naturalism in Science, Law, and Education* (Downers Grove, Ill.: InterVarsity Press, 1995).

2. See George M. Marsden, *The Soul of the American University: From Protestant Establishment to Established Nonbelief* (New York: Oxford University Press, 1994).

3. *Steady-State Economics* (San Francisco: W. H. Freeman Co., 1977; Washington, D.C.: Island Press, 1991).

4. Sam Pizzigati, *The Maximum Wage* (New York: Apex Press, 1992).

Chapter 14   A Biblical Economic Principle and the Sustainable Economy

1. C. J. H. Wright, *An Eye for an Eye: The Place of Old Testament Ethics Today* (Downers Grove, Ill.: InterVarsity Press, 1983), 112.

2. A. B. Cramp, *Economics in Christian Perspective*, mimeo, p. IX/26.

3. Robert B. Coote and Mary P. Coote, *Power, Politics, and the Making of the Bible: An Introduction* (Minneapolis, Minn.: Fortress, 1990).

Chapter 15   Sustainable Development

1. The term "maximize" should not be taken to imply any precise mathematical solution of an ethical problem. It is a convenient way to bring efficiency into a problem of serving more than one value. There are three values in play: sufficiency, sustainability, equity. Efficiency, treated in the text as a fourth value, is really a derivative value in that its goodness derives from its ability to permit a greater degree of attainment of any one of the three basic goals, given some set level of attainment of the other two.

2. The current discussion on "biodiversity" would, in my opinion, be more fruitful if it were framed in terms of the ever-increasing takeover of total life space by one species, rather than in terms of the number of different species that can remain viable in the ever-shrinking total habitat left over for them as the human niche expands. Continued human expansion means that other species will disappear or become domesticated like cattle (or zoo specimens) for their instrumental value.

References Cited in Text

Abramowitz, M. 1979. "Economic Growth and Its Discontents." *Economics and Human Welfare*, edited by M. Boskin. New York: Academic Press.

Ahmad, Yusuf J., Salah El Serafy, and Ernst Lutz, eds. 1989. *Environmental Accounting for Sustainable Development*. Washington, D.C.: The World Bank and United Nations Environment Programme.

Barnett, Harold, and Chandler Morse. 1963. *Scarcity and Growth*. Baltimore: Johns Hopkins University Press.

Birch, C., and John Cobb. 1981. *The Liberation of Life*. Cambridge: Cambridge University Press.

Boulding, Kenneth. 1945. "The Consumption Concept in Economic Theory." *American Economic Review*, May 1945, 2.

———. 1949. "Income or Welfare?" *Review of Economic Studies* 17, 79.

———. 1964. *The Meaning of the Twentieth Century*. New York: Harper and Row.

Brown, Harrison. 1970. "Human Materials Production as a Process in the Biosphere." *Scientific American*, September 1970, 194–208.

Brown, Lester, et al. 1971. *State of the World*. New York: Norton.

CEPAR, ININMS, DHS. 1988. *Encuesta Demográfica y de Salud Familiar, 1987*. Ecuador: Quito.

Clark, C. W. 1976. *Mathematical Bioeconomics*. New York: Wiley.

Cleveland, C. J., et al. 1984. "Energy and the U.S. Economy: A Biophysical Perspective." *Science* 225.

Cobb, Clifford W., and John B. Cobb, Jr. 1994. *The Green National Product: A Proposed Index of Sustainable Economic Welfare.* Lanham, Md.: University Press of America.

Cook, E. 1982. "The Consumer as Creator: A Criticism of Faith in Limitless Ingenuity." *Energy Exploration and Exploitation* 1, no. 3:194.

Costanza, R., and Herman E. Daly. 1992. "Natural Capital and Sustainable Development." *Conservation Biology* 6 (March): 37–46.

Culbertson, John M. 1971. *Economic Development: An Ecological Approach.* New York: Knopf.

Daly, Herman E. 1980. "The Economic Thought of Frederick Soddy." *History of Political Economy* 12, no. 4.

———. 1985. "The Circular Flow of Exchange Value and the Linear Throughput of Matter-Energy: A Case of Misplaced Concreteness." *Review of Social Economy* 43, no. 3:279–97.

———. 1991. *Steady-State Economics.* 2d ed. Washington, D.C.: Island Press.

Daly, Herman E., and John B. Cobb, Jr. 1994. *For the Common Good.* 2d ed. Boston: Beacon Press.

Ehrlich, P., and A. Ehrlich. 1981. *Extinction.* New York: Random House.

El Serafy, Salah. 1989. "The Proper Calculation of Income Depletable Natural Resources." *Environmental Accounting for Sustainable Development*, edited by Yusuf J. Ahmad, Salah El Serafy, and Ernst Lutz. Washington, D.C.: World Bank.

Fearnside, P. M. 1986. *Human Carrying Capacity and the Brazilian Rainforest.* New York: Columbia University Press.

Fisher, I. 1935. *100% Money.* New York.

Fleck, A. 1957. "Frederick Soddy." *Biographical Memoirs of Fellows of the Royal Society* 3:203–16.

Foy, George. 1989. "Public Wealth and Private Riches: Past and Present." *The Journal of Interdisciplinary Economics* 3:3–10.

Georgescu-Roegen, Nicholas. 1971. *The Entropy Law and the Economic Process.* Cambridge, Mass.: Harvard University Press.

———. 1979. "Comments on the Papers by Daly and Stiglitz." In *Scarcity and Growth Reconsidered*, edited by V. Kerry Smith. Baltimore: RfF and Johns Hopkins University Press.

Gever, J., et al. 1986. *Beyond Oil.* Cambridge, Mass.: Ballinger.

Global 2000 Report to the President. 1980. Washington, D.C.: U.S. Government Printing Office.

Gore, Al. 1992. *Earth in the Balance.* Boston: Houghton Mifflin.

Hartwick, J., and A. Hageman. 1993. "Economic Depreciation of Mineral Stocks and the Contribution of El Serafy." *Toward Improved Accounting for the Environment*, edited by Ernst Lutz. Washington, D.C.: World Bank.

Hawken, P. 1983. *The Next Economy*. New York: Ballantine.

Hicks, J. R. 1946. *Value and Capital*. 2d ed. Oxford: Oxford University Press.

Hirsh, F. 1976. *Social Limits to Growth*. Cambridge, Mass.: Harvard University Press.

Hueting, Roefie. 1980. *New Scarcity and Economic Growth*. Amsterdam: North Holland Publishing Co.

Ise, J. 1925. "The Theory of Value as Applied to Natural Resources." *American Economic Review* 15 (June): 284–91.

Jackson, Tim, and Nick Marks. 1994. *Measuring Sustainable Economic Welfare—A Pilot Index: 1950–1990*. Stockholm: Stockholm Environmental Institute. Published in cooperation with the New Economics Foundation, London.

Keynes, J. M. 1930. "The Economic Possibilities for Our Grandchildren." *Essays in Persuasion*. New York: Norton.

———. 1936. *The General Theory of Employment, Interest, and Money*. New York: Harcourt Brace.

Knight, F. H. 1927. "Review of *Wealth, Virtual Wealth, and Debt*." *Saturday Review of Literature*, 732.

Landázuri, H., and C. Jijón. 1988. *El Medio ambiente en Ecuador*. Quito: ILDIS.

Lauderdale, J. M. 1819. *An Inquiry into the Nature and Origin of Public Wealth and into the Means and Causes of Its Increase*. 2d ed. Edinburgh: Archibald Constable.

Ledec, G., R. Goodland, J. Kirchner, and J. Drake. "Carrying Capacity, Population Growth, and Sustainable Development." In *Rapid Population Growth and Human Carrying Capacity*, edited by D. Mahar. Washington, D.C.: World Bank.

Leipert, Christian. 1986. "Social Costs of Economic Growth." *Journal of Economic Issues* 20, no. 1:109–31.

Leontief, Wassily W. 1977. *The Future of the World Economy*. New York: Oxford University Press.

Marshall, Alfred. 1961. *Principles of Economics*. 9th ed. New York: Macmillan.

McCracken, Paul W. 1975. *Wall Street Journal*, 17 September 1975, 16.

Meadows, D. H., et al. 1972. *The Limits to Growth*. New York: Potomac Associates.

Millikan, R. A. 1930. "Alleged Sins of Science." *Scribner's Magazine* 872:119–30.

Nordhaus, William. 1991. *Science*, 14 September 1991, 1206.

Odum, E. P. 1969. "The Strategy of Ecosystem Development." *Science*, April 1969, 262–70.

Pearce, D. W., A. Markandya, and E. B. Barbier. 1989. *Blueprint for a Green Economy*. London: Earthscan.

Perrings, Charles. 1987. *Economy and Environment: A Theoretical Essay on the Interdependence of Economic and Environmental Systems*. Cambridge: Cambridge University Press.

Pesek, B. P., and T. R. Saving. 1967. *Money, Wealth, and Economic Theory*. New York.

Pigou, A. C. 1970. *The Economics of Welfare*. London: Macmillan.

PNUD/FAO/SFN. 1979. "Capacidad de Uso de los Suelos, Uso Actual y Tendencias, y el Desarrollo del Sector Forestal." Documento de Trabajo no. 30:13, 20.

Reich, R. B. 1983. *The Next American Frontier*. New York: Penguin.

Repetto, Robert. 1987. *Natural Resource Accounting for Indonesia*. Washington, D.C.: World Resources Institute.

Russell, A. S. 1956. "F. Soddy, Interpreter of Atomic Structure." *Science*, 1069–70.

Schumpeter, Joseph. 1954. *History of Economic Analysis*. New York: Oxford University Press.

Silverman, A. G. 1927. "Review of *Wealth, Virtual Wealth, and Debt*." *American Economic Review*, 275–78.

Simon, J. 1981. *The Ultimate Resource*. Princeton, N.J.: Princeton University Press.

Simons, H. 1948. *Economic Policy for a Free Society*. Chicago.

Sinsheimer, Robert L. 1978. "The Presumptions of Science." *Daedalus*, 23–35.

Soddy, Frederick. 1920. *Science and Life*. London.

———. 1922. *Cartesian Economics: The Bearing of Physical Science upon State Stewardship*. London: Hendersons.

———. 1924. *The Inversion of Science*. London.

———. 1926. *Wealth, Virtual Wealth, and Debt*. London. Reprinted by Omni Publications, Hawthorne, CA, 1961.

———. 1933. *Money Versus Man*. New York.

———. 1934. *The Role of Money*. London.

———. 1943. *The Arch Enemy of Economic Freedom* (pamphlet). Oxford.

———. 1949. *The Story of Atomic Energy*. London.

Tanzi, V., ed. 1983. *The Underground Economy in the United States and Abroad.* Lexington, Ky · Heath.

Thurow, Lester. 1980. *The Zero-Sum Society.* New York: Penguin.

Tinbergen, Jan. 1952. *On the Theory of Economic Policy.* Amsterdam: North Holland Publishing Co.

Tobin, J. 1965. "Money and Economic Growth." *Econometrica*, October 1965, 33.

Turner, F. 1984. "Escape from Modernism." *Harper's*, November.

Vitousek, Peter M., Paul R. Ehrlich, Anne H. Ehrlich, and Pamela A. Matson. 1986. "Human Appropriation of the Products of Photosynthesis." *BioScience* 34, no. 6:368–73.

Wilkinson, Richard. 1973. *Poverty and Progress: An Ecological Perspective on Economic Development.* New York: Praeger.

World Bank. 1988. "Ecuador: Country Economic Memorandum 1988." Washington, D.C.: World Bank.

Index

Library of Congress Cataloging-in-Publication Data

Daly, Herman E.
  Beyond growth: the economics of sustainable development / Herman Daly.
    p.   cm.
  Includes bibliographical references and index.
  ISBN 0-8070-4708-2 (cloth, alk. paper)
  ISBN 0-8070-4709-0 (paper)
  1. Sustainable development.   I. Title.
  HC79.E5D324   1996
  333.7—dc20
                                                        95-51311